GET BIGGER, STRONGER, AND FASTER
FOLLOWING THE PROGRAMS OF TODAY'S TOP PLAYERS

FOOTBALL TRAINING LIKE THE PROS

CHIP SMITH

New York   Chicago   San Francisco   Lisbon   London   Madrid   Mexico City
Milan   New Delhi   San Juan   Seoul   Singapore   Sydney   Toronto

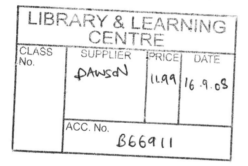
Library of Congress Cataloging-in-Publication Data

Smith, Chip.
    Football training like the pros : get bigger, stronger, and faster following the programs of today's top players / Chip Smith.
        p.   cm.
    Includes index.
    ISBN-13: 978-0-07-148868-6 (alk. paper)
    ISBN-10:   0-07-148868-5 (alk. paper)
    1. Football training.   2. Physical fitness.   I. Title.

GV953.5.S65   2008
796.33207'7—dc22
                                          2007020140

1 2 3 4 5 6 7 8 9 10 11 12 13 14 15 16 17 18 19 20 21 22 23 24 25 VLP/VLP 0 9 8 7

ISBN 978-0-07-148868-6
MHID   0-07-148868-5

Interior design by Rattray Design

McGraw-Hill books are available at special quantity discounts to use as premiums and sales promotions, or for use in corporate training programs. For more information, please write to the Director of Special Sales, Professional Publishing, McGraw-Hill, Two Penn Plaza, New York, NY 10121-2298. Or contact your local bookstore.

This book is printed on acid-free paper.

To Jesus Christ, my Lord and Savior,
who not only has given me eternal life
but has blessed me with an abundant life!
May this book honor Your Name.

CONTENTS

FOREWORD

In 1999 I was a senior playing safety at the University of New Mexico. I had a couple of good seasons at UNM and was told that I might have the physical tools and mental discipline to play in the National Football League. I went through the agent selection process and decided on Steve Kauffman from Malibu, California. Looking for the right fit for me, Steve made calls to all of the top sports performance coaches. He called me one night and was really excited about a conversation he had had with Chip Smith of Competitive Edge Sports in Atlanta, Georgia. Steve asked Chip to give me a call and discuss how his program would prepare me for the rigors of my private workouts at UNM, the Senior Bowl, and, ultimately, the NFL combine.

I'll never forget that first conversation with Chip. We talked for over an hour about my personal and professional goals. I've always made my workouts a priority, and I couldn't imagine working out any harder or with any more intensity. Chip quickly assured me that I could go harder. In fact, he thought that I could add another 25 to 30 pounds of muscle to my 6′4″ frame. That conversation was all I needed to see what was possible in terms of my development and performance. I made the decision right then and there to train with him in Atlanta.

I showed up at 235 pounds, running the forty-yard dash in the 4.6s. My body fat composition was 11 percent. Two months later, my body fat was down to 7 percent and I weighed in at 262 pounds. In addition, I shaved my forty-yard time into the low 4.5s. Needless to say, I was sold on Chip's program. I was voted MVP of the Senior Bowl. I had a great workout at the NFL combine. And I was taken as the ninth pick by the Chicago Bears in the 2000 NFL Draft. I then went on to become the National Football League's Defensive Rookie of the Year.

Over the last seven years, I have seen a dramatic increase in the size and speed of the young players coming into the league. I have had to stay up on all the newest training techniques and am constantly modifying my workout regimen. To stay on top of my game, I use Chip's speed and strength program. For example, the chapter on our experience training at high altitude in Lake Tahoe will demonstrate how thorough and creative Chip is at designing programs that fit his athletes' particular needs. Some of the stuff he comes up with is incredibly intense, and that's exactly the way I like to play! This book will guide you through the training process at its highest levels. It will give you that competitive edge that you're looking for.

One remarkable thing that you'll learn about Chip from this book is that he not only wrote the training program, but he also invented the actual training equipment he uses. He understands precisely what movements need to be emphasized. He shows you how each piece of equipment works to train that movement. And he shows you how that movement transfers easily to game-play situations. As an ex-player and coach, he knows the game of football inside and out. He understands the responsibilities of each player and position on the field.

This program will increase your athleticism. It will enhance your performance each day you train. Chip's program uses a multitude of training aids, which means it's never monotonous and predictable. You'll train specifically for your position. You'll work your butt off, but Chip knows how to keep the training techniques fresh and fun.

This book is a must-read for those looking to take their game to the next level or for professional trainers looking to give their athletes the edge. It's an inside look at the methods and techniques used by more than six hundred current NFL players and scores of college and high school athletes across the country and around the world. You'll learn the secrets of the pros and read some of Chip's insights into what it takes to make an NFL-caliber player. When you are paid to make a living with your body, you can't afford to trust your abilities to anyone but the *best*! And the simple fact is, "Chip-aroo" is the best! Here's to your success.

Brian Urlacher
Six-Time Pro Bowl Honoree
2005 NFL Defensive Player of the Year
2000 NFL Defensive Rookie of the Year

PREFACE

Man is so made that whenever anything fires his soul, impossibilities vanish.

—Jean de la Fontaine

While the inspiration for my training technique was the revolutionary ideologies and methodologies that I learned in the 1980s from the Soviets, the inspiration for my training philosophy is relationships. Anyone who knows me knows that my priorities are faith, family, and friends, in that order. All the methods, all the equipment, all the experience, and all the athletic ideology are not what motivate me to do what I do. I do what I do because of the sincere love I have for the players that I train.

My coaching philosophy is this. The way to get the maximum out of a player is to encourage him and to genuinely care about him as a person. My coaching style uses positive reinforcement as a primary motivation. It makes no difference to me if I'm working with a first-round draft pick or a hopeful free agent; I coach them all the same. I want to affirm my players in every way that I can. I want to show them appreciation. I want to shower them with positive attention and feedback. And I want to be affectionate with them. I put my arm around their shoulders. I hug them. I shake their hand with my two hands and slap them on the back while I laugh with them.

I'm not just looking to make players better at their position. I'm not just trying to help them with their strength-training technique, their speed, quickness, agility, and flexibility. Testing and evaluation are not my main concerns. I don't just want to make players bigger, faster, and stronger. The most important thing, what I live for, long for, strive for, and crave, is establishing relationships with the young men I work with. Young men who may or may not have a male role model in their life. Young men who are moldable clay. Diamonds in the rough that I can help to polish and tilt toward the sun so that they sparkle. I get the privilege, the opportunity, the awesome responsibility of coaching these young men.

Nothing thrills me more than sharing in their successes and their heartaches. I get their wedding invitations and birth announcements in the mail. I love what I do; it is my passion. It's much more than just my job. It's not just my vocation, it's my avocation. I feel that it's what God put me on the earth to do. I want to make every day count. I want to make every contact with every young man a priority. I don't believe in luck or happenstance. I know that everything happens for a reason. I believe in divine providence. I believe that to whom much is given, much is required. And I believe I've been given much. I know that one day I will answer for how I've spent my time and my opportunities. I want to spend them well.

ACKNOWLEDGMENTS

I would like to thank McGraw-Hill for dropping the opportunity to write this book in my lap, totally unsolicited, fulfilling a concealed lifelong dream. "Every good and perfect gift comes down from the Father above."

Thank you to my beautiful wife, Joy, for continuing to pray Psalm 20:4 for me. You're my secret weapon. All of our challenges have only strengthened our love. You are my inspiration and my soul mate.

Thank you to my children, Tripp, Cody, and Zach, my *Wild at Heart* sons, and to my baby girl, Summer. Y'all are my most treasured possessions in this world. I love you dearly. Tripp, you have shared in my dream of impacting the lives of athletes. Cody, you have taught me not to judge but to look at the heart. Zach, you have shown me what motivation and work ethic really look like. And Summer, you melt my heart and make me sing "Butterfly Kisses."

Thanks to my dad and mom, Reverend Dr. Carlton E. Smith Sr. and Jane Smith, who have believed in me and supported me throughout my athletic and professional career. Mom, your passion for sports motivated me to strive for excellence. Dad, you are the original "CES" and you are my hero. I can hear you saying, "Only one life will soon be past; only what's done for Christ will last!"

Thanks to my friend and associate, Robby Stewart. You have been a trusted confidant, an exemplary family man, and the best strength coach in America. Thanks for your help with the strength chapter. I appreciate you for staying the course and believing in what I started fifteen years ago.

Thank you to my staff at Competitive Edge Sports, who have believed in my program. Thanks to Aaron Roberts, CES senior sports performance coach, who helped me with the reaction and position resistance chapters; Ben Barrick, sports performance coach and the computer genius who helped me with the charts and graphs; Tripp Smith, my favorite trainer, who helped me with the stretching chapter; Bryant Appling, Maria Melts, T. J. Sellers, Dr. Brad Hodgson, and all the part-time staff that has become part of the CES family. You all have blessed me with your loyalty and your dedication to CES.

Thank you to all of my sponsors. Under Armour, the products are undeniable! Shannon, you and all your staff have been so much fun to work with; thanks for making me part of the Under Armour family. To Joseph at EAS supplements, I appreciate you for believing in my program and supporting my players with the best nutritional products in the country. To Bruce at UBS Financial Services, thanks for your friendship and support for the past ten years. Mercedes-Benz, a big thank-you for supporting me and CES.

Thank you to Coach Roger Theder. You have given me some amazing insights into the game of professional football. I think you have forgotten more than most coaches know. You have been a mentor, and I am honored to call you my friend.

To all the agents who have sent me clients over the past fifteen years, thanks to each of you for placing your trust in my ability to make your players better. I truly appreciate you!

To all the high school coaches who have participated in the CES training program, I thank you. Coach Dexter Wood and Coach Jess Simpson at Buford High School, Buford, Georgia, the ultimate model of a high school football family, you have made me feel like I played a small part in your incredible success and that we're now forever bonded. Coach Lee Shaw and your staff at Flowery Branch High School, and Coach Tim Coleman and your staff at Colonial Forge High School in Stafford, Virginia, I thank you for your trust, encouragement, help, and support. Tim, I love you like a brother. To my special friends in Maryland, Coaches Dave Dolch and Steve Luette, you have been more that just friends—you have treated me like one of your own. To Coach Quinones and your staff in Lovington, New Mexico, thanks for making me feel like an honorary member of your program. To all my friends in Truckee, California, Coach Bob Shaffer and your staff at Truckee High School, and Gary Lewis and your family, you have shown me genuine hospitality.

To Coach Speedy Faith at Shallowater High School, Shallowater, Texas, and Coach Don Rodie, thanks for your friendship and for all the fun times we've had working the Brian Urlacher Football Camp. To the many, many other coaches who are my friends, who have dedicated your lives to impacting young men, I salute you!

To all the NFL football players I have trained who have touched my life in such a positive way, without you this book would not be possible. Y'all have enriched my life in such a profound way. I could never express all the love and admiration I have for each of you. Brian and Casey Urlacher; Matt and Jon Stinchomb; Whit Marshall; Chris Combs; Billy Granville; Gannon Sheppard; Terrance Newman; Adam Meadows; Bobby Hamilton; Nate Wayne; Karon Riley; Roger Robinson; Keith Brooking; Hannibal Navies; E. J. Johnson; David Green; Drew Olsen; Roy Manning; Champ, Boss, and Ron Bailey; Charlie, Nick, and Chris Clemens; Jon and Jeremy Myers; Donnie Klien; Marcus Vick; Mike Williams; Charlie Whitehurst; Nick Ferguson; Shawn Bryson; Leonard Weaver; Brandon Spoon; Vonnie Holliday; Ryan Cook; Mark Setterstrom; Will Allen; Cody Douglas; Cosey Coleman; Fred Weary; Spence Fischer; Alvin Cowan; Brian Wilmer; Philip Daniels; Bryant Robinson; Marcus Stroud; Jonas Jennings; Eric Zier; and the hundreds of others that I have trained over the past fifteen years—you have brought me such pride and joy watching you develop into outstanding young men. You have all become my adopted sons.

FOOTBALL TRAINING LIKE THE PROS

1

The Russian Experience

Train like You Play

One day in 1986 I was riding a stationary bike in a health club. Someone had left a magazine in the rack on the bike I was riding, so I picked it up. As I looked through the magazine, I read an ad in the back looking for coaches and sports medicine practitioners who might be interested in studying abroad in the fields of sports training or sports medicine.

I answered the ad and was delighted to find out that the study abroad program was going to be held in the former Soviet Union at the world-renowned Soviet Sports Institute in Moscow. In order to be considered for the opportunity, I had to write a paper on why I should be selected to study abroad. After submitting my paper, I was notified that I had been selected to travel with a distinguished group of American and Canadian coaches, trainers, and sports medicine personnel.

A few of the notable coaches who went with me were Dana LeDuc, the head strength and conditioning coach with the St. Louis Rams; Brad Roll, former head strength coach with the Tampa Bay Buckaneers; E. J. "Doc" Kreis, the head strength and conditioning coach at UCLA; Lebarron Crauthers, former head strength coach of the New England Patriots; Dr. Jim Wright, former editor of *Muscle and Fitness Magazine*; and John Greeley, one of the top personal trainers in New York City.

From Theory to Practice

In this book, I will explain my training philosophy as it pertains to the preparation of professional athletes. What it won't be is a static technical summary of all the Soviet training methods. What I hope to accomplish, however, is to give you an inside look at training techniques that I use with the pros based on those principles. There are three simple training techniques on which I have built my program. The first is movement resistant training. The second is movement overspeed training. And the third is reaction training. If you use these three principles of my training program, you can train any sport or movement necessary to play that sport with my guarantee these principles will enhance your performance on the field. The principles of this book revolve around these three methods of training. I will show you how to structure these three components into a preseason program that will make you bigger, faster, and stronger!

When I was in school in the U.S.S.R., Dr. Yuri Verhoshansky, "the father of plyometrics," gave a seminar on how the Russians would train American football players if given the opportunity. Of course it would be hypothetical, since the Russians don't play American football. But from this lecture, I developed my six-week program to enhance sports performance for football and would like to share this information with you.

Periodization and the Team Approach

To prepare their athletes, Russian trainers would develop a year-round program using a periodization training model. Periodization is simply dividing the year up into different phases and microcycles. The Russians would divide the training year up into a number of periods of time, each with specific performance goals. The Soviets broke down their system into four preparation phases:

1. Postseason (transitional)
2. Generalized preparatory
3. Specialized preparatory (precompetitive)
4. Competitive (in-season)

They also believed that it was most efficient to use a team approach in coaching, so they assigned each coach responsibilities for the training cycles.

1. Biomechanist—technique expert and position coach
2. Conditioning expert/exercise specialist—speed and strength
3. Physiologist
4. Psychologist
5. Team physician

The biomechanist would be responsible for developing the skills portion of the training model. He would study each movement and then break down each of the movements into position specificity. He would then structure the training program to isolate each movement, as well as teaching the correct skills of each movement. This sounds like the very first job description for a sports performance coach, does it not?

The conditioning-exercise specialist would play a vital role in the physical development of each player. Based on the player's physical capabilities, the conditioning expert, along with the biomechanist, would work together developing a training program that would mimic the actual movements that the player performed on the field at his position (again, sport-specific with position-specific training). Each player would then focus on his position. For quarterbacks, this means working on their three-, five-, and seven-step drops and redirect. Defensive backs would work on their backpedal, breaking at a 45-degree angle, and so on.

The physiologist would be responsible for the testing and evaluation of each player. He would gather baseline information for flexibility, body composition, the forty-yard dash, the vertical jump, the 225-pound bench rep test, the short shuttle 5-10-5, the three-cone drill, the broad jump, the sixty-yard shuttle drill, and any other drill that can be measured and tracked. With this baseline information, each test would give the conditioning coach a quantitative way to address each area of need. In other words, a low vertical jump or short broad jump would indicate a lack of hip explosion. From this information, a planned program would be developed to closely duplicate the actual skill technique needed by the different positions.

The sports psychologist would work on reaction-type training, along with motivation, visualization, and other types of autogenic training. Autogenic training translates to "self-regulation or generation" and refers to the way your mind can influence your body to balance the self-regulative systems that control circulation, breathing, and heart rate. This process allows you to control stress by training your autonomic nervous system to become relaxed.

The Four-Phase Training Cycle

The Soviets believed that there could be little success if the athlete did not possess good overall fitness levels. General fitness levels are paramount for the athlete to achieve the next level of training—in this case, specialized speed and strength training. The Soviets also believed that merely playing a sport would not increase the overall fitness levels of the athlete. So their theory was that you must limit the actual playing time, especially at the professional level. Following are discussions of the four phases of the training cycle.

Postseason (Transitional)

This phase would begin after the postseason bowl game or after the last game of the year. The players would remain active, playing other sports to maintain the gains made during the off-season. This informal activity would keep their flexibility, power, strength, and reaction, as well as any other skills previously acquired, sharp and recallable. During this phase, sports such as racquetball, handball, and basketball are routine activities. These sports would enhance hand-eye coordination as well as maintain quickness, reaction time, foot skills, and general fitness levels. These other sports would also force the body to adapt to different skills not learned in football. A variety of informal sports would enable the nervous system to relax, allowing the athletes some variation in their routine and preventing burnout. The Soviets did not believe in playing only one sport. To the contrary, their philosophy was that specializing in only one sport would hinder the development of all the attributes of physical development. They thought that playing multiple sports when young would help in the development of an all-around athlete. The strength development of this phase would consist of mostly Olympic lifts, power cleans, hi-pull, snatches, push press, and other lifts that are explosive in nature. Again the Olympic lifts were taught at an early age and were the cornerstone of all Soviet athletes' strength training. Assistive lifts were also done in this phase. The postseason would last for one to two months for the teams that did not go to a postseason bowl game and four to six weeks for teams that were involved in postseason playoffs and bowl games. At the conclusion of this period, the generalized preparatory would begin.

Generalized Preparatory

In this phase, the conditioning-exercise coach would be busy developing individualized programs to focus on total conditioning. This program would focus again on the areas that were tested, and weaknesses that had been identified would be addressed. During this phase, strength, flexibility, speed, agility, cardiorespiratory, endurance, reaction, and other qualities that are associated with the athlete would be developed. The volume of work done in this phase would be very high but the intensity would be low.

The strength workouts would be general in nature with emphasis on the joints. Strength training involves compound movements such as bench press, incline press, and decline press along with lateral pull-downs, one-arm rows, bent rows, upright and seated rows, biceps and triceps work, shoulder work, front raises, side laterals, seated dumbbell press, standing barbell press, and neck work. Exercises for the core include crunches, sit-ups, Russian twists, knee-ups, hanging leg raises, hyperextensions, and other low back exercises.

To address lower body development, key exercises include squats, step-ups, leg extensions, leg curls, straight leg dead lifts, toe raises, abduction, adduction, and other assistance exercises. Flexibility work would also be included at this time with most of the flexibility training being passive or with a partner. The Soviets work more on dynamic flexibility, which, as you will see later on, plays a major role in my training program. Cardiorespiratory endurance work is mostly done thru LSD (long slow distance) training. However, for bigger athletes the decision to assign distance work is based on the position they play, so that offensive linemen, among others, do not participate.

The position-specific work would mainly focus on general football skills. This would include receivers running routs, offensive linemen working pass sets, linebackers working pass drops, quarterbacks working three-, five-, and seven-step drops, defensive backs working on the backpedal, and defensive linemen working on their swim and rip techniques. These sessions would be broken down into position groups kept as small as possible.

The generalized preparatory phase would last three to four months and would finish after spring practice. The Soviets believed that the higher the level of player, the less time should be spent on this phase of training with more time spent on the specialized preparation phase.

Specialized Preparatory

In this period, the exercises closely duplicate the actual movements done on the field. This phase is often called the period of specificity and is the critical phase that I have been doing with my professional athletes for the past sixteen years. There is no better way to make our athletes better at the skills they use on the field than through movement-specific training. During this phase, the intensity of the exercises increases and the volume of work decreases. The change from high volume–low intensity to low volume–high intensity occurs over a period of time at the end of the generalized preparatory phase. This adjustment in training is called transition.

Specialized strength work in this period would be geared toward the specific movements performed on the field. For example, we would use the Vertimax (explained in detail in Chapter 10) for lower body explosion, along with step-ups for hip drive, explosive squats, plyometrics, and other drills that mimic position specificity. Each position would have exercises that are designed to enhance a player's movement. Some of the kettle bell movements popular today were used for position movements such as throwing action for the quarterbacks or the hang pull to the top of the head with a toe raise. Again, all the strength movements would resemble the player's actions on the field.

Another technique used by the Soviets is drop, or strip, sets. On the bench press, for example, an athlete would load the bar with 110 percent of the determined max and then decrease the weight incrementally on the down phase 10 to 15 percent and include the concentric or muscle shortening type contraction. Upon the athlete reaching the bottom position,

30 percent of the weight would be stripped off and the bar held for a six-second count, after which the bar would be pressed up at 80 percent of the determined max for the concentric contraction. This type of strength work can be used for most compound lifts.

In this phase, specialized agility exercises would be used. Most of the agility work would consist of multiple changes of direction that include acceleration and deceleration, as well as backward, forward, and diagonal movements. Again, by working the body in a 360-degree circle, you are forcing the body to adapt to multiple movement patterns. Flexibility in this phase would consist of both dynamic and static stretching. Dynamic ballistic flexibility is used to warm up the core, and static stretching is used to cool down after exertion. Speed work would be introduced in this phase. It would include acceleration, deceleration, sprints, and linear and interval training. Some types of endurance work would be included; however, most of the work would be dedicated to speed development. Most of the high-intensity work would be done toward the end of the specialized preparation phase.

The most exciting portion of this phase of the Soviet training program was the power (speed-strength) training. This type of training would be phased in over a short period of time. The athlete must have a good power base for this type of training. Some of the exercises used in this phase are box jumps, jumps out of the squat, and jump downs. These exercises would be done holding dumbbells or an Olympic bar. After several weeks, explosive movements such as depth jumps, also known as plyometrics, would be incorporated.

The word *plyometric* is derived from the Greek word *plethyein*. This word means to increase strength and isometric tension. Plyometric training develops the ability of fast-twitch muscle fiber to produce powerful movements. It works on utilizing the stretch reflex reaction in a muscle. Many athletes have great strength; however, they can't seem to transfer that strength to the playing field. The physiological principle of plyometrics is founded on the idea of making the muscle lengthen and shorten quickly, resulting in a much stronger contraction than if the muscle had started in its normal resting position. This type of stretch-shortening action causes the muscles to store more elastic energy. Due to this action, the transfer from the stretching phase to the lengthening phase happens very rapidly, in turn producing more power. In other words, as soon as the athlete lands, hits, or catches, he immediately jumps, pushes away, or throws. With this foundation of all-around specialized training, athletes would be prepared to play at the highest level.

Competitive (In-Season)

During this period, no additional work would be done to enhance strength or speed. However, the in-season workouts should be of high enough intensity to maintain the work gained in the off-season and the general preparatory phase. The Soviets are firm believers in restorative-rehabilitative programs. They believe that this type of training is as important as the speed-strength cycles of training. Some of the methods that are used with their athletes are steam, hot and cold therapy, massage therapy, saunas, and hyperbaric chambers. The connection might be made that the Soviets would treat their athletes like thoroughbred race horses.

Russian Debriefing

As I left the U.S.S.R., I had a definite clarity of mind and purpose about what I needed to do in terms of training my athletes. It made so much sense to me. Train like you play! If you want to be explosive, you must train explosively. Sport and position specificity was the answer. The Russians had already figured that out. I just needed to figure out how to incorporate these Russian training principles into my own performance training equation.

One Sunday after church, I sat down and wrote out a six-week speed and strength program based on what I had learned in Russia. Little did I know that after sixteen years working with more than six hundred NFL players, I would still be using that basic training program to get maximum results from my athletes. With my Russian-based training program, I've had the opportunity to impact, influence, and affect the lives and careers of scores of NFL, college, and high school players.

2

The Ballistic Warm-Up

Getting Yourself Ready to Play

Trying to work muscles that are not properly stretched can result in a variety of undesirable effects. Two of the more critical areas of concern involve hindering the range of motion and preventing an athlete from achieving maximum potential. By incorporating flexibility training into your daily workout, you're making your muscles more pliable and less likely to strain, or even tear, when they are in a torque position.

The following comparison is the best example I can give for the effects of a cold muscle placed immediately under athletic duress. If you leave a rubber band in the refrigerator overnight and then take it out the next morning and immediately start stretching the band past its normal range of motion, the rubber band will certainly snap. But if you gradually start stretching the band a little at a time, it will begin to warm up. Over a short period of time, you can stretch the rubber band way past its normal range of motion. This principle is called muscle viscosity. As the blood flow to the muscle increases, it will warm the muscle up and make it more flexible.

Dynamic Flexibility

Before you start any sports activity, workout, or competition, you must go through a warm-up and flexibility period. This will increase your range of motion and reduce your chance of sustaining injury. The objective is to become warmed and flexible and, at the same time, to improve your athletic skills through rehearsing the activities you do on the field.

The motions of the flex runs and skips also teach your body the correct mechanics of fast motion. Dynamic flexibility is a series of bounds, hops, skips, runs, and ballistic stretches that warm up the core. The order of exercises should begin with the most basic of low-intensity exercises and steadily progress to the more complex movements that replicate actual practice or sport-specific movements.

Start with a gradual progression of dynamic movements (detailed later in this chapter), such as joint mobility (ankle bounds, arm swings, walking lunges, arm sweeps, etc.), and progress to ballistic stretches (knee hugs, Russian walks, Frankenstein walks, etc.). Then you'll move on to flex runs and skipping (high knee skips, fast skips, skip and paw, back skips, form runs, etc.). Next, I suggest working on multidirectional movements (carioca, tapioca, side skips, lateral shuffle, etc.) and finishing with work on power and compound moves (lateral bounds, skater bounds, step squats/tapioca, etc.).

In other words, make sure you break a sweat! This type of warm-up is what I recommend for all my athletes to use before workouts and game situations.

Program Implementation

A multitude of factors dictate how much and how long the dynamic and ballistic warm-ups last. I will adjust the drills, time, and intensity of the dynamic warm-up based on the age and general conditioning of the athlete I'm training. It typically takes between fifteen and thirty minutes from start to finish. On cold days, I might take a little longer. On linear speed days, I might add a few more dynamic drills to warm the muscles that keep your sprint flexibility.

On Tuesdays and Fridays, I add a training aid that I invented called the Chip-O-Meter. It adds resistance effects to the extension of the leg and overspeed effects on flexion of the leg. I will explain the Chip-O-Meter later in this chapter. On heavy resistance days, I might use an X-vest to load the body during the warm-up phase. The presence of added weight in the X-vest, which slips on the athlete like a regular vest, teaches the body to respond to increased resistance. The added weight also quickly warms up the core. I always finish the drills with contrast. That's where you take off the training aid (such as a vest) and do a combination of movements without the added weight. Basically, we trick the brain into thinking that the muscles have to fire harder to overcome the added resistance. Your body will respond by recruiting fast-twitch fibers that will fire sooner, making you quicker and stronger over time.

I also will add partner ballistic drills on cold days. I usually attach a short cord to both players. One player does the drill down the field one way, and his partner does the same drill back. Each player gives minimal resistance with the cords. When we have completed all of the drills, we add contrast and you get the same effect as you do with the weight vest. Following is the order of ballistic stretches I recommend.

Note: All these dynamic drills should be done at a distance of twenty-five yards each way. You can condense this area to quicken the warm-up by going down one way with a drill and coming back with another.

1. Ankle Bounds

Purpose: To flex the ankles and prepare the body to become sprint-flexible

Drill: The athlete will keep his legs locked and bound out using only the flexion of his ankles. He will swing both arms up and out at the same time, taking little bunny hops.

Chip's Tips

1. *Keep legs straight and flex at the ankles (bunny hops).*
2. *Pump your arms up.*
3. *Dorsey-flex your toes.*

2. Knee Hugs *(See Figure 2.1.)*

Purpose: To warm the hips and shoulders and stretch the hamstrings, glutes, quads, and shoulders

Drill: Knee hugs are performed with the athlete exploding off his front foot driving the opposite knee up to his chest while grabbing the knee and pulling the knee tight, creating separation. This drill works on stride lengthening.

Chip's Tips

1. *Pressing on the ball of your foot, lift and pull the opposite knee to the chest as high as possible.*
2. *Grab your knee and pull it up tight.*

Figure 2.1. Knee Hugs

3. Walking Lunges *(See Figure 2.2.)*

Purpose: To stretch the hip flexors, hamstrings, quads, glutes, and calves

Drill: Walking lunges are performed by alternating each step out at a 90-degree angle. The trail knee should lightly touch the ground, alternating legs on each step. Make sure the knee does not extend over your toes.

Chip's Tips

1. *Make sure you keep your knee in a straight line at 90 degrees. Do not let it extend over your toes.*
2. *Keep your hands behind your head when you stride out.*
3. *Drive your knee up as high as possible and out on the extension of your leg.*
4. *Keep your head up and your back straight.*
5. *Stand up, pressing your hips forward, and repeat the motion.*

4. Russian Walks *(See Figure 2.3.)*

Purpose: To stretch the hamstrings, low back, and shoulder

Drill: This drill starts by having the athlete march with his legs moving only from the hip. When the front leg swings out, the athlete will clap his hands under the swing leg, alternating with each step.

Chip's Tips

1. *March like a Russian solider, with a clap under your hamstrings.*
2. *Keep your extended leg as parallel as possible to the ground.*
3. *Explode off your front foot.*

Figure 2.2. Walking Lunges with Shackles

Figure 2.3. Russian Walks

Figure 2.4a. Walking Sweeps   b.   2.5. Frankenstein Walks

5. Walking Sweeps *(See Figures 2.4a and 2.4b.)*

Purpose: To stretch the glutes, hamstrings, hip flexors, low back, and shoulders

Drill: This drill is performed much like walking lunges with the exception that each lunge step is done after taking two steps and instead of having your hands locked behind your head, you will sweep the ground with both hands in sync with your lunge.

Chip's Tips

1. Keep hips low to the ground.
2. Take slow, long steps while sweeping the ground with your hands.

6. Frankenstein Walks *(See Figure 2.5.)*

Purpose: To warm up the hip flexors and shoulders

Drill: The athlete starts out by keeping his hands in front of his body while he alternates driving his knees up and down outside the body.

Chip's Tips

1. Keep your hands out straight, like Frankenstein.
2. Drive your leg up on the outside of your hands.

7. Power Skips *(See Figure 2.6.)*

Purpose: To warm the hip flexors in a ballistic manner; form skip with high knee action and long arm swings

Drill: On this drill, the athlete will explode off the front foot, propelling him up and out as far as he can while exaggerating his arm swings.

Chip's Tips

1. Drive your lead leg up as high as possible.
2. Exaggerate your arm swing.
3. Concentrate on height instead of distance.
4. Be as explosive as possible.

Figure 2.6. Power Skips

8. Fast Skips

Purpose: To teach the body how to move more efficiently

Drill: Fast skips are done much like power skips with the exception that the skips are short and fast with rapid arm swings while staying on the balls of your feet.

Chip's Tips

1. Take short skips at a fast pace.
2. Land lightly on the balls of your feet.
3. Rapid arm swing and elbow snap help with knee lift and drive.

9. Butt Kicks

Purpose: To warm the quads and start the ballistics stretch of the running motion

Drill: The athlete uses a fast run while exaggerating the rapid leg action, bringing the heel up to the butt while maintaining a quick arm action.

Chip's Tips

1. Use rapid leg action and a heel to butt motion.
2. Use quick arm action and swing arms from cheek to back pocket.

Figure 2.7a. Back Skips   b.   c.

10. Back Skips *(See Figures 2.7a, 2.7b, and 2.7c.)*

Purpose: To warm up the hip flexors, quads, and calves

Drill: While moving backward, the athlete will drive his hips up, out, and down while alternating each leg and taking a short skipping action.

Chip's Tips

1. Open your hips out and down in a backward motion.
2. Stay on the balls of your feet.

11. Side Skips with Crossover *(See Figures 2.8a and 2.8b.)*

Purpose: To stretch the abductors, adductors, low back, quads, glutes, and hips

Drill: Side skips are done much like the carioca step (see page 17), but they are done with a lateral skip and crossover step while swinging your arms across your body, keeping your center of gravity low.

Chip's Tips

1. Keep your center of gravity low.
2. Skip laterally, crossing the left over the right.
3. Work on hip rotation by swinging your arms across your body.
4. Keep your shoulders square.

Figure 2.8a. Side Skips with Crossover

b.

Figure 2.9. Skips and Kicks

12. Skips and Kicks *(See Figure 2.9.)*

Purpose: To teach the body to process multiple movements quickly; kick out while skipping and pawing the ground

Drill: This drill is performed much like the fast skip, with the exception that the lead leg will paw the ground toward you, prancing like a horse. Alternate your arm swings, opposite foot, opposite hand.

Chip's Tips

1. Cycle your lead leg, pawing the ground toward you.
2. Use butt-kick action on the cycle leg.
3. Always alternate your legs.
4. Do not karate kick; prance like a horse.

13. Form Runs *(See Figure 2.10.)*

Purpose: To mimic proper running mechanics and to stretch your hip flexors, hamstrings, glutes, calves, and quads

Drill: The athlete will maintain a good forward lean while driving the knees up and down in a slow, controlled running motion. He should drive his elbows in a fast cheek-to-back-pocket arm action.

Chip's Tips

1. Use good forward lean.
2. Use fast arm action and swing arms from cheek to back pocket.
3. Use explosive hip drive, like a piston.

14. Carioca *(See Figures 2.11a and 2.11b.)*

Purpose: To stretch the abductors, adductors, low back, quads, glutes, and hips

Drill: The athlete will start by keeping his center of gravity low while running laterally, crossing his right foot over his left foot, bringing his trail leg through and crossing his lead leg behind the trail leg. His arms should swing across his body.

Chip's Tips

1. Stand sideways, keeping your center of gravity low.
2. Run laterally, crossing your right foot over the left foot, bringing your trail leg through and crossing your lead leg behind the trail leg.
3. Try and keep your shoulders square.

Figure 2.10. Form Runs

Figure 2.11a. Carioca

b.

15. Tapioca *(See Figure 2.12.)*

Purpose: To stretch the abductors, adductors, low back, quads, glutes, and hips

Drill: The tapioca drill is performed exactly like the carioca drill except that the athlete takes as many fast short steps as he can.

Chip's Tips

1. Take as many steps as possible.
2. Take quick steps.
3. The last athlete to finish the drill wins!

16. Lateral Bounds *(See Figure 2.13.)*

Purpose: To work on lateral explosion

Drill: The athlete will bound laterally, pushing off his outside leg, landing on the inside leg.

Chip's Tips

1. Alternate leg hops, lifting knee to chest using arms.
2. Push off the outside leg, landing on the inside leg.
3. Work on balance; hit, get set, and explode again.

Figure 2.12. Tapioca

Figure 2.13. Lateral Bounds

17. Form Runs and Sprint

Purpose: To work on sprinting mechanics with multitask

Drill: This drill is the same as form runs except that after fifteen yards of doing form runs, the athlete will sprint the remaining distance.

Chip's Tips

1. Use good high-knee leg and arm action for five yards, and then sprint for ten more.

Ballistic Warm-Up: The Bottom Line

Remember, warm up to stretch, and don't stretch to warm up. A good ballistic warm-up will enhance your body's ability to process the speed and change of its movements by:

- Increasing the core body temperature and reducing muscle tightness
- Increasing your range of motion by dynamically stretching the hips and the muscles that move you in a complete circle
- Increasing muscle and ligament elasticity
- Increasing your neural facilitation (i.e., your brain's ability to fire rapidly by forcing your body to move in different patterns)

A few years back, I was training a current NFL player who passed out during the ballistic warm-up. When he came to, he said, "That's the hardest workout that I've ever done." I didn't have the heart to tell him that he had only completed the warm-up.

The Chip-O-Meter: Training Aid of the Pros

The Chip-O-Meter is a harness that fits over your shoulders and attaches to your feet. It was named by the Duke University athletes who first experienced the pain and performance results it provided them. It has adjustable tubing that goes from the back of the foot to your lower glutes. Through the combination of the foot and glute connecting points, the Chip-O-Meter forces you to stay on your toes for the duration of the exercise. This concept is a lot like strength shoes but without the stress on your Achilles tendon. It also keeps you in a stretch reflex by shortening the Achilles, so when you take off the Chip-O-Meter after a period of use, your feet basically explode off the ground. This action is a result of the overspeed in the flexion of the hamstring. Overspeed is the process of training your body to go beyond its normal maximum speed by forcing faster motions through a variety of unnatural activities: running downhill, being pulled by a bungee cord, or using any other artificial means. Training with overspeed creates muscle memory so that your body learns to expect faster motions. By doing set patterns and increasing the level of difficulty, you also force a specific neuromuscular response. Another positive benefit of the Chip-O-Meter is that it helps warm your core muscles and lower body by creating muscle viscosity, which is the warming of the muscles by providing greater blood flow to an area in a short amount of time.

The Chip-O-Meter and Your Sport

Warm-ups and on-field drills can be done with the Chip-O-Meter. Linebackers can do their pass drops, scrapes, fills, and backpedals. Use your imagination with your athletes. You can find new creative ways to make them work harder and smarter, with a decided emphasis on harder. As Matt Stinchcomb, lineman with the Tampa Bay Buccaneers and a frequent user of the Chip-O-Meter, has so eloquently stated, "Please burn the Chip-O-Meter!"

3

Quick Foot Ladder Drills

Fine-Tuning Coordination

The quick foot ladder works on the principle of developing general athletic skills, which are then transferred to sport-specific skills. At Competitive Edge Sports, my trainers and I time these ladder drills. Over the years, we have tested a host of players and have seen some exceptional times for certain drills. One of the drills that I will discuss in this chapter is the Icky shuffle. The pattern for this drill is in-in-out, in-in-out. Champ Bailey is the fastest football player I've ever clocked in the forty-yard dash. His time was 4.27 seconds. Champ also holds the Icky shuffle record at CES for football players, with a time of 5.4 seconds. This drill is universal for most football players. However, the benchmark time set by any athlete was 5.0 seconds by Jason Moore, a sixteen-year-old high school soccer player. Jason went on to play with the 1996 Olympic soccer team and currently plays professional soccer in the major leagues. I can't tell you how many players have challenged Champ's and Jason's times over the years to no avail.

One critical element to improving overall athletic performance is teaching the neurological system to activate more motor fibers. The more motor fibers a muscle uses, the more force it will have during contraction. A stronger muscle contraction equates to greater power output for speed and quickness and aids in a variety of functions that include joint stability, proprioception, movement dynamics, coordination, agility, and mobility. The ladder works by forcing your neurological system to send recruitment information to the muscles at a higher rate of speed, recruiting more motor fibers. This will create a quicker, faster, and more agile athlete, as well as contribute to the overall general conditioning of the athlete.

These ladder drills are very functional in teaching athletes comprehensive movement skills, and they're fun to do as well. I use a building block system of skill development that is important to the success of training with the quick foot ladders. Ladder drills should be mastered from a slow, controlled, beginning skill level and then increased gradually to a more advanced skill level. The movements should progress from smaller, quicker movements to a full range of movement skills. I progress my athletes from slow, controlled movements to fast, explosive movements as a teaching and learning progression. You'll have quicker success training with the ladder using this method. As soon as the drill becomes reflexive in nature, it's time to advance to the next ladder progressions.

Four Basic Movement Skills

We emphasize four basic movement skills with the ladders: runs, skips, lateral shuffles, and hops/jumps. When I train athletes on the ladders, I always start with these progressions. The ladder in question has plastic rungs held together with nylon webbing, much like an escape ladder. It is placed on the floor so that the space between and outside the rungs is the primary exercise area. Taped-out boxes measuring twelve inches by twelve inches could suffice as an adequate substitute. I begin the training program using a full range-of-motion runs and skips. When an athlete does these first, his body's muscle memory system learns to accept these basic skills. Once the skill is learned, the athlete can then work on improving the speed of the drill. Athletes must always remember to learn the skills slowly and then add speed with control. Once control is lost, the athlete is no longer developing skill but rather is practicing for performance failure. It is crucial to practice all four basic skills for the simple fact that athletes need stimulus variation. Each skill aids in varying motor fiber recruitment and is important to the learning process.

Program Implementation

By breaking your ladder workout into reps and sets, you are maximizing your skill and athletic movement. Make sure that you follow the prescribed order of drills. Random order is not beneficial. Progression of movement is significant. For linear drills, I have my players go up the ladder and back down, practicing the same drill. That constitutes two reps: one up and one back. It usually takes an athlete a couple of times to learn the basic foot patterns. At that point, most athletes will master the drill and can move on to increasing the speed of the drill. For lateral foot drills, four repetitions is ideal because each side of your body should be unilaterally trained using two reps. Down and back is one rep for lateral foot drills because each side of the body has to be trained to complete the movement cycle. I use the quick foot ladders four days per week. Typically, I select a minimum of two drills out of the four basic skill sets for the player's training session. And in reality, one set of each drill is usually sufficient.

Position-Specific Application of the Quick Foot Ladder

For position-specific work on the ladders, I try and match the foot patterns with those used on the football field. In other words, the movements you do at your position on the field are duplicated with the movements on the ladder.

For athletes who spend most of their time on linear movements (this would include wide receivers, running backs, tight ends, and defensive backs), I place emphasis on form runs, skips, resistance runs with cords, hand weights, weight vest, and Chip-O-Meters. I also have players spend time doing sprints into and out of the ladders. This works on stride frequency by forcing the player to take short, choppy steps. Players work on stride lengthening by sprinting out of the ladder. Foot quickness is developed by having the player use different foot patterns, limiting the amount of time the foot is actually touching the ground. In other words, step lightly and quickly. This reinforces positive foot interaction with the ground.

For football positions that focus on lateral movements (this would include defensive linemen, linebackers, and offensive linemen), I would place most of the emphasis on lateral movement and agility drills. These positions depend on short bursts of intense speed. The player should work on first-step explosion drills, for example, one in from the side. The player would concentrate on driving the lead foot into the ladder box and staying under control while moving laterally. This particular movement would simulate a drive or angle block on a defender.

Quick Foot Ladder Drills

1. Ankle Bounds/Bunny Hops *(See Figure 3.1.)*

Purpose: To work on ankle flexibility with balance and to warm up the upper body with fast arm swings

Drill: Perform two-foot jumps in each of the ladder squares, keeping feet together as if one and making sure the heels never touch the ground.

Chip's Tips

1. *Explode off the balls of your feet.*
2. *Keep your center of gravity over the ladder.*
3. *The faster your hands move, the faster your feet will move; make sure both hands move together to minimize foot contact time.*
4. *Bound out and not up.*

2. High Knee Skips *(See Figure 3.2.)*

Purpose: To teach the body to move explosively with proper mechanics

Drill: Start with feet together. Skip into the first ladder box with lead foot keeping good forward lean; alternate feet throughout drill, driving each foot up and down in an explosive manner.

Chip's Tips

1. *Make sure to use a rapid arm motion; this will help with knee lift and drive.*
2. *Make sure your arm drive is in an opposite hand–opposite leg motion.*
3. *Stay on the balls of your feet.*
4. *Fast hands make for fast feet.*

3. Fast Skips *(See Figure 3.3.)*

Purpose: To teach rapid hand-foot motion and body control through a range of activities

Figure 3.1. Ankle Bounds/Bunny Hops with Chip-O-Meter

Figure 3.2. High Knee Skips with Chip-O-Meter

Figure 3.3. Fast Skips with Chip-O-Meter

Drill: This drill is the same as the high knee skip except the skip is only two to three inches off the ground and the arms are used in a rhythm with the feet, in a fast motion. Maintain good forward lean and stay light on the balls of your feet.

Chip's Tips

1. Concentrate on an explosive arm drive. Snap your elbows as quickly as possible in rhythm with your feet.
2. Keep a good forward lean.
3. Keep your step close and low to the ground.
4. Keep your knee over your toe.

4. Form Runs with One Foot In

Purpose: To warm the body up, increase flexibility, and decrease the chance of injury

Drill: Facing the ladder, sprint through the ladder with each foot striking every other box. Keep your knee lifted to midheight, stay light on your feet, and move your arms in a rapid motion.

Chip's Tips

1. Stay on the balls of your feet.
2. Keep a good forward lean.
3. Make sure you complete the drill, don't skip rungs, and stay under control.
4. Remember, the faster your arms move, the faster your feet will move.

5. Form Runs with Two Feet In

Purpose: To teach the body proper running mechanics at a fast pace (These runs will improve general athletic skills.)

Drill: Start by facing the ladder in the same direction as high knee form runs. Instead of one foot in every other box, both feet will strike the same box. Always lead with the same foot, followed by the trail foot. The cadence is in-in, in-in.

Chip's Tips

1. Slow the tempo until you find the right rhythm.
2. Pump your arms in rhythm with your feet.
3. Keep your head up and eyes straight ahead.
4. Sprint out after the last box.

6. Lateral Runs with Two Feet In *(See Figures 3.4a and 3.4b.)*

Purpose: To move the body in a lateral motion, working on adduction and abduction (You are forcing the body to move laterally and under control.)

Drill: Start by facing laterally, with one foot in the box and one foot out. Step into the next box with the lead foot, bringing the trail foot into the box the lead foot just left. Continue to the end of the ladder. The cadence is in-in-out-in-out-in, in-in-out-in-out-in.

Chip's Tips

1. Make sure that your hands are moving front to back as you move your body laterally.
2. Stay on the balls of your feet.
3. Keep your center of gravity in the center of the box.
4. Never cross your feet.

7. Lateral Runs with One Foot In *(See Figure 3.5.)*

Purpose: To train the feet to respond to forward explosive movements from a lateral position

Drill: Start by facing the ladder from the side. Step in the first box with one foot. Use an explosive exaggerated step with the lead foot as the trail foot stays outside the box. The cadence is in-out-out, in-out-out.

Figure 3.4a. Lateral Runs with Two Feet In with Chip-O-Meter

b.

Figure 3.5. Lateral Runs with One Foot In with Chip-O-Meter

Chip's Tips

1. Concentrate on keeping your hips low.

2. Move your hands front to back in rhythm with your feet.

3. You determine your lead foot by the direction you go—that is, step right–go right, step left–go left.

8. Icky Shuffle *(See Figures 3.6a, 3.6b, and 3.6c.)*

Purpose: To teach complex foot patterns and to force a neuromuscular firing to teach the feet to respond to complex instructions from the brain through multifoot contacts and multiple change of direction

Drill: Stand and face the end of the ladder on either the right or left side. Step in the first box with the lead foot followed by the trail foot stepping in the same box. Repeat the motion to the end of the ladder. When starting on the right side, step with the right foot. When starting on the left side, step with the left foot. The cadence is in-in-out, in-in-out.

Chip's Tips

1. Stay light on your feet.

2. Cut in a zigzag motion.

3. This cadence is the basis for any on field change of direction.

Note: In case you haven't noticed, I'm giving you specific verbal cadences for each complex foot pattern drill. It's extremely important that you use these word cues by repeating them aloud each and every time you do the drills until your feet have mastered the drills. This is a way to verbally command your feet to master the drill.

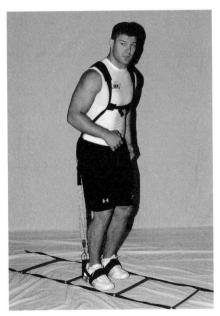

Figure 3.6a. Icky Shuffle with Chip-O-Meter

b.

c.

9. Crossover Icky *(See Figures 3.7a, 3.7b, 3.7c, and 3.7d.)*

Purpose: To increase hip rotation and flexibility and to work on coordination and balance

Drill: Start by facing the ladder on either the right or left side. Step across the ladder and into the box with your outside foot. Then step outside the box with your trail foot followed by the lead foot. Repeat the pattern for the length of the ladder. This complex movement is like a dance step. The cadence is in-out-out, in-out-out.

Chip's Tips

1. Rotate the hips while staying under control.
2. Drive the arms across the body to enhance hip rotation.
3. Stay in rhythm throughout the drill.
4. Work on driving the hips up and down explosively.

10. Two In from the Front *(See Figures 3.8a, 3.8b, 3.8c, and 3.8d.)*

Purpose: To increase hip rotation and flexibility and to work on coordination and balance by moving in a linear motion

Drill: Start by facing the middle of the ladder. Step into the first box with the lead foot followed by the trail foot into the same box. Step outside the ladder with the lead foot and step outside

Figure 3.7a. Crossover Icky with Chip-O-Meter   b.   c.   d.

Figure 3.8a. Two In from the
Front with Chip-O-Meter

b.

c.

d.

the ladder with the trail foot. Step back into the second box with
the lead foot followed by the trail foot into the same box and so
on. The cadence is in-in-out-out, in-in-out-out.

Chip's Tips

1. Maintain good forward lean.
2. Stay light on the toes.
3. Focus on speed of stride frequency.
4. Fast hand movement equals fast foot movement.

11. Slalom

Purpose: To improve lateral speed and foot quickness

Drill: Start by facing the ladder with one foot inside the first box
and the other foot outside the box. Jump to the next box in a
diagonal pattern, alternating the outside and inside foot. Zigzag
the length of the ladder as if snow skiing.

Chip's Tips

1. Keep your hips low.
2. Stay on the balls of your feet.
3. Use your arm swing to propel you forward.
4. Stay under control.

12. Quick Hips

Purpose: To develop flexibility, hip explosion, and foot quickness

Drill: Face the side of the ladder with your lead foot in the first box and your trail foot outside the box. Swivel your hips and replace the lead foot with the trail foot in the box. The lead foot will land outside the box. Swivel your hips in the opposite direction and alternate foot placement.

Chip's Tips

1. Stay on the balls of your feet.
2. Rotate your hips by using your upper body momentum.
3. Keep your shoulders square.

13. Two In from the Side

Purpose: To work on multiple foot contacts in a rapid-fire motion

Drill: Face the side of the ladder and move laterally. Step into the box with your lead foot followed by your trail foot. Take two steps into each box and two steps out of each box with the lead and trail foot. The cadence is in-in-out-out, in-in-out-out.

Chip's Tips

1. Stay on the balls of your feet.
2. Pump your arms front to back.
3. Stay light on your feet.
4. Keep your eyes focused straight ahead.

Ladder Drills: The Bottom Line

The ladder is a great training aid. I use it daily to assist me in fast-twitch muscle fiber recruitment. It's a fun tool to use for developing foot speed, agility, coordination, plyometric movements, acceleration, deceleration, cutting, first-step explosion, and general conditioning. There are no mistakes on the ladder, only new drill inventions. A lot of my drills have been developed by players who did not quite master an intended drill but improvised and created their own version. Part of the success of any drill is the fun factor. The quick foot ladders have unlimited potential for creating excitement and variety. My players love it when I crank up the music. It's amazing how many dance steps get incorporated into these drills. Every time I use the quick foot ladders, we seem to qualify a new contestant for "Dancing with the Stars."

Ladder Workout: Progressions: Six Weeks

Week 1

Days 1 and 3	Days 2 and 4
Ankle Bounds	Chip-O-Meters
High Knee Skips	Ankle Bounds
Fast Skips	High Knee Skips
Form Runs: 1 In	Fast Skips
Form Runs: 2 In	Form Runs: 1 In
Lateral: 2 In	Form Runs: 2 In
	Lateral: 2 In
	Contrast
	High Knee Skips
	Lateral: 2 In
	5 Tuck Jumps

Week 2

Days 1 and 3	Days 2 and 4
Ankle Bounds	Chip-O-Meters
High Knee Skips	Ankle Bounds
Fast Skips	High Knee Skips
Form Runs: 1 In	Fast Skips
Form Runs: 2 In	Form Runs: 1 In
Lateral: 2 In	Form Runs: 2 In
Quick Hips	Lateral: 2 In
1 In from the Side	Contrast
	High Knee Skips
	Lateral: 2 In
	5 Tuck Jumps

Week 3

Days 1 and 3	Days 2 and 4
Ankle Bounds	Chip-O-Meters
High Knee Skips	Ankle Bounds
Fast Skips	High Knee Skips
Form Runs: 1 In	Fast Skips
Form Runs: 2 In	Form Runs: 1 In
Lateral: 2 In	Form Runs: 2 In
Quick Hips	Lateral: 2 In
1 In from the Side	Contrast
Icky Shuffle	High Knee Skips
Crossover Icky	Lateral: 2 In
	5 Tuck Jumps

Week 4

Days 1 and 3
Weight Vest

Days 2 and 4
Chip-O-Meters

Days 1, 2, 3, and 4
Ankle Bounds
High Knee Skips
Fast Skips
Form Runs: 1 In
Form Runs: 2 In
Lateral: 2 In

Week 5

Days 1 and 3
Weight Vest

Days 2 and 4
Chip-O-Meters

Days 1, 2, 3, and 4
Ankle Bounds
High Knee Skips
Fast Skips
Form Runs: 1 In
Form Runs: 2 In
Lateral: 2 In

Week 6

Days 1 and 3
Weight Vest

Days 2 and 4
Chip-O-Meters
Hand Weights

Days 1, 2, 3, and 4
Ankle Bounds
High Knee Skips
Fast Skips
Form Runs: 1 In
Form Runs: 2 In
Lateral: 2 In

Days 1, 2, 3, and 4	Days 1, 2, 3, and 4	Days 1, 2, 3, and 4
Quick Hips	Quick Hips	Quick Hips
1 In from the Side	1 In from the Side	1 In from the Side
Icky Shuffle	Icky Shuffle	Icky Shuffle
Crossover Icky Slalom	Crossover Icky Slalom	Crossover Icky Slalom
	2 In from the Front	2 In from the Front
	2 In from the Side	2 In from the Side
Contrast	Contrast	Contrast

Day 1	Day 1	Day 1
Fast Skips	High Knee Skips	Form Runs: 1 In
Icky Shuffle	Icky Shuffle	1 In from the Side

Day 2	Day 2	Day 2
High Knee Form Runs	High Knee Form Runs	Icky Shuffle
Lateral: 2 In	Lateral: 2 In	Lateral: 2 In
	Release Hand Weights	Release Hand Weights

Day 3	Day 3	Day 3
1 In from the Side	Icky Shuffle	High Knee Skips
Crossover Icky	High Knee Skips	Form Runs: 2 In

Day 4	Day 4	Day 4
High Knee Skips	Form Runs	High Knee Skips
Icky Shuffle	Lateral Runs: 2 In	Lateral Runs: 1 In from the Side
	Release Hand Weights	Release Hand Weights

4

Stretching and Flexibility

Getting Warm, Then Loose

Stretching and flexibility are an integral part of my training program. In this chapter, I will discuss different types of stretching as well as the implementation of each. However, static partner stretching will be my main focus. Although there are numerous stretching varieties, I implement two of the more common and user-friendly types. Dynamic and static stretching, when used together, have given my athletes tremendous results with increased range of motion, flexibility, and injury prevention. I use a systematic approach to flexibility training that is time-efficient and is in synch with the design of my overall speed and strength program. One of the common problems I notice with my college and professional athletes is that they're usually very tight in the hips and hamstrings. I attribute this tightness to heavy lifting (that is, squats) with little or no stretching afterward to lengthen the heavily contracted muscles. Over time heavy contraction of a muscle reduces the range of motion and invites tightness. Eliminating this tightness and increasing range of motion can greatly increase speed and quickness, while reducing the chance for injury.

Dynamic Stretching

A dynamic stretch is a movement or an exercise that gradually increases the range of motion of a certain muscle or muscle group while also increasing core body temperature, muscular temperature, and blood flow to the extremities. I touched on this type of stretching in the ballistics chapter. I use dynamic stretching as a warm-up before beginning a running program. Dynamic stretching, unlike certain other forms of stretching, can be used every day during training. Dynamic stretching should be performed until a light sweat is broken, which indicates the athlete is warmed up and ready to run. It's important to remember that when performing dynamic stretches, the athlete should start out doing slow and small motions, gradually increasing to larger and faster ones. An example of this method would be performing Russian walks. The athlete is going to kick the leg out in front of the body until a slight stretch is felt in the hamstring. These kicks should increase in height as the muscle is loosened up and more range of motion is achieved. Moving too fast too quickly can cause injury, so it's very important to start out slow and work at a comfortable pace.

Static Stretching

A static stretch is actually holding a stretch in a given position for a given amount of time. When I use static stretches with my athletes, I usually hold each stretch between eight and fifteen seconds. This time varies due to flexibility in the muscle stretched as well as feedback from the athlete. Breathing is very important when doing static stretches. Proper breathing relaxes the body and helps remove toxins from the muscles. When performing static stretches, the athlete must exhale and relax as he is eased into the hold position. Static stretches should always be done after a thorough warm-up.

I usually implement static stretches following my running sessions. This is a great time to assist my athletes in the mental and physical demands of their transition into the weight room. The static stretching transition time accomplishes many goals. Here are two examples of the many. First, it allows for a cool-down period immediately following intense running and speed exercises. This is an important phase for the body to rid itself of as much lactic acid and other wastes produced during intense anaerobic activity as possible. Second, I stretch my athletes after running and before lifting so that the body is prepared to be as limber and flexible as possible for the intense lifting in the weight room.

The Stretching and Flexibility Routine

The following paragraphs discuss how to properly perform partner stretches and the benefits each stretch will provide. I follow the same routine, every time, with every player. This is important for a number of reasons. I want to make sure that each muscle can be stretched to the farthest point without other muscles inhibiting the range of motion. For example, if I'm going to stretch my chest without stretching my arms first, then my arms may be a limiting factor in how much range of motion I can achieve in my chest. When stretching after an intense running workout, many of the smaller "limiting" muscles are already loose and do not need as much attention. For example, the lower back and hips should be fairly loose due to all the agility movements; so they will not be as much of a limiting factor as they would at other times. The same applies for the calves and many of the other smaller muscle groups.

When performing partner stretches, it's just as important that the partner knows how to stretch to reduce the chance of injury. Here are a few simple rules and guidelines to follow to ensure maximum results with minimal risk.

Chip's Tips for Proper Stretching

1. **Communicate with your partner often.** Pay attention to what your partner is saying and to his body language relating to the stretch. If he screams, let off. If he asks you to push harder, then apply more pressure.

2. **Never use rapid, forceful movements.** This will hurt and can cause serious injury.

3. **Always ease into and out of a stretch.** Increase force gradually and evenly until desired stretch is achieved, and then start the eight- to fifteen-second count. When letting off of a stretch, it is just as important to release evenly and gradually into the relaxed position.

4. **Stretching should *not* be painful.** Always stretch to a point of comfortable tension. Remember that the point at which maximum stretch is felt may increase as flexibility and range of motion increases.

5. **Remember to breathe.** As I stated earlier, breathing will help remove toxins and relax the muscles.

6. **Use common sense.** Stretching is not rocket science, but injuries can occur if done improperly.

The following stretches should be done in the order they are listed. When two athletes are stretching each other, it's important for one athlete to complete the whole series of stretches first and then switch with the partner.

Lower Body and Back Stretches

1. Sit and Reach Stretch (low back, hamstrings, hips)

Athlete: Sit with both feet together, out in front of the body. Focus on keeping the chest out and the back straight. Reach as far as possible toward the toes without pain. Keep your knees as straight as possible.

Partner: While kneeling behind the athlete, place both hands in the middle of his back and gently push forward until he feels a comfortable stretch. To reduce the chance of low back strain, do not put hands higher than the middle of the back. Hold the stretch for eight to fifteen seconds, and then slowly release into a relaxed position.

2. Seated "V" Stretch (low back, hamstrings, hips)

Athlete: While seated, spread legs into a wide "V" shape. Lean toward the right leg while reaching for the right foot with both hands. Keep the back straight and chest out. Repeat same for the left leg. For the middle, place both hands between legs, reaching as far as possible while keeping correct posture.

Partner: Place your hands in the middle of the athlete's back and push him down toward his foot to a comfortable hold position. Remember to start counting when a comfortable hold position is achieved.

3. Butterfly Stretch (groin, hips, glutes) *(See Figure 4.1.)*

Athlete: While sitting, bring legs into the crotch as far as possible, with the soles of your feet together. Sit upright with hands holding feet together and elbows resting on the inside of the thighs. The glutes can be stretched if the athlete leans the body forward, as if he were going to put his nose on the ground.

Figure 4.1. Butterfly Stretch

Partner: Kneel behind the athlete and place hands on the inside of the athlete's knees. Apply gradual, increasing pressure on the knees toward the ground until a comfortable hold position is achieved. While stretching the glutes, the partner should move his hands from the athlete's knees and place them on his middle back, pushing the athlete's body forward toward the ground. It is important to communicate vocally, given that you are facing the athlete's back and cannot read facial expressions or body language.

Figure 4.2. Lying Hamstring Isolation Stretch

4. Lying Hamstring Isolation Stretch (hamstring)
(See Figure 4.2.)

Athlete: While lying on your back, raise the right leg as far back as it will go on your own power. Keep the left leg straight and hips flat on the floor. Slightly bend the right knee. Repeat same for the left leg.

Partner: While kneeling in front of the athlete, place one hand on the heel of his raised leg and the other hand on the opposite thigh, making sure that it does not raise off of the ground. Push his raised leg toward his head until a comfortable hold position is achieved. A bent knee is OK in this stretch as it will actually isolate the hamstring much better. Repeat same for the opposite leg.

5. Lying Knee to Chest Stretch (groin, hips, glutes)
(See Figure 4.3.)

Athlete: While lying on your back, bring your knee into your chest as close as possible.

Partner: Place the foot of the leg being stretched in the center of your chest. Hold the thigh of the opposite leg flat on the ground. Using your chest and bodyweight as leverage, slowly drive the athlete's knee into his chest until a comfortable hold position is achieved.

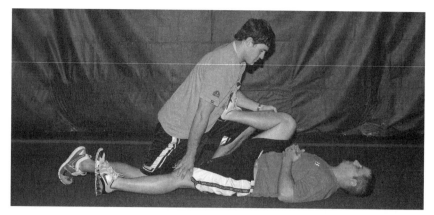

Figure 4.3. Lying Knee to Chest Stretch

6. Cross Body Hamstring and Hip Stretch (hamstring, hips, iliotibial band, glutes, low back) *(See Figures 4.4a and 4.4b.)*

Athlete: While lying on your back, cross your right leg across your body. Keep your hips and back flat on the ground. Keep your left leg straight.

Partner: With the athlete's right leg across his body, place your left foot on the floor just above his left kneecap. Put the athlete's right Achilles just below your right kneecap. Simply walk your foot up toward his head, keeping the leg straight. When the athlete's leg reaches the hold position, use your bent knee to fine-tune the appropriate hold angle. Hold this position for eight to fifteen seconds, as you stretch mostly the hamstrings and low back. Next, slide the athlete's Achilles down your shin until your ankles are touching, isolating the hips and iliotibial band. Hold this position for eight seconds. Then place the athlete's right foot against the inside of your right knee. Use your knee to drive the athlete's knee across and into his chest to isolate the groin and glutes. Hold this for eight to fifteen seconds. Repeat the same steps for the opposite leg.

Figure 4.4a. Cross Body Hamstring and Hip Stretch   b.

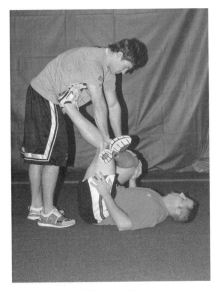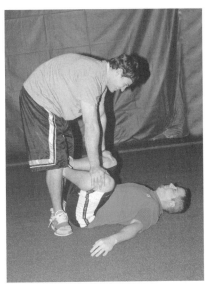

Figure 4.5. Piriformis Stretch   Figure 4.6. Birthing Stretch

7. Piriformis Stretch (glutes, low back, hips) *(See Figure 4.5.)*

Athlete: Lying on your back, cross your right leg and place your foot on top of your left thigh. (Your legs should be in a figure 4 shape.)

Partner: Lift the athlete's left leg and place the sole of his left foot into your stomach. Use your body weight to drive both his right and left legs into his chest. Use your hands to hold the right leg in place. Drive the leg into his chest until a comfortable hold position is achieved and hold for eight to fifteen seconds. Switch legs and repeat on the opposite leg.

8. Birthing Stretch (groin, hips) *(See Figure 4.6.)*

Athlete: While lying on your back, pull your knees up and put the soles of your feet together. Bring your feet into your groin as far as possible, and place them on the inside of your partner's knees.

Partner: Place the athlete's feet on the inside of your knees and drive his feet into his groin. Place your hands on his knees and push lightly outward. This should make it look as if the athlete is giving birth. Drive into the groin until a comfortable hold position is felt, and hold for eight to fifteen seconds.

9. Quad Stretch (quadriceps, hip flexor)

Athlete: While lying on your stomach, curl your heel up to your butt. Try to keep both hips on the ground at all times.

Partner: Push the athlete's heel toward his butt at the same time, holding the hip down to the ground. If the athlete's heel touches his butt and maximum stretch is not felt, then lift his knee off the ground until maximum stretch is felt. At this maximum position, hold the stretch for eight to fifteen seconds.

Upper Body Stretches

1. Chest and Shoulder Stretch (pectorals, deltoids)

Athlete: Sit with both legs out in front of your body. Try to touch your hands together behind your back.

Partner: While kneeling behind the athlete, grab both wrists and bring them together as if the backs of his hands were going to touch. Next, raise his arms up toward his head until a comfortable hold position is achieved. Be careful not to force his arms because severe shoulder injury can occur.

2. External Rotation (shoulder) *(See Figure 4.7.)*

Athlete: With your partner kneeling behind you, sit with your legs out front and place your right elbow on your partner's knee. Keep your right arm at a right angle with fingertips pointing toward the ceiling. Repeat the stretch with the left arm.

Partner: While kneeling behind the athlete, raise the knee of the shoulder to be stretched. Place the athlete's elbow on top of your

Figure 4.7. External Rotation

Figure 4.8. Internal Rotation

Figure 4.9. Torso Stretch

thigh, keeping the arm bent at a right angle. Without forcing the arm, slowly rotate the arm backward until a comfortable hold position is achieved. Take extra care not to force the arm because serious damage can occur.

3. Internal Rotation (shoulder) *(See Figure 4.8.)*

Athlete: Sit in the same position as for external rotation except point your arm and fingers toward the ground. Repeat the stretch with the left arm.

Partner: Kneel in the same position as for external rotation but with the athlete's arm pointed toward the ground. Slowly rotate his arm backward toward the hip. Keep his arm locked in a right angle. Do not force the arm backward. Find a comfortable hold position.

4. Torso Stretch (back, abs, torso) *(See Figure 4.9.)*

Athlete: Sit with both legs out in front of you and your hands locked behind your head. Sit up straight and relax your torso.

Partner: Stand behind the athlete and reach around his arms. You should be able to connect your hands behind the back of the athlete. Slowly twist his arms and body left and right until a comfortable hold position is achieved. Be careful not to force the stretch because serious spinal injury can occur.

Stretching and Flexibility: The Bottom Line

These stretches are the staple stretches that I use with my athletes. However, I'm never limited to these stretches because in certain circumstances, a more specialized stretch may be necessary for an athlete. For example, if an athlete has tight hips and hamstrings, I may spend more time on these areas to try to correct the problem. If an athlete has an injury that may prevent him from getting into a proper stretching position, I may have to use an alternative stretch to achieve the same goal. The key to stretching is frequency. The only way to achieve maximum benefits from stretching is to do them often. The number of times a week may vary from athlete to athlete, but the bottom line is that it must be done on a regular basis. For optimum results, stretching every day will greatly improve flexibility.

I suggest that my athletes stretch during workouts and again in the evening before bed. Stretching before bed does a number of things that are helpful for recovery. Stretching increases blood flow and circulation to the muscles. Blood flow carries the nutrients and building blocks needed to repair and recover fatigued muscles. By stretching before bed, the muscles are flooded with nutrient-rich blood. These nutrients help repair the muscles during sleep. Another reason I suggest my athletes stretch before bed is to simply sleep better. Stretching releases pleasure chemicals called endorphins. These endorphins are what make you feel relaxed and loose after a good stretch. Endorphins also help you sleep better. The more relaxed and limber your body is, the faster you will fall asleep and the better sleep you will enjoy. My athletes have experienced tremendous results following this routine.

5

Resistance Training

Make It Tougher and Get Better

The greatest concern among athletes today, especially in football, is how to improve speed. The purpose of this chapter is to show you how you can increase your speed by training with resistance. It's important to train movements with resistance without impeding the actual mechanics of the movement. Resistive speed is a complex process that is controlled by the brain and nervous system. The brain and nervous system must be taught to handle faster movements with added resistance. By mimicking what you do on the field and adding resistance to that movement, you are recruiting explosive muscle fibers. When the subsequent resistance is removed from a particular movement, the muscles fire explosively to overcome the phantom resistance. The muscles are tricked, so to speak. That resistance can be from a variety of apparatus such as resistive cords, weight vests, medicine balls, sleds, parachutes, or any other training aids that provide resistance to a particular movement. The results are improved first-step explosion and immediate change of direction. Improving your playing speeds, including acceleration, deceleration, change of direction, sprinting, reaction, and delivering and avoiding a blow, depend on a complete balanced approach to this unique conditioning program.

Developing Quickness Through Resistance

Without adequate speed and quickness, athletes in most sports will find it nearly impossible to achieve personal goals. The resistance program at Competitive Edge Sports applies different methods of sport-loading techniques to help athletes develop speed, agility, and quickness. Resistance is used for linear, lateral, diagonal, and vertical drills. Football is a game of inches, and developing quickness is a key element. Resistance training can improve your game and give you that extra edge needed to win. This chapter presents a collection of resistance drills that I use to give our athletes the edge on the field.

Moving Up and Back with Four Patterns

This drill is designed to work multiple movements in virtually every direction while incorporating rapid changes of direction. The equipment needed for this drill will be eight cones, bungee cords, and belts. The cones will be set up five yards apart from each other, and the coach should set them up in four sets. (See Figure 5.1.) The patterns used on this drill are shuffle out and back, turn and run out with a tapioca back, sprint out–sprint back–pedal back, and backpedal out–sprint up. The athlete will perform the given movement on each set of cones until he has completed them all. When the athlete has finished the fourth set of cones, he will rest for about twenty seconds before returning to the starting point, performing the same pattern coming back the other way.

After the athlete has completed the pattern on the first set of cones, he must transition up to the next set. The transition is different depending on the given pattern. Another person should act as an anchor for the athlete

Figure 5.1. Setup for Moving Up and Backs

Figure 5.2. Anchor Setup for Moving Up and Backs

doing the drill. This anchor should be five yards away from the closest cone and should move accordingly with the athlete performing the drill. To start the drill, have the athlete and the anchor pair up together and put on a D-ring belt. The bungee cord is then doubled up and looped through a ring on each person's belt to attach them. (See Figure 5.2.) The anchor moves out to the appropriate distance and stays there until instructed to move. The athlete is given the pattern and assumes an athletic position, ready to move when told.

Pattern 1: Shuffle Out and Back

On this pattern, the athlete will slide out laterally until he has reached the outer cone and then slide back to the inside one. (See Figures 5.3a and 5.3b.) Instruct him to keep the cones in front of him the entire way out and back so he can guide himself and so he doesn't step on or knock them over. Once he gets back to the inside cone, he must then go around it. Don't cut through on the inside. You will then transition up to the next set. The transition on this pattern will be a rapid sprint forward to the next inside cone. The anchor thus far would have remained motionless during the lateral movement but should move forward on pace with the athlete performing the pattern during the transition. Instruct the anchor not to move inward during the lateral slide to the outside cone so as to keep adequate tension on the bungee cord. (See Figure 5.4.) Make sure the athlete is keeping his hips low during the slide to lower the center of gravity. Also, the athlete should keep a wide base with the feet during the slide and shouldn't let his feet get closer than six inches to each other. During the transition, make sure the athlete is bursting quickly to the next set of cones and completely breaking down by lowering the hips and chopping the feet to transition into the next slide.

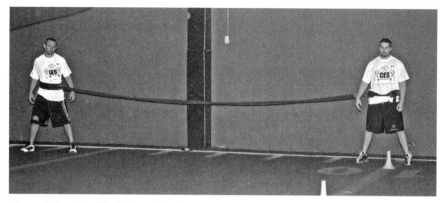

Figure 5.3a. Shuffle Out and Back

b.

Figure 5.4. The Anchor Provides Tension

Pattern 2: Turn and Run Out (Tapioca or Shuffle Back)

On this pattern, the athlete will start by facing the inside cone and assuming an athletic stance. Once the drill starts, he will turn and run toward the outside cone. Once he reaches the outside cone, he will then break down and square up on it. The athlete should then tapioca back toward the inside cone and get ready to transition to the next set. The transition is the same as in the previous drill, with a rapid sprint up to the next cone with a complete breakdown.

Coaching tips for this drill are to make sure the athlete maintains a good forward lean on his sprint outward and uses good arm drive. Also, on the tapioca portion of the drill, make sure the athlete keeps his hips low and rapidly turns his feet and hips. Making sure the athlete goes around the inside cone is essential to help him work on change of direction and body control. Again, the anchor will remain motionless during the sprint out and tapioca back while moving forward on pace with the athlete on his transition.

Pattern 3: Sprint Out and Backpedal Back

On this pattern, the athlete will start by facing toward the outside cone, with the inside cone on his right side. Once the drill starts, the athlete will then sprint as fast as possible to the outside cone and then decelerate to a complete stop once he's reached it. Once this has taken place, the athlete then transitions into a backpedal returning toward the inside cone. The athlete must then transition to the next set of cones by going around the inside cone and then lateral sliding until he reaches them. This will be completed all the way down on every set and then done again coming back in the opposite direction.

Coaching tips for this drill are to make sure the athlete maintains a good forward lean and arm drive on the sprint until he reaches the outside cone. He should chop his feet and lower his hips during the deceleration and change of direction phase. On the backpedal, the athlete must maintain a good posture of having his shoulder over his knees with a good elbow drive backward, remaining on the balls of his feet. The transitional slide should be with low hips and a wide base. Again, the anchor remains motionless until he needs to move on the transition phase.

Pattern 4: Backpedal Out and Sprint Back

On this pattern, the athlete starts out with his back facing the outside cone and the inside cone on his left side. Once the drill starts, the athlete will then backpedal as quickly as possible to the outside cone. (See Figure 5.5.) Once he reaches it, he then transitions into a sprint forward back toward the inside cone. The transition to the next set of cones will be the same as in the previous drill, with a rapid lateral slide to the left until he reaches them, and then he should repeat the pattern. Again, make sure the athlete goes around the inside cone on the transition to work on change of direction and body control.

Coaching tips for this drill consist of the athlete keeping his shoulders over his knees, pushing off the ball of the foot, and using good elbow drive on the backpedal. When the athlete transitions from the backpedal to the sprint, he should use a cycling motion with his feet to rapidly and effectively change his direction back into the forward sprint. On the transitional slide, he should maintain a wide base with his feet and keep his hips and center of gravity low. The anchor, of course, remains motionless until the transition phase to the next set of cones.

These drills are to be done as fast as the athlete can complete them with good changes of direction. Allow for appropriate rest between repetitions to achieve the maximum benefit of conditioning and sport-specific training. Each pattern should be done down and back on the four sets of cones one time during the training session. The coaches should watch carefully to help athletes maintain good form on the drills, keep athletes from getting injured, and ensure that athletes get all the benefits possible from the workout. This drill is used once a week.

Figure 5.5. Backpedal Out and Sprint Back

Training Apparatus: Increasing Resistance

There are numerous training aids available to add resistance in a movement. Here is a closer look at some of the current resistance training aids.

Shackles and Punch Belt

The shackles and punch belt are two training devices that, when used together, will improve lateral speed, agility, and hand and foot quickness. The shackles have two ankle cuffs that are connected by a small piece of surgical tubing. (See Figure 5.6.) Shackles allow athletes to keep a proper base while providing safe resistance with full range of motion. When the athlete steps in a certain direction, the cord stretches, forcing the trail foot to follow. The shackles isolate the adductors, abductors, hip flexors, and hip extensors.

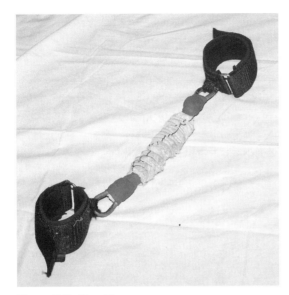

Figure 5.6. Shackles

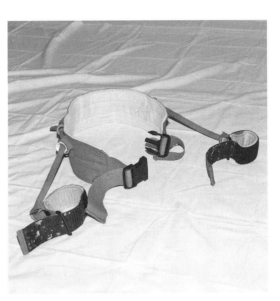

Figure 5.7. Punch Belt

The punch belt is a training device that I invented so I could add resistance during any type of extension of the hands and arms. It is a belt with surgical tubing connected to the back; the tubing is fed through a ring device that connects to wrist cuffs in front. The tubing in the back has an adjustable setting so you can adjust it according to an athlete's height and wingspan. (See Figure 5.7.)

The role of the punch belt is to provide resistance in punching, catching, hand placement, and multiple hand techniques. The punch belt also provides resistance for arm drive, which is used to stabilize the torso so that power can be generated and efficiently transferred through the hips. I originally developed these for offensive linemen to provide resistance in the punching motion during their pass sets. Over the years, the punch belt has been adapted to many different player positions and multiple hand movements. The shackles and punch belt are used two days out of the week with a distance up to twenty yards for each drill. To increase intensity in drills, use a weighted vest, sandbags, or medicine balls depending on the athlete's age, weight, gender, or sport. The drills I use at CES include walking lunges, backward lunges, high knee marches, step squat punches, step squats at 45s, high knee skips, shuffle punches, lateral bounds, skater jumps, and volleyball skips.

• **Walking lunges.** This is the same warm-up activity described in Chapter 2 but with added resistance. The shackles will apply the resistance to the lunge, working the lower body. Athletes should try to stretch the shackle as far as possible. The punch belt provides resistance on the extension of the arms. Remember, speed is a product of stride length and stride frequency, which, in turn, are partly determined by fast arm action.

• **Backward lunges.** The backward lunge is performed in exactly the same manner as the forward lunge, but instead of stepping forward, you'll step backward. The forward lunge works balance and hip flexibility. The backward lunge focuses more on isolating the quadriceps, hamstrings, glutes, calves, and lower back.

• **High knee marches.** Marching is a basic form used before skipping and should be performed deliberately with body control. Your heels should not touch the ground on this exercise. Drive your right knee to hip level, with your thigh parallel to the ground on each stride. You should dorsi flex your right foot (pulling up your toes toward your shins) at the top of the knee drive. Your right ankle should be directly under or slightly behind your right knee, which should be at 90 degrees or less. Rise on the ball of your left foot and extend the left ankle and knee as your body passes over the right foot during the walking stride. Make sure you use proper arm drive motion. Remember to use counter arm and leg movement. Swing your arms slowly and deliberately in a mock running motion in rhythm to marching strides. Repeat this action, raising your left knee to hip level with your right leg moving through a normal walking stride into a full extension on the balls of your feet. (See Figure 5.8.)

Figure 5.8. High Knee Marches

• **High knee skips.** The high knee skips follow the same format for posture and limb mechanics as marching. Although skipping is a more advanced motor skill and requires more coordination and control compared to marching, the speed of skipping is faster and the frequency of foot strike and arm motion is faster as well.

• **Steps/squats/punches.** Start out standing sideways in the direction you're going. Take your right leg and step, keeping your left leg stationary. Make sure to lift the stepping leg high out to the side. When you step, keep your head up and your back straight while keeping the tube stretched. Slowly descend until your upper legs are parallel to the ground. While in a squatting position, you will use a punching motion. Keeping the hands close together, you will punch out from your body, keeping the thumbs up. The punch technique should be done with good explosion. Slowly take your left leg and bring your feet back together. Continue stepping to the right for twenty-five yards and make sure you face the same direction coming back, with the left leg leading. (See Figure 5.9.)

Figure 5.9. Steps/Squats/Punches

• **Steps/squats/punches at diagonal 45 degrees.** The step/squat/punch at 45 degrees has similar mechanics as the step squat but will focus more on the hips, glutes, and quadriceps. Start facing backward in the direction you are traveling. Take your right leg and rotate your hip out, placing your body and foot at a 45-degree angle. The left foot should turn slightly to 45 degrees while the hip opens to the right. Try to lift the stepping leg high when opening the hips. Both your feet should be flat on the ground. From the 45-degree position, lower into a squat position and use the punch technique, using the same form as in the step squat. Make sure to keep your weight back so that your knees don't extend past your toes. Slowly bring the left foot together with the right. Repeat the same process with the left hip and foot. (See Figures 5.10a and 5.10b.)

• **Shuffle punches.** Begin in a lateral position in the direction of travel. Keep your knees bent and your butt low. Step into the lateral movement with your right leg and follow with the left. Whatever pace you set for your forward foot will determine the speed in which the trail leg follows. Without crossing your feet or allowing them to touch, keep the cord stretched out as far as possible. Make sure to keep your knees bent and keep your shoulders facing laterally as you shuffle. Begin the punch technique with every third step while maintaining your shuffle. Start with your arms crossed, open them up wide for the second step (each step is counted by the movement of the lead leg), and allow the motion to lead into the punch for the third step. (See Figure 5.11.)

• **Lateral bounds.** The lateral bound is designed to develop the explosive leg power required in starting lateral movement. Assume a semisquat stance. Push off with your left foot to propel yourself and use your right leg to force your hips up and out. As soon as you land on the right foot,

Figure 5.10a. Steps/Squats/Punches at Diagonal 45 Degrees   b.

Figure 5.11. Shuffle Punches

drive off again with the left foot in the same direction. During the bound phase, try to control your body. Don't worry about speed, stress, lateral distance, or height. As your experience in bounding progresses, you can increase the intensity by adding weight and increasing the number of repetitions.

• **Skater jumps.** The skater jump is a basic bound at a 45-degree angle. Face forward and, in a single motion, drive your right leg up and jump from your left leg, landing on the right. Try to balance your footing without taking extra steps. Repeat this same motion, using your momentum to carry you for distance and height. Remember if you're bounding to the right, you're landing on the right. If you're bounding to the left, you're landing on the left. By using solid hips and good knee drive, an athlete can have better results while bounding.

• **Contrast.** Then do high knee skips and lateral shuffles for twenty yards each.

Progressive Resistance

Progressive resistance may be one of the most important aspects of my training. I use two drills to accomplish this: liner resistance direction and sport-specific resistance. Resistance runs will address the issue of speed verses quickness. Speed is the measure of how fast an athlete can sprint in a short distance. Coaches and players both know that, even though some individuals have the capability to run at high speeds, they still lack the explosive power to accelerate, change directions, or get the entire body to move rapidly. Quickness refers to the ability to perform highly specific movements in the shortest time. It also stimulates the nervous system to process and produce rapid contractions and relaxations of the muscle fibers. When training the first five to fifteen yards of a sprint, heavy resistance training is the best way to accomplish the most explosive movement. Heavy resistance develops superexplosive starts, while light resistance increases acceleration speed. This can be accomplished by using a three-ring belt, an apparatus with long cords that can attach to a pole or an anchor system.

I train using heavy linear resistance two days a week. The best way to train linear resistance is to use sprint loading work. This is accomplished with a weighted vest, cords, and cuffs. Linear resistance training depends on the athlete's size, age, and strength. A beginner will start out with a single long cord. An advanced athlete will start with two. After two weeks of sprint loading, more resistance can be applied, depending on how the athlete handles the load. Following the two weeks of loading, a third cord can be applied to elite athletes by placing cuffs on the biceps and attaching a split short cord device to the cuffs, which will be anchored with a long cord. (See Figure 5.12.) This setup will now have two long cords connected to the three-ring belt and one long cord connected to a split short cord connecting to the cuffs on the arms, giving you a three-cord setup.

The following week, a weight vest is applied to the runs. After completing the progression resistance for four to six weeks, the final phase of sprint loading is presumed if the athlete is healthy and making progress. The last load will have four long cords and a weighted vest. Two cords will connect to the three-ring belt with the other long cords connecting to the cuffs. Regardless of the setup you choose, use a load that allows proper form. Too much weight will cause you to lose form and prevent explosive movements. The distance applied for linear runs is fifteen yards with three sets of six repetitions.

No two athletes run exactly the same way. Therefore, when sprinting with linear resistance, an athlete must use good mechanics to gain the optimal results of the drill. The first phase of a linear resistance run is perfecting stance. The start can be performed from a toe lean first step, a forty start, or a position start. (See Figure 5.13.) Coaches should instruct players to accelerate in a straight line, driving their knees straight up for fifteen yards. Make sure that as an athlete, your arms work in opposition to the legs, with the right arm and left leg coming forward as the left arm and right leg go backward and vice versa. As you sprint, make sure that you keep your feet underneath your hips. If your stride extends out in front of your hips, you're in a breaking motion, which will slow you down. After each rep, make sure that you carefully turn around and walk back to the starting position to repeat the next rep. Form running shouldn't be overdone, just controlled. Remember, explosion and acceleration are key!

I train my players using position-specific resistance. It's a great alternative for progressive training. With position specificity, the resistive load is usually lighter. Do not add so much weight that you impede the mechanics of the movement. Remember, heavy resistance develops superexplosive starts, while light resistance increases acceleration speed. Regardless of your position, there are five ways to improve your playing speed and quickness: increase the length of your stride, increase the number of steps

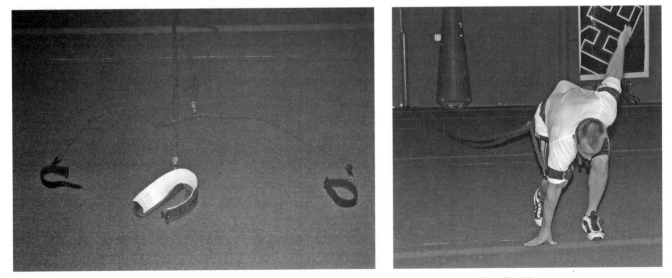

Figure 5.12. Training Aids

Figure 5.13. Starting Position

you take per second (that is, stride faster), improve your quickness and starting ability, improve your acceleration time (that is, reach your full speed faster), and improve speed endurance. The start is usually from a toe lean first step acceleration or position start. The equipment setup for position-specific resistance is identical to linear resistance. The max load for position-specific progressive resistance is two long cords. Beginners should only use a single long cord for this drill. The distance used for position-specific resistance is fifteen yards with five sets of four repetitions. During the first set, the player will accelerate as fast as he can for fifteen yards. (See Figures 5.14a and 5.14b.) On the second set, the player will face laterally and shuffle five yards, turn, and sprint for ten yards. On the third set, the player will face his left side and shuffle for five yards, turn, and sprint ten yards. The forth set is four backpedals for fifteen yards. The last set includes two repetitions of backpedaling, two to the right and two to the left. The player should turn and sprint for ten yards after opening his hips. And at the end of every sprint, the player should turn around and walk back for the next set or repetition. In contrast, substitute two sprints for forty yards.

The Black Widow

The black widow is a two-person running device used for resistance training. The black widow develops strength and power for acceleration. The unit comes with four adjustable cuffs, two for the arms and two for the legs, with surgical tubing attaching to each cuff and an attachment handle at the end. The cuffs for the arms fit directly on the bicep of the arm. The cuffs for the legs fit below the kneecap. (See Figure 5.15.) This allows the arms and legs simultaneously to move with full range of motion while

Figure 5.14a. Acceleration   b.

a coach applies the resistance needed. The black widow can be used for sprints, backpedals, and position work. I use the black widow once every three weeks. The distance used for the widows are twenty-five to thirty yards for two sets of five repetitions with twenty-five seconds between each run.

Before the player begins, make sure the anchor for the widow pulls the remaining slack out of the cords. The runner should stand tall with both feet together and fall forward, driving his lead leg down quickly. (Coaching tip: Make sure your player runs in a straight line, not in a wide running gait.) Players should not run as if they are pulling dead weight. However, good resistance needs to be applied by the anchor, allowing full range of motion with good form. Too much resistance will cause the runner to lose form. While sprinting with the widow, get a full range of motion with your arms. If you are lazy with your arm action with the resistance applied, you are limiting your potential for speed. Range of motion with the arms should generally be hip to cheek. If your arms fall outside of this range, your running mechanics will be negatively affected. In short, you'll run slower and get tired faster. The backpedals have similar mechanics. The cuffs and surgical tubing are placed in front of the runner. (See Figure 5.16.) The distance and sets are still the same. For contrast, sprint the same distance without any equipment attached for two repetitions.

Release Harness

The harness is a two-person setup that works by adding resistance in the running motion and assists in sprint technique. The release harness consists of a belt and a release handle and is used for resistance and contrast training. I use the release harness for linear speed and position-specific

Figure 5.15. The Black Widow for Forward Movement

Figure 5.16. The Black Widow for Backpedals

work. The breakaway cord has two handles. The big handle is used for manually resisting another runner. It typically is a little longer than the second handle. The leash cord connects to the back of the belt. Two athletes of similar body weight and power should use the same release harness. The lead runner should begin by standing tall and falling. The mechanics should be similar to the action used with the black widow. When starting the drill, the coach will hold the large handle while letting the small handle lay on the ground. Anchors should give light resistance, allowing the runner to keep good form. (See Figure 5.17.) The athlete's speed levels should be close to 90 percent of his maximum speed with distances of twenty to thirty yards for two sets of six repetitions and twenty-five seconds of rest between each set. The athlete should finish the drill using contrast of the same distance as the drill.

To release the runner from resistance, the anchor or coach will grab both handles, pulling slightly on the smaller handle, while the runner runs. The anchor will hold the bigger handle closer to the body with his dominant hand while holding the smaller handle in the other hand farther away from the body. The runner will start with a normal toe lean first step and accelerate as fast as possible. When the runner accelerates for ten yards, the anchor will pull the smaller handle, releasing the runner without resistance. (See Figure 5.18.) Runners should keep running through the distance that is marked. If done correctly, the runner should have a marked change in speed.

Meadow Harness Drill

The Meadow harness drill is used to train in a multidirectional plane. The drill is great for all positional training in football. I use the Meadow harness drill to work on lateral resistance and reaction. This drill adds

Figure 5.17. Release Harness with Light Resistance

Figure 5.18. Releasing the Runner

a new dimension to training. When I originally came up with this drill, I used five short cords for resistance. Over the years, those five cords have evolved into one massive short cord with a harness. The drill also includes five cones, which are placed seven steps away from the runner or five to six yards in an arc formation. The cord or cords attach to an anchor system. The harness attaches to the other end of the cords or cord. Have runners partner up in groups of two or three. Runners should be grouped based on their weight and skill level. One player will put on the harness, while the second player stands in front of the cones, points, and gives directions. Before the first player starts, make sure that all the slack is pulled out of the cords or cord. As the second player points to a cone, the runner will sprint as fast as possible, driving his knees and arms while maintaining good forward lean. (See Figure 5.19.) As the runner reaches the cone, he will break down and decelerate and then backpedal to his original starting position as fast as possible without standing up. When the runner reaches his starting point, the pointer will point to another cone, and the runner will accelerate to this next cone.

I tell players that it is very important to stay low on their backpedal for safety purposes. I have my athletes work on the Meadow harness drill with resistance once every two weeks. The sets are three or four with eight repetitions, depending on the skill level and conditioning level of the athlete. Intensity can be adjusted by adding more cords or subtracting cords for beginners or lightweight players. You should never exceed five cords. For contrast, do six reps.

Up-Back Drills

As a coach, I know the importance of lateral movement in football. When I train a player in lateral movements, my objective is to have him be

Figure 5.19. Five-Cone Drill

explosive in all directions. Remember, velocity multiplied by force equals power. The more power generated, the more explosive the player. Explosiveness helps with acceleration, and increased acceleration transfers to game speed. In the up-back drill, the player works in a linear and lateral direction with very little rest. The equipment needed is one long cord doubled up with two belts. The players will face the same direction, with the runner being anchored by his partner, who will provide resistance. The players will secure the belt over their hips so that the cord comes off the back of the runner and is positioned directly in the front of the anchor. (See Figure 5.20.) The distance used for this drill is fifteen yards, with the runner standing on the ten-yard line and the anchor standing on the five.

The runner will begin the drill by performing a predetermined movement to the fifteen-yard line, while the anchor stays stationary for the entire drill. There should be slight tension on the cord before the drill begins. There are three different patterns in this drill: sprint, shuffle (right and left), and backpedal, with multiple sets. With each set, the players will alternate being the anchor and doing the drills. (After the first athlete completes the shuffle, the two athletes quickly change positions and reverse roles.) The sets go as follows:

- 4 sets of 8 repetitions with 2 minutes of rest
  1. 1 set of 8 reps sprinting
  2. 1 set of 8 reps shuffling to the right
  3. 1 set of 8 reps shuffling to the left
  4. 1 set of 8 reps backpedaling
- 4 sets of 6 repetitions with 1 minute, 30 seconds of rest
  1. 1 set of 6 reps sprinting
  2. 1 set of 6 reps shuffling to the right
  3. 1 set of 6 reps shuffling to the left
  4. 1 set of 6 reps backpedaling

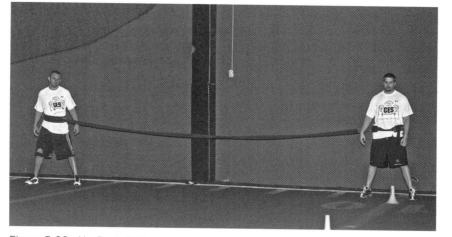

Figure 5.20. Up-Back Drill

- 4 sets of 4 repetitions with 1 minute of rest
    1. 1 set of 4 reps sprinting
    2. 1 set of 4 reps shuffling to the right
    3. 1 set of 4 reps shuffling to the left
    4. 1 set of 4 reps backpedaling
- 4 sets of 2 repetitions with no rest
    1. 1 set of 2 reps sprinting
    2. 1 set of 2 reps shuffling to the right
    3. 1 set of 2 reps shuffling to the left
    4. 1 set of 2 reps backpedaling

Note: Contrast with four repetitions without any resistance.

Sprinting

On command, the lead runner will sprint for five yards and backpedal as fast as possible. Remember, the cord applies resistance when sprinting and overspeed in the backpedal phase. I make sure players maintain good posture by having their shoulders over their knees, with a good elbow drive backward, while remaining on the balls of their feet. The anchor must stay stationary the entire time while the other partner is performing the pattern.

Shuffling

The second and third patterns are shuffling to the left and right. The runner will secure the cord so that it will extend out from the side of his body toward the anchor. The anchor will stay stationary while providing resistance directly to the side of the lead runner. Both athletes will stay in a straight line while performing the shuffle patterns. On command, the lead runner will shuffle for five yards and shuffle back for the predetermined repetitions. Make sure that players stay low with their knees bent and butt low. Make sure that they do not cross their feet or let their heels touch while shuffling. (See Figure 5.21.)

Backpedals

The two athletes will be facing each other throughout this drill. The runner will secure the cord so that the strap extends from the player's abdomen back to the anchor runner. The anchor will be providing resistance from directly in front of

Figure 5.21. Shuffling

the runner. The runner will backpedal for five yards and sprint forward as fast as possible for the predetermined repetitions. Emphasize proper form. Keeping the hips low will help athletes backpedal. (See Figure 5.22.)

Note: If the runner cannot perform the pattern using proper form, the coach or training partner should reduce the amount of resistance placed on the runner. This drill is used once a week.

Weight Vest

The weight vest is another piece of equipment that I use on heavy resistance days. The vest can be safely utilized by all ages and adapted to all positions in football. The weight vest is used during ballistics, ladder and resistance drills, and position work. Speed training with the weight vest results in more explosive fiber recruitment. It builds lower leg power, acceleration, and endurance while training. I have found that I can easily use the vest for various applications during different periods of training. I also use the vest during the summer to acclimate my players to the weight of their football equipment. Avoid using the vest with precision drills to prevent injury and to enhance skills. If the vest is used correctly, skill level will improve.

Figure 5.22. Backpedaling

Sandwich Drill

For the athlete who needs superior lateral movement and quick reaction, I use the sandwich drill. The sandwich drill is a multidimensional drill allowing athletes to enhance lateral quickness through resistance, deceleration, and change-of-direction skills. The drill includes two long cords and a three-ring belt, two anchors, and a coach to give direction to the runner. Wrap two cords around the waist and anchor it to the belt, with the belt in the center. Have one anchor with a cord attached to the right and another anchor with a cord attached to the left, providing resistance from both sides to the runner. (See Figure 5.23a.) Have the player center with the coach assuming the ready position. (See Figure 5.23b.) The player should react to the coach's cues by shuffling or turning and running toward the direction he points. (See Figure 5.23c.) As the runner begins to move laterally, the anchors should pull the cord slightly to prevent the runner from getting his feet tangled in the cords. The sets and repetitions for the sandwich drills are three sets with eight to ten changes of direc-

Figure 5.23a. Sandwich Drill   b.   c.

tion. This drill strengthens adductors, abductors, hip extensors, and hip flexors—all the muscles that move you laterally and diagonally. It also improves first-step quickness, acceleration, and deceleration, while teaching athletes to have greater body control and balance. I typically use this drill twice a week The contrast should be one set with seven changes in shuffling directions.

Long-Tow Drill

The long-tow drill is a basic two-person linear resistance drill. The purpose of the long tow is to develop the strength and explosive power necessary for acceleration and speed endurance. A basic long cord is needed with a two-belt setup. The belt positions over the hips and can fit any size waist. The design of the belt allows the user to quickly change the position of the belt, thereby making transitions from drill to drill more efficient and maximizing training time. In this drill, both athletes will face the same direction, with the trail runner providing resistance for the lead runner. Both athletes will secure the belt over their hips so that the bungee cord comes straight off the back of the lead runner and is positioned directly in front of the trail runner. The trail runner will be directly behind the lead runner. (See Figure 5.24.) There should be a slight tension in the cord to begin the drill. A slight tension reduces the risk of injury that could result from a sudden jarring or jerking. On command, the lead runner will run a predetermined distance, with the trail runner providing resistance with his body weight. The lead runner must emphasize a strong knee drive and arm action while maintaining an erect posture and keeping the feet pointing straight ahead. If an athlete cannot perform the run using proper form, his partner should reduce the amount of resistance placed on the runner. At the end of the run, the two runners can quickly change roles by simply rotating the belts around their hips. The former lead runner will now be in position to provide resistance to the former trail runner. The long-tow exercise should be done over a distance of forty to sixty yards. The long tow is usually performed once every two weeks. Beginners should start with only one cord. Depending on the player, some will be able to handle a two-cord setup. Advanced athletes may be able to use a weighted vest with a two-cord setup. Repetitions for the long tow are one set of six repetitions with thirty to forty-five seconds between each run.

Figure 5.24. Long-Tow Drill

Resistance: The Bottom Line

In conclusion, resistive running can be used to improve linear, lateral, and position speed. Just remember that any movement on the football field could and should be trained with resistance. By adding different loads to any movement, the body will tear down and build back fibers in the same way as from using progressive resistance in the weight room. Two days a week is optimal for resistance training in both linear and lateral work. The fun thing about training with resistance is watching the expression on a player's face when he takes the resistance off and takes his first steps in contrast. His eyes light up, his mouth opens in an "O," and his whole countenance says, "Wow!" It's very gratifying to me as a coach to watch the physiological transformation that takes place in the player. But even more impressive is the boost in his confidence and self-esteem as he realizes the progress that he has made. I love it!

Position Resistance Drills for Offense

Quarterbacks

1. Quarterback Drops

Purpose: To add resistance to a quarterback when he gets into his drop and to help his footwork and drop quickness

Equipment: A resistance cord and a D-ring belt. To progressively load this drill over time, the quarterback can also use ankle shackles, a weighted vest, and extra cords for more resistance.

Drill: On this drill, the quarterback will use three-, five-, and seven-step drops. The quarterback will need to attach a resistance cord to himself. The cord should be in front of him to give resistance in the proper drop-back motion. After each repetition, the quarterback should return to the starting spot and repeat the drill until he completes the desired reps. (See Figure 5.25.)

Chip's Tips

1. *The quarterback should hold a ball, to simulate the play as realistically as possible.*
2. *The quarterback should also have some tension in the cord so that there is resistance from the very first movement.*
3. *In addition, once the quarterback has reached his drop depth, he should then move in the pocket as necessary.*

Figure 5.25. Quarterback Drops

2. Rollout/Option

Purpose: To give resistance to a quarterback during a rollout or option situation (this will help him get out faster)

Equipment: A resistance cord, a D-ring belt, and some cones. To progress this drill over time, the quarterback can also wear a weighted vest, use extra cords, and even wear a Chip-O-Meter.

Drill: On this drill, the quarterback will have a cord attached to him with a belt. The cord should be on his hip to begin with to give resistance in whatever direction he is rolling out. The quarterback should work both directions equally. As the drill progresses, the belt should allow the cord to move from his hip to his back as the quarterback rolls out.

Chip's Tips

1. *The quarterback should sprint out with good running form (that is, a good forward lean, knee drive).*
2. *He should also be holding a ball. Setting a cone up for him to get out around helps to make the drill more realistic.*

Running Backs

1. Zone Run

Purpose: To give resistance to a running back during a zone run to a certain side of the field

Equipment: A resistance cord, a belt, and some cones. This drill could also be done with a release harness or a black widow. To progressively load this drill, a weighted vest or extra cords can be used.

Drill: On this drill, the running back will have a resistance cord attached to him from the back of a belt to provide resistance in the proper direction. The running back will simply take a lateral step to the side of the field he is running to and then burst forward toward the line of scrimmage. The running back should work both sides of the field with a total sprint of about ten to fifteen yards.

Chip's Tips

1. Make sure the running back starts in his usual stance, holding a ball, and has some light tension in the cord before starting.
2. Also, he should simulate bouncing the run inside or out to make the drill as realistic as possible.

2. Cutting and Switching

Purpose: To give a running back resistance while he changes direction and switches the ball to the opposite hand

Equipment: A resistance cord, a belt, and some cones. This drill can also be done using a release harness or a black widow. To progressively load this drill, you can also use a weighted vest and extra cords.

Drill: On this drill, the running back will have a cord attached to him by a belt with the resistance behind him. Four cones must be set out in front of him in a zigzag pattern about five yards apart from each other. The running back will then burst forward up to the first cone, break down on it, and then sprint off toward the next cone, sprinting upfield. Every time the running back reaches a cone, he should switch the ball to the other hand.

Chip's Tips

1. The running back should start in his normal stance. While holding a ball, he should run with a good forward lean, changing directions as sharply and quickly as possible.

Receivers

1. Resisted Routes

Purpose: To resist a receiver while he gets off the line of scrimmage and runs his route

Equipment: A long resistance cord, a D-ring belt, and some cones if the field is unmarked for certain routes.

Drill: On this drill, the receiver will have a resistance cord attached to him from behind using a belt. The receiver chooses the routes he would like to run. The routes should be no more than thirty yards in length due to the limitations of the cord.

Chip's Tips

1. *The receiver should work on stutter stepping and swimming off of a defensive back to make the drill more realistic.*
2. *Also, the receiver should run good clean routes and have a ball thrown to him on each one.*
3. *Tight ends should come from their normal stance as well and mimic releasing off the block.*
4. *To progressively load this drill, the receiver can also wear a pair of quick hands or hand shackles and an extra cord.*

2. Quick Hands

Purpose: To train a receiver's reaction time and ball-catching skills while resisting his hands at the wrist

Equipment: A pair of quick hands and either a live quarterback or a Jugs Ball Throwing Machine.

Drill: On this drill, the receiver will wear a pair of quick hands while catching passes from his coach or a Jugs machine. The receiver should stand about twelve to fifteen yards away at the beginning of the drill and take a small step forward every time he catches a ball. (See Figure 5.26.)

Figure 5.26. Quick Hands

Chip's Tips

1. *Change the location of the ball on every throw and the angle the receiver may have to catch it from (for example, over the shoulder, right side, left side, high, low).*
2. *To progressively load this drill, change the velocity of the throw and tighten the quick hands for more resistance.*

1. Resisted Pass Sets

Purpose: To resist a lineman through his pass-setting technique

Equipment: A belt, a resistance cord, and some cones. This drill can also be done with a black widow.

Drill: On this drill, the lineman will wear a belt with a resistance cord attached to him from the front to provide the proper resistance. The lineman should start in his normal pass set stance with tension already in the cord. He then will kick step back to his normal depth of a pass set.

Chip's Tips

1. The lineman should set with the proper technique, as quickly as possible.
2. The lineman should also set properly according to his position on the line; guards and centers will usually set more laterally as opposed to getting depth, whereas a tackle will usually get more depth.
3. All positions should also incorporate a redirect on their set. This consists of setting a certain direction and then quickly coming back the opposite way to simulate field situations.
4. To progressively load this drill, the lineman can also wear a pair of ankle shackles, a weighted vest, and more cords. A pair of quick hands can also be used for when the lineman punches out during his set.

2. Super Heavy Resisted Pass Sets

Purpose: To resist the pass set but with a massive amount of resistance

Equipment: A pair of quick hands, three long cords, and cord anchor points.

Drill: On this drill, the lineman will wear a pair of quick hands with three doubled-up long cords attached to him to simulate a 325-pound defensive lineman. The cords are attached to the belt by various rings sewn onto it and then attached to anchors at 45-degree angles in front of, and on each side of, him.

Chip's Tips

1. The lineman should set as quickly as possible and with great technique.

2. Also, the lineman should set to the specific style of his position and punch out with his hands during the repetitions.

3. To progressively load this drill, the lineman can also wear a pair of ankle shackles and a weighted vest.

Position Resistance Drills for Defense

Defensive Backs

1. Pass Drops

Purpose: To give resistance to a defensive back during his backpedal and his turn and run

Equipment: A long cord, a D-ring belt, and some cones.

Figure 5.27a. Backpedal for Defensive Backs

Drill: On this drill, the defensive back should have a long resistance cord attached to him with a belt, with slight tension already in the cord. The defensive back should start in a normal stance with the cord in front of him to provide the proper resistance. The defensive back should begin the drill with a backpedal and should then turn and run when he has dropped to the desired depth. He should continue running for ten to fifteen yards. He should do this equally to the left and right sides. (See Figures 5.27a and 5.27b.)

Chip's Tips

1. The defensive back should backpedal with good form, keeping his hips low during the turn and run. He should also use an arm swing to help turn the hips and shoulders rapidly on the turn and run.

2. The defensive back can also work on coming out of the turn and run and break back, toward the line of scrimmage.

b. Backpedal Turn and Run

2. Backpedal and Weave

Purpose: To give resistance to a defensive back while he drops back with an extended backpedal and weaves back and forth

Equipment: A long cord and a belt. This drill can also be done with a black widow, with more work coming from the arm attachments as well.

Drill: On this drill, the defensive back will have a resistance cord attached to him by a belt with the cord in front of him to give proper resistance. With tension already in the cord, the defensive back will backpedal and then weave side to side in a zigzag pattern, as if drifting from different zones, for about fifteen to twenty yards.

Chip's Tips

1. The defensive back should backpedal with good form and with good elbow drive, especially if he is doing this drill with a black widow.

Linebackers

1. Pass Drops

Purpose: To add resistance to a linebacker during his pass coverage drops

Equipment: A D-ring belt, a resistance cord, and some cones.

Drill: On this drill, the linebacker will have a resistance cord attached to him in the front to provide the proper resistance during the pass drop. With tension already in the cord, the linebacker will turn his hips and run back at an angle to his left, right, or straight back into his pass coverage zone. Once the linebacker is back deep enough, he will then turn back toward the line of scrimmage and settle out into his zone. (See Figure 5.28.)

Chip's Tips

1. The linebacker should get his hips open as quickly as possible and keep his head turned back toward the backfield.

Figure 5.28. Pass Drops for Linebackers

2. Once the linebacker settles into his coverage zone, he should keep
   his feet moving.
3. To progressively load this drill, a weight vest can be added.

2. Scrape and Fill

Purpose: To add resistance to a linebacker while he shuffles down
the line of scrimmage and then comes forward to fill the gap

Equipment: A D-ring belt, two resistance cords, cones, and an
extra person to help anchor.

Drill: On this drill, the linebacker will have
a resistance cord attached to him from
behind and then another on the opposite
side, to which he'll be shuffling. Cones must
be set up to simulate the gaps or holes in
an offensive line. With tension already in
the cords from the side and behind, the
linebacker shuffles laterally toward the
hole he is instructed to fill and then comes
forward to fill it. To work the other side, the
lateral resistance cord has to be moved to the
opposite side. (See Figure 5.29.)

Chip's Tips

1. The linebacker needs to stay low on his
   lateral movement and then burst forward
   with a good lean when filling the hole.
2. To progressively load this drill, a weighted
   vest can be added.

Figure 5.29. Scrape and Fill

Defensive Linemen

1. Rip and Swim

Purpose: To add resistance to a defensive lineman on his get-off
and rip or swim techniques

Equipment: A resistance cord, a D-ring belt, some cones, and a
bag or dummy.

Drill: On this drill, have the lineman take his normal stance, with
a resistance cord attached to him from behind with a belt. The
lineman should then come out of his stance and use a ripping or
swim motion, continuing upfield for three to four yards. Having

Figure 5.30a. Rip and Swim   b.

a bag or someone to act like an offensive lineman is very helpful
in making the drill as realistic as possible. (See Figures 5.30a and
5.30b.)

Chip's Tips

1. *The lineman should fire out low and work both directions equally
   with each technique.*
2. *To progressively load this drill, a weighted vest, extra cords, and
   quick hands can be added.*

2. Two-Gap

Purpose: To add resistance to a defensive lineman who plays in a
two-gap situation

Equipment: A resistance cord, a D-ring belt, and a bag or person.

Drill: On this drill, have the lineman come from his normal
stance, with a resistance cord attached to him from behind. The
lineman should line up on a bag or person and have a running
back in the backfield to make the drill as realistic as possible.
The lineman should then fire out, engage the person or bag, and
wait for the running back to move in the direction he is headed.
Once the back makes his move, the lineman should then shed the
blocker and go into the proper gap.

Chip's Tips

1. The defensive lineman needs to fire out quickly to engage the offensive lineman and extend his arms to keep his opponent at arm's length.

2. To progressively load this drill, a weighted vest, extra cords, and quick hands can be added as well.

3. Attack and React

Purpose: To add a large amount of resistance to a defensive lineman to help simulate a bull rush or a two-gap play

Equipment: Three long resistance cords, a pair of quick hands, and a large dummy or bag.

Drill: On this drill, the lineman will have a pair of quick hands on and attach a doubled-up resistance cord on each of the three rings attached to the belt anchored behind him. The lineman will come out of his normal stance and either punch out and bull rush on a bag or play a two-gap situation. The doubled-up cords will help make the defensive lineman feel like he is going against a large offensive lineman.

Chip's Tips

1. Make sure the lineman fires out low and locks his arms out with the quick hands while coming upfield.

2. You can load this drill even further with a weighted vest, but the number of cords already in use is usually enough.

Overspeed Training

Breaking the Speed Barrier

In 1987 one of the first things I learned during my educational experience in the Soviet Union was the principle of overspeed training. I'll never forget the illustration on this concept that was presented at the Soviet Sports Institute. Do you remember when you were a child and you ran downhill at an extremely fast pace? You ran out of control, but you didn't fall. Your brain was firing on overtime, telling your hands and feet to react quickly to its neuromuscular commands. The Russians had a theory that if you were able to train your body to go beyond its normal maximum speed, you could delay the onset of muscular fatigue. By training at maximal speeds and maintaining the speed for as long as possible, the Russians felt that they could push an athlete's natural speed barrier even further. They used another similar illustration to describe this phenomenon. If you ever saw Carl Lewis sprint in a one-hundred-meter race, you might have noticed that at the fifty-meter mark, it looked like he accelerated past his competition. In actuality, Carl just maintained his natural speed and the rest of the field decelerated, making it look like he was running away from them.

By forcing your muscles to fire faster through artificial means, you can teach the muscles to continue the firing action for a longer period of time. This firing of muscle fiber will create muscle memory and cause your body to expect faster motions. With overspeed training, it's possible to increase your maximum speed by 20 percent more than your natural running speed. I've timed players in the 4.6 range in the forty-yard dash. Then the same athlete is trained with an overspeed cord and actually lowers his time into the 3.6 to 3.7 range using the cord. In a relatively short period of time, typically six to eight weeks, I have seen unbelievable improvement. The characteristic results show an improvement varying from 0.03 to 0.06 of a second for elite-level athletes. There is the potential for even greater results with the untrained athlete.

Training Options for Overspeed Techniques

There are three ways that I know of to train with overspeed. The first is running downhill. This is the very first way that I used overspeed when I returned from the Soviet Union in 1988. I would incorporate overspeed training two days per week and quickly found out that the stress of over-striding was very taxing on an athlete's hamstrings. The athlete needs to have at least forty-eight hours of recovery time before training with overspeed again. This guideline for recovery is what I continue to use with overspeed training.

The second way to train with overspeed is modeled directly from the Russians. They used an electric wench to pull the athlete in the direction of the run, reeling in their sprinters about 10 to 15 percent faster than they could naturally run. The wench had to be hooked up to a stationary object and could be used by only one athlete at a time—not a very practical way to train athletes today. Nevertheless, it worked quite well for them. Along the same lines is the use of a high-speed treadmill. The treadmill forces the athlete to run at speeds faster than their natural gait. Some of these treadmills run at speeds upwards of twenty-five to thirty miles per hour. Personally, I'm not a fan of this technique, primarily because you don't play your sport on a treadmill. It's just like players who do their training on a track. I've always felt that you should train on the surfaces on which you play. Don't get me wrong—if the high-speed treadmill is the only tool available to you for overspeed training, by all means use it. It is still very beneficial and provides the same neuromuscular benefits.

The third way to train overspeed is to use elastic rubber cords. The great thing about using these cords for training is that they gradually increase speed, allowing you to regulate the amount of speed that is generated over a particular distance. The tighter the cords are stretched, the more explosive your first step will be. The looser the cords, the more gradual the overspeed rate is applied. One of the critical things you must understand is that it can be dangerous to use naked tubing. I realized this early on in my overspeed training as I was constantly being whipped with broken tubing. To solve this problem, my equipment builder and I came up with some nylon sheathing to encase the naked tubing. This safety feature eliminates a lot of the potential for injury.

The Particulars of Overspeed Training

One of the most positive aspects of using elastics is the fact that I can train groups of players simultaneously. The second benefit of the elastics is their versatility. Elastics allow us to train two specific movements: assistance and resistance. Assistance is overspeed. Resistance is used for position-specific work. By alternating assistance and resistance, I am able to train my players at high speeds by loading the muscles with the effects of the elastics and training speed and agility at maximum capacity. Another great benefit of using the cords is that while one group anchors, the other group is running. This allows the anchor group to recover while the other group is working.

I use elastics for position-specific work. On overspeed days, I not only work on linear speed, but I also work with players on position-specific overspeed. By adding overspeed techniques to position training work, I'm able to force the player to train at maximum speeds that they could not achieve without an aid. Because the cords are pulling you at roughly 115 percent of your natural speed, your body has no recourse but to respond by moving faster. The simple fact is that over a six- to eight-week period, repeatedly forcing your body to move faster than your natural speed will result in increased speed. This happens because fast-twitch muscle fibers are transformed in two unique ways. The fibers you have are firing harder, and new muscle fibers are being activated. It doesn't matter whether you are running linearly, diagonally, or backward—the end result is increased speed and quickness in all directions.

Chip's Overspeed Program

I train with overspeed two days per week, Tuesdays and Fridays. On overspeed days, I train my players with position-specific overspeed and linear overspeed. The combination of these two applications depends on the needs of the player. If the player needs to decrease his forty-yard dash time, I have him spend more time on linear work. I will have him do two sets of five reps of ten-yard dash overspeed starts. The distance needed to do the drill is ten to fifteen yards. In addition, I add two sets of five reps of forty-yard overspeed runs. For position overspeed, I have the player start out with two sets of position overspeed movements. This set could consist of up to three movements per position. As the body adapts to the position overspeed, I'll gradually increase the number of sets the player does to achieve maximum results.

Linear Overspeed Program

1. Ten-Yard Overspeed Start

Purpose: To increase the drive phase of the forty-yard dash

Equipment: Two belts with an eight-foot elastic cord.

Drill: You will perform this drill with a partner who stands fifteen yards in front, holding the end of the elastic cord. Come out of a forty-yard start stance being pulled by your partner. (See Figure 6.1.) Sprint for a distance of ten yards, continuing to accelerate until completing the ten-yard distance. Make sure that you do not throw on the brakes. Decelerate after you have run ten yards.

Chip's Tips

1. Keep 80 percent of your weight on the ball of your foot.
2. Your back foot should be four to six inches behind your front foot.
3. Keep your head down.
4. Inhale and stay tight.
5. Explode off both feet.
6. Your front hand should be on the starting line, and your back should be in a cocked position.
7. Explode out for seven steps, or approximately ten yards.

Figure 6.1. Ten-Yard Overspeed Start

2. Forty-Yard Overspeed Drill

Purpose: To teach the motor units to fire faster over a forty-yard distance (The forty-yard dash is the standard by which football speed is measured. Because most of the players that I train are getting ready for the NFL combine or are already in the league as unrestricted free agents who will have to run a forty for a prospective team, I will spend considerable time with the player on the forty-yard dash technique.)

Equipment: Two belts with a twenty-five-foot elastic cord.

Drill: The drill is performed with a partner. The end of the elastic cord is hooked to the front of both players. Note: My overspeed cords are manufactured at a length of twenty-five feet, which will stretch to a length of seventy-five feet, or twenty-five yards. The anchor player will back up twenty-five yards from the runner, facing him. (See Figure 6.2a.) The stance will not be an overspeed start but an upright stance to increase the amount of pulling resistance. The runner will stand tall and fall into an explosive first drive step, sprinting forty yards at maximum speed. (See Figure 6.2b.) As the runner is sprinting, the anchor will be reeling in the runner's cord. (See Figure 6.2c.) The runner will continue a natural stride through the finish line and should not throw on the brakes. At the end of the forty yards, the runner will return to the start line and repeat the drill. Caution: Because of the explosiveness of this drill, it is extremely taxing on the quadriceps and hamstrings. Therefore, if the athlete feels either of them tightening up, stop immediately. I have a saying that I share with all my athletes: "Whenever you feel tightness, it's better to stop now so that you can live to run another day."

Figure 6.2a. Forty-Yard Overspeed Drill   b.   c.

Chip's Tips

1. Stand tall and fall.

2. Stay on the balls of your feet.

3. Alternate elbow snaps with opposite leg drive.

4. Fast arms equal fast legs.

5. Keep a good forward lean, chest over knees, and accelerate through the drill.

6. Keep your legs under your hips.

7. Partner is to reel in the cord.

Sample Linear Overspeed Program. Over a six-week span, I would have my athletes focus on their ten-yard overspeed starts and forty-yard overspeed drills to further develop their linear speed on overspeed days. For the ten-yard starts, I would have them run two sets of five reps with twenty seconds of rest during weeks 1 and 2, then progress to three sets of five reps for weeks 3 and 4, followed by three sets of eight reps for the final two weeks, maintaining the same rest time throughout. For forty-yard drills, weeks 1 and 2 would be one set of five reps with forty-five seconds of rest, in weeks 3 and 4 athletes would progress to two sets of five, and they would finish up weeks 5 and 6 with two sets of eight. Your rest time between sets is actually the time it takes to walk back to the starting position. Rest two minutes between exercises.

Overspeed Alternate Drills. In addition to the ten-yard overspeed starts and the forty-yard overspeed drill, there are three other drills that can be used for linear overspeed training. You may select one of these to interchange with the two aforementioned drills for variety. The first is the long overspeed progressive run, the second is the short cord partner tow, and the third is the suicide run progression.

1. Overspeed Progressive Run

Purpose: To force the body to move multidirectionally and explosively, with different movements

Equipment: Two belts with a twenty-five-foot elastic cord.

Drill: Much like the linear overspeed forty-yard runs, there will be an anchor partnered with a runner, the cord will be stretched thirty yards, and the distance of the run is forty yards. However, with the overspeed progressive run, you will add three new movements to the forty-yard run. To start the drill, run two forty-yard sprints, walking back to the start line after each sprint. Then you will face laterally and shuffle ten yards, turn 90 degrees, and sprint straight through the finish line. Repeat two of these drills to the right and two to the left. The next progression is to backpedal ten yards from the start line, flip your hips to the right, and sprint the remaining thirty yards. Repeat one to the right and one to the left. The last progression is for the runner to start in a kneeling position. The coach will grab the cord about three to four yards from the runner and pull him into his sprint explosively. The runner will then complete the forty-yard sprint.

Chip's Tips

1. Keep your feet together, and stand tall and fall.
2. Keep your chest over your knees.
3. Make sure to use fast arm action as you sprint.
4. When decelerating, keep your feet under you and under control.
5. Drop your hips when decelerating.
6. During the lateral shuffles, keep your center of gravity low.
7. Don't cross your feet during lateral shuffles.
8. On the backpedal, keep your chest over your knees.
9. When you turn to the right on your backpedal, rip your arm to the right, forcing your hips to open in that direction. Use the same action on the left side.

2. Short Cord Partner Tow

Purpose: To work on first-step explosion and fast foot turnover rate, as well as to minimize ground time

Equipment: Two belts with an eight-foot elastic cord.

Drill: This is a partner drill with a short eight-foot elastic cord. The cord is hooked to the front of your belt and the back of your partner's belt. Your partner is ten yards in front of you, facing the same direction. On the coach's command to go, both partners will sprint ahead. Your partner will sprint ten yards, and you will sprint twenty yards. The tension of the stretched cord will tow you to sprint faster than your partner, who is pulling you, and then you will slingshot past him for the last ten yards of your sprint.

Chip's Tips

1. Stagger your feet like a forty start, but stand tall.
2. Remember to use explosive arm drive. The faster your arms move, the faster your feet will move.
3. Stay light on the balls of your feet.
4. Accelerate all the way through.

3. Suicide Run Progression

Purpose: To work on speed endurance

Equipment: Two belts with a twenty-five-foot elastic cord.

Drill: This can be a partner drill or you may use a fence or post as an anchor. You will use a twenty-five-foot elastic cord attached to the front of your belt and anchored at the opposite end, with four cones spread out at five-yard intervals, from ten to twenty-five yards out from the start line. For your first progression, you will back up to stretch the cord out to twenty-five yards. Then sprint twenty-five yards to a cone, rapidly decelerating under control as you reach the cone. After reaching the cone, you will skip backward to the starting position. This back skip will be with resistance. For the second progression, you will sprint twenty yards to a cone, decelerating under control as you reach the cone. After reaching the cone, you will skip backward to the starting position again. For the third progression, you will sprint fifteen yards to a cone, decelerating under control as you reach the cone. After reaching the cone, you will skip backward to the starting position again. For the fourth progression you will sprint ten yards to a cone, decelerating under control as you reach the cone. After reaching the cone, skip backward to the starting position.

Chip's Tips
1. Stand tall and fall.
2. Make sure you maintain good forward lean.
3. Keep your chest over your knees on your backpedal.

General Overspeed Drills

The following drills are appropriate for all players, regardless of their position.

1. W Drill

Purpose: To work on multiple changes of direction, acceleration, and deceleration at high speeds

Equipment: Two belts with a twenty-five-foot elastic cord.

Drill: The W drill is done with a partner. Both players are hooked up to a twenty-five-foot elastic cord. Place six cones five yards apart in a diagonal arrangement. The player who is doing the running first will start on the first cone facing his partner. The partner will move laterally with the athlete as he starts to run to each cone. The first pattern I will have the player perform is sprint, backpedal, sprint, backpedal, sprint, backpedal, and sprint. This drill is great for defensive backs and linebackers. The next drill I will have the player do is shuffle-turn-shuffle for the distance of the cones. This is a great drill for offensive linemen, as they can work on their slide step as if they were practicing pass protection. The last drill in this progression is the sprint, plant, sprint, plant, sprint, plant, and sprint. This drill is great for all skill positions. It teaches the athletes how to step, plant, and push off of the outside foot, which is so important in cutting and changing direction.

Chip's Tips

1. Stay under control.
2. Keep your center of gravity down.
3. Drop your hips down on change of direction.
4. Cycle your feet on your backpedal.
5. Keep your eyes straight ahead.
6. Move your arms fast.

2. Stride Ladder Drill

Purpose: To improve stride length through the acceleration phase of a forty-yard dash (I use the stride ladder to teach positive reinforcement of the strides for the first ten yards. I have broken down the forty-yard dash into three phases. The first phase is the drive phase, where I teach my players to take what I believe to be optimal stride lengths for the exercise. The stride length should be seven strides in the first ten yards. If a player is taking more than seven strides in those ten yards, he is spinning his wheels and is taking time off the clock by spending too much time on the ground. If the player is taking fewer than seven strides, he is overstriding and can't generate enough power to achieve top end speed. Stride length is primarily an effect of genetics; however, the Soviets proved that stride length and stride frequency could be improved through practice of proper technique. Remember, speed = stride length $\times$ stride frequency.)

Equipment: Stride ladder or paint sticks.

Drill: The player will stand tall and fall, driving his lead foot into the first rung of the ladder. He will accelerate all the way out of the ladder, staying in a straight line and keeping his hips over his knees. I usually do two sets of ten reps for this drill, and I do this drill on overspeed days.

I had my equipment builder make my stride ladder, using an optimal stride length. I previously used paint sticks from a home improvement store. They were free, but I hated picking them up at the conclusion of the workout. I would lay them out in this stride frequency sequence for ten yards. If you do not have access to a stride ladder, the paint sticks will work just as well.

Chip's Ideal Stride Frequency Sequence

Pro Strides	Beginner Strides
2' 10"	2' 4"
6' 5"	5' 2"
10' 9"	8' 6"
15' 7"	12' 2"
21' 1"	16' 2"
27' 0"	20' 5"
33' 5"	24' 11"

Chip's Tips

1. Stand tall and fall.
2. Keep your hips over your feet.
3. Keep your eyes straight ahead.
4. Make sure to use fast arm swings as you run.
5. Stay on the balls of your feet.
6. Keep your strides inside shoulder width.

3. Seven-Cone Pattern Run

Purpose: To work on acceleration, deceleration, change of direction, and speed cutting

Equipment: Seven disc cones.

Drill: The seven-cone progression runs start with the cones set up like a box, ten yards square, with four cones on the corners and one cone in the middle. The other two cones are placed five yards from the front two cones perpendicularly. The athlete starts on the middle cone. The drill starts when the coach gives a direction to the player: right or left foot. The player then drops his hips and runs to one of the back cones. The next time the athlete is up, the coach will give the player a right or left signal, and the athlete will run to the back cone, around, and back to the middle cone. The next progression is for the athlete to react to the coach's direction either right or left, where the player will run around the back cone and break down on the middle cone. Just as the player starts to break down, the coach will give the player a right or left signal, and the player will sprint up to the front cone, breaking down on the cone. The next progression is for the athlete to go through the same sequence, except when the player gets to the front cone, he will shuffle out laterally to the last cone. The final progression is the full run plus; when the player shuffles out to the last cone, he will sprint forward five yards.

Chip's Tips

1. Stay under control.
2. Keep your hips low on the change of direction.
3. Stay light on your feet.
4. On your backward movement, drop your hips and explode in the direction you are going.
5. Make sure to use fast arm swings as you run.
6. Keep your eyes straight ahead.

4. NFL Short Shuttle

Purpose: To measure lateral quickness, speed, coordination, and explosion

Equipment: Three cones.

Drill: This drill is called the 5-10-5. You start by straddling the five-yard line with either your right or left hand touching the line. You may choose to go to either the right or left side to start the drill. Let's say you run to your right first; you must touch the goal line with your right hand and then turn and sprint to the fifteen-yard line, touching the line with your left hand. After touching the line, you must turn and sprint back past the five-yard line where you started. Just remember you have to touch the line with your hand and not your foot.

Chip's Tips

1. Keep your center of gravity low.
2. Stay inside the box, and reach and touch the line with your hand.
3. Get your hips turned on the transition from the hop to the sprint.
4. Make sure you run through the line as you finish.
5. On the start, put all your weight on the ball of your front foot.
6. Point your foot in the direction you are going to start.
7. Try and stick to taking seven to nine steps for the whole drill. If you take more than that, you are spinning your wheels; anything less than seven and you are overstriding.

5. L Drill

Purpose: To measure multiple changes of direction, acceleration, deceleration, cutting ability, flexibility, and body control

Equipment: Three cones.

Drill: The L drill starts by placing three cones five yards apart in the shape of an "L." The L portion is always to the right. If you start on the five-yard line, you will start in a forty-yard stance; you will run five yards and touch the ten-yard line with your right hand. You then will turn and run back to the five-yard line, touching the line again with your right hand. You will then turn and sprint around the second cone. After running on the outside of the second cone, you will do a figure eight around the third cone, staying as close as you can to the inside of the second cone. Finish by sprinting past the cone that you started beside.

Chip's Tips

1. Keep your center of gravity low.
2. This drill works on explosive change of direction, so keep your center of gravity low.
3. Reach for the line—don't run past the line.
4. Remember, you are competing against yourself.
5. Try and travel five yards in two steps with no wasted effort.

6. Star Drill

Purpose: To work on sprinting, deceleration, coordination, backpedaling, and change of direction

Equipment: Five cones.

Drill: As the name of this drill implies, you will be running in a star pattern. Five cones are set five yards apart in a star pattern. The progression starts with a forward sprint to the middle cone, followed by a backpedal at 45 degrees, followed by a sprint back to the middle cone. You will work yourself around the star pattern by sprinting, then backpedaling, until you are back to where you started.

Chip's Tips

1. Keep your center of gravity low.
2. Stay light on your feet.
3. Keep your chest over your knees on your backpedal.
4. Remember, fast arms equal fast feet.
5. Explode out of the break.

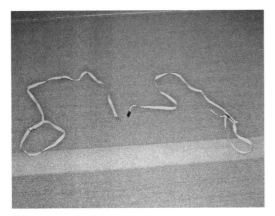

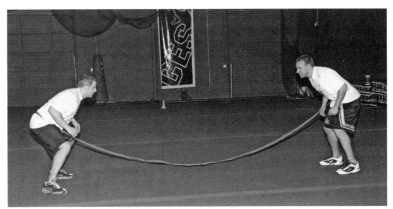

Figure 6.3a. Reaction Belt

b. Reaction Belt Drill

Reaction Belt Drill. The purpose of the reaction belt drills is to teach the athlete reactive, explosive speed and multiple changes of direction. The reaction belts required are waist belts that are connected by a strap of Velcro. (See Figure 6.3a.) Each partner places a belt around his waist and connects the belt by hooking the fastening clips together. The Velcro is then connected between the two athletes. Athletes can play different games using these simple training devices to increase interest and variance. (See Figure 6.3b.)

1. Mirror Drill

Purpose: To work on lateral reaction

Equipment: Two reaction belts with Velcro.

Drill: Two athletes stand facing each other, wearing the reaction belts fastened at the waist. Two cones are placed twenty yards apart. One athlete is the leader and the other athlete is the follower. On the coach's command to start, the leader tries to juke the follower by moving laterally as fast as he can. The follower tries to keep the leader from breaking the Velcro as he mirrors the leader. If the leader breaks the Velcro, he wins. However, if the follower keeps the Velcro from breaking, he wins. The drill will last for ten seconds, followed by a role reversal between the leader and the follower. The drill times are ten seconds on and fifteen seconds off. This is a great drill for defensive backs and offensive linemen.

Chip's Tips

1. Keep your eyes on your partner's belly button.
2. Stay within arm's length of each other if you can.
3. Keep a low center of gravity.
4. Keep score.

2. Partner Tag Drill: Coleman Progressions

Purpose: To work on reaction in a multidirectional plane (Each of these progressions teaches the body to move and react in different positions. These progressions force the body to react to the motion of the other competitor.)

Equipment: Two reaction belts with Velcro.

Drill: There are four different progressions to this drill. The first is what we call get-ups. With the belts connected to the leader's back and the follower's front, both are seated cross-legged. The leader jumps up as quickly as he can and tries to sprint ahead of the follower and break the belt. The follower will react as quickly as possible to the leader and try and keep up with the leader so that the belt does not break. If the leader breaks the Velcro, he wins. If the follower stays with the leader, he wins. The point system I use is this: You get one point if you break the Velcro and one point if you keep from breaking the Velcro. If you are in the back, you can receive another point by tapping your partner on the back before he crosses the line at the twenty-yard cone. The second progression is for both athletes to start from a push-up position. The leader will be facing straight ahead on all fours. The follower will be facing the same direction, also on all fours. The leader will jump up and start sprinting and the follower will react to the movement of the leader. The same point system is in effect as the seated partner tag. The third progression is with both athletes on one knee, facing the same direction as they did in the push up drill. The athlete in the back reacts to the athlete in the front. The last progression will have both athletes lying on their backs. Both athletes are facing in the same direction. The athlete in the back will react to the athlete in the front as he rolls over and starts to sprint. The points system stays the same for all these drills. The drill will last ten seconds, switching each time you change ends.

Chip's Tips

1. Stay light on your feet.
2. Have fun.
3. Keep score.
4. Try and match your speed and skill with someone who is equal.

Position-Specific Overspeed Program for Offense

Quarterbacks

1. Three-Step Drops

Purpose: To work on foot quickness

Equipment: Shackles and a belt with a twenty-five-foot elastic cord.

Drill: The quarterback will take a quick three-step drop.

Chip's Tips

1. Stand tall.
2. Keep the football at shoulder height.
3. Don't crouch.

2. Five-Step Drops

Purpose: To increase foot speed and quickness

Equipment: Shackles and a belt with a twenty-five-foot elastic cord.

Drill: The quarterback will take five quick drop steps.

Chip's Tips

1. Stand tall.
2. Keep the football at shoulder height.
3. Don't crouch.
4. Keep your feet moving.

3. Seven-Step Drops

Purpose: To increase foot speed and quickness, so as you drop quicker, you can read your throwing progression faster

Equipment: Shackles and a belt with a twenty-five-foot elastic cord.

Drill: The quarterback will take seven quick drop steps.

Chip's Tips

1. Stand tall.
2. Keep the football at shoulder height.

3. Don't crouch.
4. Keep your feet moving.
5. Don't overstride on your drops.

4. Redirection

Purpose: To teach the quarterback to read and react to his surroundings

Equipment: Shackles and a belt with a twenty-five-foot elastic cord.

Drill: The redirect drill is a drill I have all my quarterbacks do every day. I have the quarterback take a five-step drop. As he settles on the drop, I have him keep his feet moving. I then give him a right or left signal, where he will take a quick lateral step, either backward or sprinting laterally. As the quarterback redirects out of the pocket, I will have receivers standing on the right and left, and I will have the quarterback spot throw to one of the receivers. Because the quarterback sees the field and reacts to a visual cue given by the coach, this skill is transferred to the field. There is a sister drill that I also do with the quarterbacks that involves redirection. I have the quarterbacks give me a seven-step drop, keeping their feet moving. I will give them a quick directive point: right, left, or center. The quarterback will take one step quickly in the direction of the point, stepping right, left, or center while moving toward me. I try and keep the number of directional changes between eight and ten.

Chip's Tips

1. Stand tall.
2. Keep the football at shoulder height.
3. Don't crouch.
4. Keep your feet moving.
5. Don't overstride on your drops.
6. Stay on the balls of your feet.

Running Backs

1. Zone Runs

Purpose: To teach the running back to step in the opposite direction, to be able to see and react, plant, and cut at a fast speed

Equipment: Six six-inch half dummies, a belt with a twenty-five-foot elastic cord, and a football.

Drill: The running back will step to the right and quickly cut back to the left, sprinting upfield ten yards. He will repeat the same action in the opposite direction.

Chip's Tips

1. Start from a two-point stance.
2. Stay on the balls of your feet.
3. Keep the football tucked in your outside arm.

2. Bag Drill

Purpose: To teach the running back control over change of direction, cutting, acceleration, and deceleration

Equipment: Six six-inch half dummies, a stand-up dummy, a belt with a twenty-five-foot elastic cord, and a football.

Drill: This drill is set up by placing six of the quarter bags about one yard apart, three bags on the right and three bags on the left. The running back will start on one side of the first bag. The first part of this drill is to have the running back step over the bags in a diagonal pattern. His foot contact cadence is in-in, out-out. Repeat this pattern to the end of the bags, where the player will then sprint straight ahead for five yards. The next bag drill involves six half bags and a stand-up dummy. The setup for this drill is to lay the half bags in a row with the pop-up dummy about five yards in front of the bags. The running back will line up on the right side of the bags about seven yards in front of them. He will run high knees over the bags. The coach is behind the pop-up dummy. As the player comes over the last bag, the coach will push the pop-up dummy to the right, and the player will break hard to the left.

Chip's Tips

1. Stay on the balls of your feet.
2. Keep a good forward lean.
3. Explode on your change of direction.
4. Always keep the ball tucked in your outside arm.

3. Zigzag Cone Drill

Purpose: To teach balance, coordination, explosive change of direction, acceleration, and deceleration

Equipment: Eight cones, a belt with a twenty-five-foot elastic cord, and a football.

Drill: This drill requires eight cones that are lined up in a straight line with two feet in between each cone. The running back will be running in a zigzag pattern through the cones. The steps will be short and explosive. The cadence for this drill is step-step-plant, step-step-plant, diagonally through the cones, followed by a sprint of five yards.

Chip's Tips

1. Concentrate on your outside foot plant.
2. Stay on the balls of your feet.
3. Keep a good forward lean.

Wide Receivers

1. Running Routes

Purpose: To teach the wide receiver how to create space between himself and the defensive back, explosive change of direction, hand quickness, and reaction to the ball

Equipment: A belt with a twenty-five-foot elastic cord.

Drill: The wide receiver will actually run routes from the right side and from the left side of the field. The routes are run off of a route tree.

Chip's Tips

1. Stay on the balls of your feet.
2. Keep your head on a swivel.
3. Keep your hips down on your break.
4. Concentrate on the ball.
5. Catch the ball with your hands as opposed to your body.
6. Catch it, tuck it, and get upfield.

2. Quick Foot Get-Off Drill

Purpose: To teach the wide receiver to move his feet quickly and to separate himself from press coverage

Equipment: A belt with a twenty-five-foot elastic cord and two cones.

Drill: For this drill, there will be two cones set up, one on the right and one on the left. The wide receiver lines up on the inside of the left cone in a two-point stance. He will chop his feet and use his hands in a swim technique, getting to the outside of the cone and then upfield ten yards. He will then run a hitch pattern. The coach will feed him the football. He will catch it, tuck it, and get upfield five more yards. Repeat this drill to the right side.

Chip's Tips

1. Chop your feet as fast as you can.
2. Get your hands moving quickly.

3. Quick Hands Drill for Wide Receivers

Purpose: To teach the player's hands to react quickly, catching the football from different angles

Equipment: Quick hands and a football.

Drill: The wide receiver will be wearing a training aid that I invented called the quick hands. This training aid adds resistance to both of the player's hands, giving resistance in the movement of catching the football. The aid does not impede the actual catching movement. The coach will throw the football at different angles. I like to throw the ball in an "around-the-world" motion. The wide receiver will shoot his hands out to catch the football away from his body. The duration of this drill is three minutes.

Offensive Linemen

1. Pass Set Drill

Purpose: To teach the offensive lineman to be explosive in his pass sets and to be able to defend against the bull rush

Equipment: Shackles and a belt with a twenty-five-foot elastic cord.

Drill: The lineman will work in three directions on this drill. He will start out by moving diagonally with three slide steps. The next movement will be two hops backward. The last movement is three slide steps diagonally in the opposite direction.

Chip's Tips

1. Stay low on your pass set.
2. Keep your head up and your back straight.
3. Sit back on your haunches.
4. Keep a wide foot base.
5. Keep your hands up.
6. Keep your eyes focused straight ahead.

2. Pulling Drill

Purpose: To teach the offensive lineman how to drop step, open his hips, and run laterally

Equipment: Five cones and a belt with a twenty-five-foot elastic cord.

Drill: Place three cones about five yards apart in an equilateral triangle pattern; place the remaining two cones to the right and left of the base of the equilateral triangle. The lineman will line up facing the middle cone. He will drop step his outside leg, open up his hips, and turn and run in a semicircle around the outside of the cone. Then he will turn and run up the field.

Chip's Tips

1. *Keep your hips down.*
2. *Keep the weight on the balls of your feet.*
3. *Rip your elbow open in the direction of the pull to force your hips to open.*
4. *Keep pressure off your hand that is on the ground.*

3. Lateral Shuffle and Punch

Purpose: To teach the offensive lineman to stay in a lateral posture while using his hands against his opponent

Equipment: Two cones, shackles, and quick hands.

Drill: Place two cones five yards apart. The lineman should shuffle laterally between the cones, making sure his feet do not cross while keeping his foot base wide. He should alternate hand punches, left and then right.

Chip's Tips

1. *Stay on the balls of your feet.*
2. *Keep your center of gravity down.*
3. *Keep your back straight and your head down.*
4. *Keep your hands up.*

4. Drive Block Drill

Purpose: To work on hip and hand explosion

Equipment: A Meadow harness (five-cord training aid), quick hands, and a blocking shield.

Drill: This is a partner drill. The lineman's partner will need a hand shield. He will stand about one yard in front of the lineman. The lineman will fire out of a three-point stance, locking his hands out on the hand shield, in a punching motion, driving his partner back five yards.

Chip's Tips

1. Stay on the balls of your feet.
2. Keep your center of gravity low.
3. Keep your thumbs up on your punch.
4. Keep a wide foot base.

5. Mirror Drill

Purpose: To teach lateral reaction, quickness, coordination, and balance

Equipment: Shackles, quick hands, two cones, and a belt with a twenty-five-foot elastic cord.

Drill: This is a partner drill. The lineman's partner will line up facing him. The lineman will mimic the same movement that his partner makes, staying in front of him. The two players should move laterally between the two cones, which should be placed five yards apart.

Chip's Tips

1. Keep your center of gravity low.
2. Keep your feet shoulder width apart.
3. Keep your hands up.

6. Quick Hands Drill for Offensive Linemen

Purpose: To train the hands for quickness (The purpose of training hands is the same as training foot speed. Hand quickness is learned in the same way that foot quickness is learned. I train the hands to react quickly to the movements in the trenches that you need to master. Hand movement is one of the most under-trained movements in football. Working on hand movements can make a mediocre player good and a good player great. On the professional level, it's all about the hands.)

Equipment: Quick hands and a football.

Drill: This is a partner drill. Both players stand facing each other. The offensive lineman starts with both of his hands on the chest of his partner. The defensive player will try to knock off one of the hands of the offensive lineman. As fast as the hand is knocked off, the offensive lineman will replace his hand back on the chest of the defensive player.

Chip's Tips

1. Keep your eyes on the football.
2. Keep your hands out in front of you.
3. Explode your hands toward the ball.

Tight Ends

1. Quick Foot Get-Offs

Purpose: To work on getting separation, creating space, and getting out into your route quickly

Equipment: A belt with a twenty-five-foot elastic cord, a blocking shield, and a football.

Drill: In this drill, the tight end will line up in a three-point stance. He will step down like he is blocking, and then he will release upfield and run a quick out route. The coach will throw to him.

Chip's Tips

1. Keep your eyes straight ahead.
2. Catch the football with your hands.

2. Quick Hands Drill

See the wide receiver drill.

3. Drive Block Drill

See the offensive lineman drill.

4. Running Routes

Purpose: To mimic the route that the tight end runs on the field

Equipment: A belt with a twenty-five-foot elastic cord and a football.

Drill: The tight end can run any route that he would normally run. He should work on running quick-release routes. He will finish the drill by catching the football, tucking the ball and turning upfield, and sprinting ten yards.

Chip's Tips

1. Stay on the balls of your feet.
2. Catch the football with your hands.
3. Explode out of your break.

5. Quick Hands Drill

See the offensive lineman drill.

Position-Specific Overspeed Program for Defense

Each movement for each position is trained with overspeed and resistance.

Defensive Linemen

1. Quick Foot Rip and Swim Get-Offs

Purpose: To teach the defensive lineman how to read and react (This improves balance, quickness, and lateral movement. It will teach the lineman how to use his hands in the rip and swim technique.)

Equipment: Quick hands, a long cord, and a pop-up dummy.

Drill: The drill has the defensive lineman react to the snap of the football. On the snap, or movement from the coach, the player will either use the swim technique or the rip technique on the pop-up dummy. He will concentrate on getting upfield quickly.

Chip's Tips

1. Keep your center of gravity low.
2. Move on the snap of the football.
3. Rotate your hips on the swim movement.
4. Make sure you concentrate on using quick hands.

2. Read and React Drill

Purpose: To work on hip explosion, quickness, change of direction, balance, and quick hands

Equipment: A pop-up dummy, quick hands, and a long cord.

Drill: In this drill, the coach will face the defensive lineman while the player is in a three-point stance. There is a pop-up dummy in front of the player. The coach has his arms spread out and will then drop one of his arms down to his side, signaling the snap of the ball. The other arm that is still pointing indicates the direction the player should go. The player will use a rip or swim technique on the dummy while getting upfield.

Chip's Tips

1. Keep your center of gravity low.
2. Explode your hands out.
3. Keep your eyes straight ahead.

3. Two-Gap Drill

Purpose: To teach the player how to rotate his hips (It will teach balance, explosive lateral movement, and hand quickness.)

Equipment: Quick hands, a long cord, and a pop-up dummy.

Drill: This drill is the same as the read and react drill, with the exception that the player will lock onto the dummy and rotate his hips in the direction that the coach points.

Chip's Tips

1. Keep your center of gravity low.
2. Lock your hands onto the dummy.
3. Explode in the direction the coach points.

4. Quick Hands Drill

See the offensive lineman drill.

5. Lateral Shuffle and Punch

See the offensive lineman drill.

Linebackers

1. Pass Drops

Purpose: To work on diagonal movement, hip rotation, backpedaling, and reaction

Equipment: A belt with a twenty-five-foot elastic cord.

Drill: On this drill, the linebacker will drop into pass coverage at a depth of eight to ten yards. The player will settle his feet and put himself into a position to react to the quarterback's movement.

Chip's Tips

1. Make sure that you drop your hips.
2. Explode off your inside foot.
3. Stay on the balls of your feet.
4. Keep your center of gravity low.
5. Keep your head on a swivel.

2. Scrape and Fill

Purpose: To work on lateral movement as you read and react

Equipment: Eight cones and a belt with a twenty-five-foot elastic cord.

Drill: The setup for this drill is eight cones, lined up in a straight line, two yards apart. The linebacker lines up five to seven yards in front of the cones. The cones to the right represent the gaps on the line, A gap, B gap, C gap, D gap. The cones on the left represent the same gaps. The coach will call out one of the gaps. The player will run straight ahead, shuffle down to the gap, do an arm rip action, and explode up into the gap. He will repeat this randomly for different gaps.

Chip's Tips

1. Keep your center of gravity down.
2. Stay on the balls of your feet.
3. Play downhill.
4. Step in the direction that you are going.
5. Stay under control.

3. Urlacher Drill

Purpose: To teach read and reaction, lateral quickness, and playing under control

Equipment: A belt with two twenty-five-foot elastic cords and eight cones.

Drill: The setup and the drill are the same as for the scrape and fill drill, with the exception of adding another cord to the player's outside hip.

Chip's Tips

1. Stay on the balls of your feet.
2. Step in the direction that you are going.
3. Keep your center of gravity low.
4. Stay under control when you shuffle.

4. Read or React Drill

Purpose: To teach multiple changes of direction

Equipment: A belt with a twenty-five-foot elastic cord.

Drill: The linebacker lines up at his position, seven yards off the ball. He will read play action by coming up toward the line of scrimmage. He will then read pass and drop eight to ten yards in the hook to curl zone.

Chip's Tips

1. Stay on the balls of your feet.
2. Explode on the change of direction.
3. Drop your hips.
4. Keep your head on a swivel.

5. Cut Block Drill

Purpose: To teach the linebacker to stay low and use his hands to fight off the cut block

Equipment: One pair of quick hands and one small dummy.

Drill: The linebacker shuffles laterally, wearing a pair of quick hands. The coach throws a dummy at the linebacker's knees, and the player blocks the dummy by forcing his hands down quickly on the dummy.

Chip's Tips

1. Stay on the balls of your feet.
2. Keep your hands out in front.

6. Quick Hands Drill

See the offensive lineman drill.

Defensive Backs

1. Backpedal Drill

Purpose: To teach the defensive back to stay low on his backpedal (He pumps his arms quickly and keeps his center of gravity down and his chest over his knees.)

Equipment: A belt with a twenty-five-foot elastic cord.

Drill: The player will backpedal in one of three directions (straight, right, or left) for a distance of fifteen yards. The player will turn and break to his right for one set, to his left for one set, and then straight back for a third, each time backpedaling in a straight line for fifteen yards.

Chip's Tips

1. Keep your chest over your knees.
2. Stay on the balls of your feet.
3. Keep a low center of gravity.
4. Maintain fast arm action.

2. Backpedal and Weave Drill

Purpose: To teach proper backpedal and weave technique

Equipment: A belt with a twenty-five-foot elastic cord.

Drill: This drill is the same as the backpedal, with this exception: the player will backpedal weave to the right and backpedal weave to the left.

Chip's Tips

1. Keep your chest over your knees.
2. Stay on the balls of your feet.
3. Keep your center of gravity down low.
4. Maintain fast arm action.

3. Backpedal and Straight Line Drill

Purpose: To teach multiple changes of direction

Equipment: A belt with a twenty-five-foot elastic cord.

Drill: Same as the backpedal with this exception: the player will break at a 45-degree angle forward and sprint ten yards.

Chip's Tips

1. Keep your chest over your knees.
2. Stay on the balls of your feet.
3. Keep your center of gravity down low.
4. Maintain fast arm action.
5. Work on cycling your feet on your backpedal transition.

4. Backpedal and 90-Degree Angle Drill

Purpose: To teach the defensive back to open his hips on change of direction

Equipment: A belt with a twenty-five-foot elastic cord.

Drill: This drill is the same as the other backpedal drills, with this exception: the defensive back will backpedal ten yards, then open his hips, and sprint at a 90-degree angle ten yards up the field.

Chip's Tips

1. Keep your chest over your knees.
2. Stay on the balls of your feet.
3. Keep your center of gravity low.
4. Maintain fast arm action.
5. Work on cycling your feet on your backpedal transition.

5. W Drill for Defensive Backs

Purpose: To work on explosive multiple changes of direction from a backpedal to a sprint

Equipment: A belt with a twenty-five-foot elastic cord and five cones.

Drill: Cones are set up five yards apart in a W pattern. The player will start off in a sprint to the first cone, then backpedal at an angle to the second cone in the W, then sprint to the third cone, then backpedal to the fourth cone, and finally sprint to the fifth cone.

1. Stay on the balls of your feet.
2. Stay under control as you transition from sprint to backpedal.
3. Cycle your feet on your backpedal and break.

Contrast Training

After any drill that has loaded the body with resistance, overspeed, or reaction (drills using elastic cords, weight vests, hand weights, etc.), you should immediately remove the training aid and repeat at least one repetition of the same drill. This technique is called contrast training. You are, in a sense, tricking the brain into thinking that it still has resistance, overspeed, or reaction influences in the specific movement that you have just performed. The muscle fibers will fire explosively to overcome the resistance, overspeed, or reaction of the movement. By recruiting explosive fibers with this method, you immediately feel the difference with your first-step explosion. That is what we call sports speed; it is a learned response.

Overspeed Training: The Bottom Line

Remember that the purpose of overspeed is to force your body to expect fast motion. That includes linear or straight line movements and all the movements that you do for your particular position. You are recruiting fast-twitch muscle fibers by enhancing neuromuscular response. It affects your brain's ability to send signals along the neuromuscular pathways. I have a saying that I repeat to all my players: "Quickness is a state of mind; to win you have got to be quick." Don't just run fast for the sake of being fast. Speed without control has no application on the football field. Speed under control will give you the competitive edge. To be successful, you must maintain your skills and technique while running fast.

7

Reaction Training

Teaching Your Body to Respond

Simply stated, reaction is a learned response. It must be trained and developed just like any other skill that pertains to football or sports in general. Every play or action on the football field starts out with each player knowing ahead of time what their actions will potentially be. To prepare for this, you can train your muscles to fire sooner and more explosively, improving your reaction time by as much as 20 percent. The most critical movement in the progression is that first movement; this is the point where typically one athlete wins and his opponent or rival loses. The end result depends on how each player reacts to what he sees and the actions he takes in response.

The training world is filled with various theories on reaction. I've seen many different articles on reaction: some that were very good, some that comprised primarily filler information, and some from sports scientists who obviously have yet to train their first athlete. I personally believe that reaction training is the one method that has been overlooked in the training world, with the exception of the Soviets.

All of the athletes that I have worked with, from Champ Bailey to Marcus Vick, have been blessed with God-given ability and I dare not try and take any credit for that talent. However, I do believe that by training reactively, you can improve on that God-given ability and enhance your sport explosiveness and reaction time. It's for that reason that I train reaction virtually every day here at Competitive Edge Sports. I believe that it can be improved upon through daily repetition, especially during the first few weeks of training. I have reaction drills designed for the general movement skills that can be useful for overall football ability. I also have position-specific reaction drills for every position on the field. I routinely use reaction drills that involve an audio and/or a visual stimulus.

General Reaction Drills

I have a standard set of reaction drills that we use in our training that will benefit any player regardless of his position. They comprise multiple movement combinations that every athlete will make on the field, including bounding, sliding or shuffling, turning and running, hip rotation, backpedaling, vertical jumps, and sprinting. The drills can easily be done in groups of varied size, including almost as many players as you want, depending on the available space. It's best to try and have two to three separate groups, which assists in providing adequate rest intervals between drills. Even separating the players by position is acceptable, though not necessary, while using the general reaction drills. Have the coach running the drill stand in front of the group performing the drill. The athletes should be spaced out properly so as not to run into one another and also so they have an unobstructed view of the instructor. Following are the drills in the order I normally use them.

1. **Lateral Bounds** *(See Figure 7.1.)*

    Purpose: To improve plyometric quickness and ballistic explosiveness

    Drill: The players should be standing ready in a two-point stance and in a good athletic position. The coach should use either his hands or some type of instrument (for example, a football) to signal direction. Using only left and right directional signals, he should point to a direction for the athletes to follow. The athletes must then react to the signal by bounding laterally out and back to their starting position as fast as possible. Bounding on this drill consists of driving off the opposite leg of the direction you were signaled (for example, if the coach signals left, push off the right leg), landing on the other, and driving off that leg back to the starting position. The players should not "hop" over, which is pushing off with both legs in the desired direction and then landing on both feet with the same movement during the recovery phase. Athletes should recover to the starting position before getting another signal. Because of the short distance covered, this drill is done fairly rapidly, allowing just enough time for athletes to get back to the ready position before the next signal comes. This is a visual cue reaction drill, with no audio involved. The

Figure 7.1. Lateral Bounds

number of reps is typically higher on this drill, usually going for about twelve to fifteen total.

Chip's Tips

1. Stay in the ready position.
2. Keep your feet shoulder width apart.
3. Bound back as fast as possible to the middle position.

2. Lateral Slides *(See Figure 7.2.)*

Purpose: To build explosive change of direction and lateral quickness

Drill: The athletes should start in the same position as in the previous drill. Again, the coach should be up in front giving the direction using only a left or right signal. Once the coach gives the signal, the athletes must then react by sliding (also called shuffling) in the given direction. On this drill, the coach can choose to use either an audio cue or another prop to signal the athlete to stop and recover back to the starting position by sliding back. The audio cue can be as simple as the coach yelling "back," blowing a whistle, or using any other sound or verbal command he decides to use. The coach can place cones five yards from the center and have the players shuffle to a cone and back. (A line on the ground can be used in place of a cone.) The distance covered by the athletes is determined by the coach (perhaps three, four, or five yards), depending on what they want to accomplish. Coaches should teach and encourage the athletes to stay low, keep a wide

Figure 7.2. Lateral Slides

base with their feet, and not cross their feet over each other. Also, the athletes should get out and recover as quickly as possible. The repetitions on this drill are usually around seven or eight because of the increased distance the athletes are required to cover.

Chip's Tips

1. *Shuffle out as explosively as possible.*
2. *Plant on the outside leg, coming back to the starting position.*
3. *Do not cross your feet on the shuffle.*
4. *Keep your center of gravity as low as possible.*

3. Sprint Out at 45 Degrees

Purpose: To increase first-step explosion, acceleration, and deceleration

Drill: This drill is started with the athletes and coach in the same position as in the previous drills. The drill uses three direction signals: left, right, and straight forward. Again, the coach can decide to use an audio cue or a prop to signal the athletes to recover back to the starting position. On the left or right direction signal, the athletes must turn and run at a 45-degree angle either to a cone or until the coach gives the audio signal, at which point they should return by backpedaling. On the straight forward signal, the coach should pull the visual cue back toward himself to help indicate the coming forward action. The athletes should recover by backpedaling to the starting position. Again, have the athletes get out and recover as quickly as possible. With the amount of distance covered, the repetitions with this drill should be around seven or eight.

Chip's Tips

1. Do not take a false step.
2. Drop your hips on the change of direction.
3. Stay on the balls of your feet.

4. Quick Hips *(See Figures 7.3a and 7.3b.)*

Purpose: To improve hip rotation, agility, and balance

Drill: This drill is also called quarter turns or quarter eagles. The drill is started with the coach and athletes in their usual positions. Once the coach gives the direction (using a left or right signal only), the athletes should turn their hips and legs out to that direction and back as quickly as possible. An athlete's feet should remain roughly shoulder width apart during the whole drill. The coach should instruct the athletes to turn the lower half of their bodies only in the given direction and to keep their shoulders square to the coach. A variation to this drill to add intensity is to have the athletes "chop" their feet (keep the feet moving, quick—chop, chop) between each signal. This drill is done fairly rapidly because no distance is covered. The repetitions on this drill are usually twelve to fifteen.

Chip's Tips

1. Stay on the balls of your feet.
2. Keep your center of gravity low.
3. Explosive hip rotation is a good drill.

Figure 7.3a. Quick Hips   b.

5. 180s

Purpose: To work on hip rotation, agility, and balance

Drill: This drill is a variation of the fourth drill (quick hips). The coach and the athletes are in their usual positions. Instead of the athletes turning their hips only in the given direction (left or right only), they will turn their whole body 180 degrees around and then recover back as quickly as possible. This drill is done rapidly with the next signal given as soon as the athletes can recover completely. No distance is covered during this drill, so the repetitions should be twelve to fifteen.

Chip's Tips

1. Stay on the balls of your feet.
2. Keep your center of gravity low.
3. Make sure to concentrate on explosive hip rotation during this drill.

6. 45-Degree Bounds

Purpose: To improve plyometric quickness and ballistic explosiveness

Drill: This drill is much like the first drill (lateral bounds), except that the direction of the bound changes. The athletes and coach are in the usual positions, and a left or right signal is used. Instead of bounding laterally, the athletes will bound forward at a 45-degree angle. Just as for the lateral bound, the athletes must land on the opposite leg they pushed off from and then push back off of that leg to recover to the starting position. This drill is done rapidly, so the coach should give the next signal as soon as the athletes recover. The repetitions should be twelve to fifteen.

Chip's Tips

1. Stay in the ready position.
2. Keep your feet shoulder width apart.
3. Bound back as fast as possible to the middle position.

7. Sprint Outs

Purpose: To increase explosive change of direction, quick reaction, acceleration, and deceleration

Drill: The positions of the athletes and coach are the same as in the previous drills. This drill uses left, right, and middle signals. The coach should use an audio cue to signal the athletes to recover to the starting position. When a left or right signal is given, the athletes should sprint forward at a 45-degree angle to the coach and straight forward on the middle signal. When the athletes are signaled to recover, they should backpedal to their starting position. The coach should give the next signal as soon as they recover and encourage them to maintain eye contact with him to receive the rapidly changing signals. Also, the athletes should stay in their backpedal until the next signal is given and then "cycle" their feet to help learn to quickly change their direction. *Cycle* means to keep your feet moving fast in a straight up and down motion. The repetitions on this drill should be seven to nine.

Chip's Tips

1. Do not take a false step.
2. Keep your hips under you during the deceleration phase.
3. Keep your eyes on the coach.
4. Never turn your back or lose sight of the coach.

Reaction Drill Progressions

We also use reaction drills that are a progression of movements added to one another until the drill is one long series of reactions and subsequent movements. The drills are a great way to simulate extended on-the-field action. These drills incorporate multiple movements on different planes that can be useful for every position. These are best done in groups of athletes to include enough rest time between each player's repetitions. These drills usually include both an audio and visual cue and incorporate equipment such as cones, mini-hurdles, and dummies or bags. There are many different setups you can use, but the following are a few of the most common ones that we use.

Reaction Drill Progression #1

This drill has five different progressions and is usually about four or five reps for each person per progression. First, set up two cones about four feet apart and then two more cones about five yards farther out at a 45-degree angle from the first set. The cones will resemble a "V" with a slightly wider base. Have the athletes form a line behind the first two cones, with one person between the cones, ready to start the drill. (See Figure 7.4.) The coach will be a little farther out from the second set of cones, standing between them and in front of the athletes, ready to give the signal. On the first progression, the coach gives a left or right signal, and the first athlete in line reacts by sprinting out toward the second cone that is diagonally placed five yards away. The athlete should concentrate on not "false stepping." False stepping is taking a step backward to be

Figure 7.4. Reaction Drill Progression #1

able to take a step forward. It's a wasted motion. He should accelerate all the way past the second cone, which is five yards away. The athlete then jogs back to the end of the line and the next person steps up between the first cones and awaits the signal. This is done until all the desired reps are completed.

The second progression starts with the athletes lined up about three yards back from the first set of cones. When the coach starts the drill, the first athlete will jog forward, jump vertically, and land between the first two cones. The coach must time the athlete's jump correctly so that he can give a left or right signal exactly when the athlete lands. The athlete then reacts to the direction given and sprints out past the proper cone. Again, the athlete goes to the back of the line, waiting for the next turn until all reps are accomplished. The coach should instruct the athlete not to false step, to get enough height on the jump, and to jump up and not out, giving the coach enough time to properly give the signal.

The third progression has the athletes starting between the first cones but facing away from the coach so their backs are completely turned. This drill incorporates an audio cue first. When the coach yells the signal, which can be "ball" or "turn" or some such, the first athlete performs a 180-degree turn and faces him. The athlete must then pick up the left or right signal and sprint past the appropriate cone. Again, the coach must emphasize that athletes are not to false step and should sprint past the cone. The coach should incorporate both directions so as not to work one side only.

The fourth progression again has the athletes starting between the first cones and facing the coach. This drill also uses an audio cue to start the drill. When the coach says "go," the athlete jogs forward quickly until he's between the second set of cones and then breaks down, coming to a stop. The coach then gives a left or right signal, and the athlete then slides (shuffles) laterally toward the cone until he is past it. The coach should instruct the athletes to break down completely between the second set of cones so they are able to change their direction as efficiently as possible and to keep the hips low on the slide. The athlete then goes to the back of the line and awaits his next turn.

The last progression starts out with the same sequence of events as the previous drill. Instead of breaking down and then shuffling out past the cone, the athlete turns and runs out past it. There are many different additions a coach can make to these progressions so they will be longer or more challenging, whatever the imagination can conjure up. The coach can do this in future workouts to help maintain variety and intensity.

Reaction Drill Progression #2

This drill is pieced together step-by-step until the athlete is performing multiple movements that last around twelve to fifteen seconds. The coach gives the athletes one step to perform and then adds another step to it once everyone in the group has finished. The coach keeps adding steps until the drill is completed. The drill requires four cones and bags, or low hurdles, to be set up in a specific pattern. The coach stands in front of the obstacle so that he can give the direction signals and occasional verbal cue. The cones are set up in a square pattern with seven or eight yards between each one, with a cone in the center for a starting point of the drill. The bags, or hurdles, are set up side by side one yard apart and just outside the front two cones. The athletes stand in a line behind the back two cones, where they will be out of the way while they're awaiting their turn. The first person will do the first segment of the drill and then go to the back of the line. The next time the athlete comes out, he will repeat the first segment and then add another and another as the coach instructs, until the full drill is complete. Here are the steps.

1. The coach uses a left or right signal. Once the signal is given, the athlete will turn and run toward the back cone. Once he reaches it, the coach instructs him to break down and come to a stop. That is the end of this segment. The athlete goes to the back of the line.

2. The athlete should repeat the first segment. Instead of breaking down and stopping on the back cone, the athlete should round it, run back to the starting cone, and break down.

3. The athlete should repeat the previous two segments. Once he comes back and breaks down on the starting cone, the coach gives him another left or right signal. Once the signal is given, the athlete will sprint forward to the front cone and break down, coming to a stop.

4. The athlete should repeat the previous three segments. Once he has broken down on the front cone, he should transition into a lateral

run over the bags/hurdles until he's over all of them, at which point he should stop.

5. The athlete should repeat the previous four segments. Once he has cleared the last bag, he should turn and run back upfield toward the back cone.

A different variation of steps 4 and 5 can be that the athlete, instead of taking lateral steps over the bags and then sprinting upfield, should turn and run over the bags and then transition into a backpedal until he reaches the back cone. One more variation to step 5 calls for a verbal cue. The athlete should backpedal until the coach says "go." The athlete then sprints forward until he is past the coach.

Position Reaction Drills

Each position has its own unique movements that can be trained using reaction. Following are some of the drills we typically use, broken down by position.

Quarterback Redirection Drill

This drill will work on the quarterback's ability to react and move when there is pressure in the pocket. The quarterback should hold a football so that the drill is as realistic as possible. He takes the desired number of steps to his drop. Once he is back, the coach must then give him a left, right, or middle signal. If the signal is left or right, the quarterback will sprint out or backpedal in that direction, depending on what hand he throws with. If the signal is in the middle, he steps up into the pocket.

Running Backs

The following drills are for running backs.

Drill #1—Zone Runs. The coach will be using a left, right, or middle signal. The running back should be in a two-point position. Once the signal is given, the back will sprint out in that direction. The drill will simulate a zone run, or it can be tailored as a blocking assignment.

Drill #2—Read and React. The backs start in a predetermined direction and simulate taking a handoff. Once the back has gained enough ground to where he would be around the line of scrimmage, the coach should give a left or right signal. The back then reacts and bounces the run outside or inside, depending on what side the run is designed for.

Receiver Get-Offs

This drill teaches the receiver how to get off the line of scrimmage. The receiver starts in his two-point position. The coach will use a left or right signal. Once the signal is given, the receiver simulates the footwork and hand drills that he has been taught to get off the line in the direction given.

Tight Ends Block Down and Release Drill

This drill works on the tight end's ability to block down and then release off the line. The coach will give a left, right, or middle signal. On a snap count, the tight end will block down in the predetermined direction. Once the signal is given, the tight end will release off in that direction.

Offensive Linemen: Guards and Centers

These are position drills for offensive line play.

Drill #1—Pass Sets. This drill will help the lineman react to whatever movement a pass rusher takes against them. The coach will use a left, right, or middle signal. The lineman will start in his pass-setting stance. Once the signal is given, the lineman will pass set in the normal technique taught for that position in the direction given. If the signal is a middle call, the lineman must simulate being bull-rushed and use the technique taught for not giving up ground.

Drill #2—Redirect. On this drill, the lineman will be given a certain direction to pass set on the starting signal. The coach will use a left or right signal only. The lineman starts in the predetermined direction, and once the signal is given, he will redirect either back the other way or continue in the same direction.

Offensive Linemen: Tackles

With this drill, the tackle will be given a signal to start setting in the direction for whatever side he plays. The coach will use a left or right signal only. The tackle will begin his pass set, and when the coach gives the signal, the tackle will either redirect in the opposite direction or continue to set deeper along the same path.

Defensive Backs

These drills enhance defensive back play.

Drill #1—Backpedal and Run. The defensive back should be in his stance and ready to move. The coach will use a left, right, or middle signal. When the coach gives the left or right signal, the defensive back will turn his hips and drop back in that direction, getting a depth of eight to ten yards. If the middle signal is given, the defensive back will backpedal straight back.

Drill #2—Backpedal and Break and 45 Degrees. The defensive back should be in his ready position. The coach will start the defensive back in a backpedal with a verbal signal. After the defensive back has covered a few yards, the coach will give a left, right, or middle signal. If the signal is left or right, the defensive back will turn toward that direction and get depth. If the signal is in the middle, the defensive back will turn and run straight back. Another version of this drill is to add a verbal signal to change the direction of the defensive back. The coach can wait until the defensive back has covered enough ground and then yell "ball." At that point, the defensive back should break down and cut back toward the coach.

Linebackers

These drills help linebackers at their position.

Drill #1—Pass Drops. The linebacker should be in his ready stance. The coach will use a left, right, or middle signal. When the coach gives the left or right directional signal, the linebacker should turn his hips and drop back into pass coverage. The linebacker should take the appropriate depth to drop into the flat coverage area and then settle into that area by squaring back up toward the line of scrimmage. On the middle signal, the linebacker drops straight back with a backpedal into the coverage area while keeping his head on a swivel, settling out at the appropriate depth. The coach should ensure that linebackers use the techniques their position coaches have taught them to properly drop into coverage. The linebackers should also keep their feet moving once they settle into their coverage area to help them change direction when necessary.

Drill #2—Scrape and Fill. With this drill, the coach will need cones or bags to simulate the gaps to be filled on the line of scrimmage. The coach will be on one side of the bags/cones and the linebacker on the other. The coach, acting as the ball carrier, starts the drill with his movement. The coach will choose his hole to run to, and the linebacker will react to him. The linebacker should slide (scrape) down the line and then step into (fill) the hole the coach has gone to.

Drill #3—Hip Switch. This drill trains the linebackers to turn their hips as quickly as possible. The linebacker should start in his defensive stance. The coach will use a left or right signal. The drill starts when the coach gives the first signal. The linebacker drops in a straight line backward, turning his hips to whatever direction the coach gives. The coach should alternate signals about every four or five yards so the linebacker works both sides over a distance of twenty to twenty-five yards.

Defensive Linemen

These drills improve the defensive line play.

Drill #1—Read and React. This drill will use either tall bags or another person to act as an offensive lineman for the defensive lineman to work off of. The coach will act as the ball carrier and move left or right only. The drill should be started with a verbal signal by the coach and then progress with his physical movement. The defensive lineman should start in his appropriate stance in front of the bag/offensive lineman. When the coach gives the signal, the defensive lineman must come out of his stance and engage the offensive lineman without penetrating too deep. When the coach makes his move to the left or right, the defensive lineman will react by shedding his blocker and getting to the runner. The runner should hesitate slightly to simulate a handoff, helping to make the drill as realistic as possible.

Drill #2—Rip and Swim. This drill will help the defensive lineman react with explosion from his stance and then rip and swim in the gap that has been given. The coach should start the drill with a left or right signal only and use a tall bag or another person to act as an offensive lineman. Have the defensive lineman take his stance in front of the bag/offensive lineman and watch for the coach's signal. The defensive lineman can choose the technique he prefers to achieve penetration through the line to get up the field into the backfield. He should concentrate on getting three or four yards upfield on each repetition.

8

Linear Speed
What It Means to Be Fast

Over the years, the forty-yard dash has evolved as the measuring stick for testing running speed in the game of football. I was told by one NFL old-timer that it was used because the distance between the running back and the free safety was about forty yards. I was also told that forty yards is about the distance the quarterback could throw to a receiver after his seven-step drop. Back in the day, colleges used the fifty-yard dash as their favored method for testing linear speed.

The title of speed performance coach is a bit of a misnomer. I'm more of a coach who trains sports movement. Less than one-half of 1 percent of the athletes that I train are training to enhance track speed. The greatest distance that most football players ever run during a game might be twenty yards, with most positions only moving two or three yards per play. The wide receiver position is most likely the only position that is required to run twenty or thirty yards at a time. Even then, these players are hardly ever running in a straight line. Football speed is completely different from track speed. In this chapter, I will break down the forty-yard dash as it applies to football combines and testing. I will displace some myths about the reality of speed. What does it mean to be fast? What is the norm for each position at the professional level? By the end of this chapter, you should have a better understanding of how to increase your forty-yard speed, as well as your position speed.

The Forty-Yard Dash

The forty-yard dash tests for explosion, power, speed, and short endurance. The player will start from a three-point stance, exploding off the line, accelerating and reaching top speed, and maintaining that speed for forty yards. (See Figures 8.1a and 8.1b.) The forty-yard dash is also subdivided into three increments, and times are recorded at the ten- and twenty-yard line as well. The ten- and twenty-yard measurements are critical for offensive and defensive linemen because those distances give a more accurate picture of what the big guys do on the field. While the players are timed by a coach with a handheld timer, the ten- and twenty-splits and the finish are timed with an electronic beam. But because there's not a touch pad at the start, this cannot be classified as a true electronic time.

Debunking the Myths of the Forty-Yard Dash

Over the last sixteen years, I've had the opportunity to time endless professional, college, and high school athletes. The forty-yard dash is the most feared, lied-about, and misinterpreted four or five seconds of agony in an athlete's drive for professional status. It also happens to be one of the most respected tests, worth millions of dollars to the athlete if he can run well.

I keep a short newspaper clipping in my office desk. The clipping is from the indoor track-and-field championships held at East Tennes-

Figure 8.1a. The Forty-Yard Dash Stance   b.

see State University in Johnson City, Tennessee. It lists the final results and times for the indoor forty-yard dash. I usually pull the clipping out a couple of times per year to show high school kids who think they are faster than they really are. The indoor forty is run on a Mondo track, the fastest surface you could ever race on. A Mondo track is a hard rubber track that grips your shoes and keeps you from sliding. The sprinters are in a controlled indoor environment where they can use track spikes, which aren't allowed at the NFL combine or pro days on college campuses. They have six of the fastest sprinters in the country running against them. It's well known among athletes that if you want to improve your speed, you should have somebody as fast as or faster than you to race against.

In the particular year of the clipping, two of the sprinters in the race were Alvis Whitted, currently playing wide receiver with the Oakland Raiders, and Tiki Barber, a premier running back with the New York Giants before retiring after the 2006–07 season. Both of these guys are NFL stars. The forty-yard dash was timed electronically on this superfast track. Can you guess what the winning time was? Alvis, who had run in the Olympic trials for the 1996 games in Atlanta, came in sixth place behind Carl Lewis and Michael Johnson, both of whom are arguably two of the greatest sprinters of all time in the one-hundred-meter and two-hundred-meter events, respectively. Alvis's official time was 4.54 seconds. Tiki finished in 4.68 seconds. These performances sound pretty slow by today's standards. After all, we regularly hear of 4.0s and 4.1s supposedly being run by today's athletes. Notice I said "supposedly"!

In 1988 at the Summer Olympic Games in Seoul, Korea, Canadian sprinter Ben Johnson set the world record in the one-hundred-meter dash with a time of 9.79 seconds, shattering the world record in this event. Ben was later stripped of his gold medal for taking the anabolic steroid stanazolol. I have seen his one-hundred-meter race broken down by track coaches into the sixty meters, the fifty meters, and the forty-yard dash. His fifty- and sixty-meter times are both faster than the current world records today. Unfortunately, the forty-yard dash does not have any official times recorded. But if there were, Ben Johnson would possibly have the fastest forty time with his 4.38 finish.

I have clocked more than six hundred elite-level football players in the past sixteen years. The fastest forty time I've ever clocked was Champ Bailey, at 4.27, during his pro day workout in Athens at the University of Georgia. Now, let me start out by telling you the difference in my timing system and the timing system used to time Ben Johnson. Ben was timed with an electronic timing device. He started with a starter firing a blank pistol, where he had to react to the sound. The pressure from his feet on the starting blocks measured his reaction time. If the pressure from his feet released before the gun, he was charged with a false start. Ben wore track spikes, which makes your ground time faster. When you run without spikes, your feet will slide just a little bit as you pull the ground toward you. If you multiply the number of foot contacts by the number of strides in a forty-yard dash, you can see how much time is taken off the clock, even in a race as short as the forty. I recommend seventeen to twenty strides in the forty-yard dash.

Ben had the fastest sprinters in the world chasing him along with a global audience staring at him, so his adrenalin was working overtime. He was running on the fastest surface in the world, in the optimal conditions, and was competing for his country in his attempt to win a gold medal, the most coveted and respected award in the universe. Based on that example, do you honestly believe that there are any high school kids in America that run in the 4.2s?

Champ and the 4.27

Champ Bailey's forty-yard dash was timed on an Astroturf fielding in high winds. He was timed by scouts, some of whom were older than sixty-five. They started their clocks on Champ's movement, while some anticipated his finish. The accepted way to time the finish is to wait until the athlete completely crosses the finish line. Some simply guessed on his start and nearly all of the one hundred scouts and coaches present had different times! There is a lesson to learn here. The forty-yard dash has no set standards for timing or for converting track time to grass time. In fact, most teams convert track times to grass times by rounding up to the nearest tenth of a second. I've been at testing days on college campuses where players have been timed in the forty-yard dash on tracks, grass fields, field turf, Astroturf, tennis courts, and weight room floors, not to mention inside hallways and gymnasiums, as well as just about any other surface where a distance of forty yards could be measured. What I am saying is that there is no exact science to timing forties. There are just too many variables in the testing process to be consistent.

The last point I want to make before I share my forty-yard dash program with you is this: the Indianapolis combine is known as a notoriously slow running surface. Just because a skill player runs a fast time does not mean that fast guys are fast and slow guys are slow. It's all entirely relative. Every year, I hear reporters make statements about players who choose not to run their forty-yard dash at the NFL combine. Instead they opt to run at their pro days, on their campus, in a familiar setting, on fast surfaces, and with extra time to train. There is another good reason why they don't run their forties, besides the benefits I just mentioned. The running surface at Indy is not kind to bigger players. That is to say, the heavier you are, the longer your foot stays in contact with the ground, which results in adding time to your forty. Conversely, the lighter you are, the less time your foot stays in contact with the surface. The thicker the surface, the slower you are. The fastest surfaces to run on are Mondo track, concrete, rubber flooring, Astroturf, and grass field. The slowest of all the running surfaces is field turf. Field turf is eight to ten inches thick with ground rubber as its base. It is extremely spongy and is also the surface that players run on at the NFL combine.

Techniques of the Forty-Yard Dash

The forty-yard dash is the shortest race that is used to measure linear speed. And just like any skill that is learned, the forty-yard dash is a skill that can be coached. By following the systematic approach presented here, you will be able to improve your linear speed. I have broken the forty-yard dash down into six movements that can be learned. You must practice over and over again to acquire these skills.

Stance

The way I teach my players to start is a pretty simple technique. Start by placing your power foot on the starting line. If you're not sure what foot to start with, have somebody stand behind you. With your eyes shut, have them push you forward. The foot that you step forward with will be your back foot, the one left behind your power foot. Once you determine which foot is your power foot, you will then place your knee in a direct line with your front foot. I want you to imagine that you are being photographed for a group picture and you are on one knee with your arms resting on your front knee. Keep your head up and your back straight. From that position, your back foot should be directly four to six inches behind the front foot when you stand up. (See Figures 8.2a and 8.2b.)

If you have your right foot back, then you would place your right hand just outside your shoulder frame and on the starting line. One of the things you will always hear me tell my players is that we want to run thirty-nine yards as opposed to forty or forty-one yards. This means you

Figure 8.2a. Forty-Yard Dash Start   b.

should crowd the starting line. Your back leg will be bent slightly with 80 percent of your weight on the ball of your front foot. Your arm should be cocked at about a 90-degree angle with your elbow slightly above your back.

Chip's Tips

1. Take a picture.
2. Keep your weight on the balls of your feet.
3. Keep your back foot four to six inches behind the front foot.
4. Inhale and stay tight.
5. Keep your elbow cocked and held high.
6. Crowd the starting line.

Posture and Position

From your stance, your hips should be cocked higher than your head. Your back should be flat, with your eyes either looking down or fixed on a point fifteen yards down the field. Stay relaxed, as tense muscles have a tendency to make you run stiff. By putting all the weight on the balls of your feet, you can feel the transfer of weight to the front foot just before you take off. You will have the sensation of falling on your face, but right before that happens, you will explode off both feet. It's something innate that keeps you from falling. The illustration that I like to use is one of comparing the first step, or the pushing off of both feet, to the cocking of a double-barreled shotgun. By cocking both hammers instead of just one hammer of that shotgun, you're getting twice the explosive power. By exploding off both feet, you're exploding violently out of your stance. To demonstrate this principle, I have my players jump off one foot to see how far they can jump. Then I have the players jump off the ground with both feet; they quickly see that they can jump farther with both feet. I believe that this pushing motion, the motion of pushing off the ground with both feet on your first step, is based on Newton's Third Law of Motion, which states that for every action, there is an equal and opposite reaction. This principle applies to running when you push off on your first step and are pushing against the ground (that is, force) and the ground propels you into a forward motion. The more force you use to push off (that is, using both feet instead of just one), the greater your initial propulsion.

Remember what I mentioned previously about the direct correlation between the forty-yard dash time, the vertical jump, and the power clean. As you drive your hips in an upward motion, whether for your push off in the forty, the upward thrust of the vertical jump, or an explosive hip drive on your power clean, you must use the ground for force to propel you forward, upward, and out! I routinely videotape my players' ten-yard starts. The one thing that I look for is whether the athlete is stepping out on his first step or if he is using both his heels to apply force toward the ground in a violent, explosive manner on the takeoff. By using the video, I can show the player what I am talking about and improve his overall start.

One often-overlooked aspect of the starting stance is proper breathing technique. I want my athletes, while in their stance, to use a breathing technique called the Valsalva maneuver. Here's the easiest way to explain this technique. Do you remember your mom coming to you because you were strong and asking you to open that stubborn jar of pickles? You grabbed that jar, held your breath, and twisted the lid until it came off. That's an example of the Valsalva maneuver. By holding your breath, you raised your blood and intrathoracic pressure, which gave you added strength and explosion. In the same light, by holding your breath and staying tight, you gain that same edge on your forty-yard dash takeoff.

Chip's Tips

1. Keep your back straight.
2. Explode off both feet.
3. Inhale and stay tight.
4. Drive your back arm.

Arm and Hand Position

On your forty start, you should place your hand on the starting line. Always remember that whichever foot is in the back, the same hand is on the front line. Some coaches teach opposite hand, opposite foot. I think it is easier to just remember, right foot back, right hand on the line, left foot back, left hand on the line. Whichever hand is not on the ground should be cocked above the back. The optimal hand position is one that is relaxed. I coach players to hold their index finger and thumb lightly together, with the arm action cheek to cheek, slightly coming across the body as if the player is zipping up his coat. Make sure you don't tense up as that will make your upper body tight and affect your turnover rate. Remember, the faster you move your arms, the faster your feet will move.

Chip's Tips

1. Use fast arm swings.
2. Run cheek to cheek.
3. Stay loose.

The First Ten Yards—The Drive Phase

The first ten yards are the most crucial in a winning forty-yard dash. It's not only the slowest portion of your race but the segment where you will generate all your power and momentum to be able to gain top end speed. As in all phases of this race, I break down the strides into optimal foot strikes. I believe that six or seven steps in the first ten yards is the best stride for most of my athletes. If you are taking more than seven strides, you are probably spinning your wheels. If you are taking fewer than six strides, you are most likely overstriding and are not able to generate and maintain any top end speed.

The first ten yards are all about explosion and acceleration. As a matter of fact, your whole forty-yard dash is pure acceleration. You really don't reach top speed until fifty-five to sixty yards. Try and maintain a straight line, staying low during the drive phase, keeping a good forward lean, and keeping your head down. I want my players to stay as close to the sideline or hash marks as possible. Make sure that you drive your lead leg straight up and down under your hips. If you step outside shoulder width, you in effect become a parachute by increasing your wind drag. You always want to remain in an aerodynamic posture. Also, without visual reference to keep you in line, you'll wander in the lane, which will cost you precious time. As I teach my players, pick an object about fifteen yards down the track and keep your eyes on that object, staying low until you reach that fifteen-yard mark. At that point, you should be in an upright position. Stay relaxed and continue to drive your arms from the elbows.

Chip's Tips

1. Explode out.
2. Keep a good forward lean.
3. Drive your elbows.
4. Keep your head down.
5. Keep your steps in a straight line.

The Second Twenty Yards—Transition Phase (Ten to Thirty Yards)

The second twenty yards is where you should be close to maximum stride length. Your turnover rate (that is, the time it takes an athlete to complete a stride) should be at peak levels. During this phase, you should be maintaining a good forward body lean and should be near your top acceleration speed. In this phase, your arm drive should be explosive and in synch with your knee drive. Again, I have found that optimum stride length is around ten to eleven strides for twenty yards. At your top end speed, your stride rate should be about two strides per five yards traveled. If my stride calculations are right, then your forty-yard dash will look like this:

0 to 10 yards	6 strides
10 to 20 yards	4 strides
20 to 30 yards	4 strides
30 to 40 yards	4 strides
Total Strides = 18	

I try and keep my athletes' strides at eighteen to twenty strides for the forty. Keep in mind that each athlete's stride depends on stride length and individual flexibility. Also, remember that the key to increasing linear speed is to increase stride length and stride frequency. One of the most effective things I can do for my players wanting to increase their speed is to make sure that I continue to work on overall flexibility. Dynamic and static flexibility will increase range of motion, joint mobility, and tendon strength. If I train a player who has no flexibility, I can probably decrease his forty time by at least 0.01 to 0.02 of a second simply by making him more flexible. On the other hand, if he has great flexibility, my goal is to increase his upper and lower body strength and focus on his running mechanics.

The Last Ten Yards—The Finish (Thirty to Forty Yards)

The last ten yards of a forty-yard dash can determine the outcome of the race. If you have not worked on increasing your strength base, this is the part of the race where you typically begin to decelerate. By training with resistance and overspeed (as covered in Chapters 5 and 6) over fifty to sixty yards, you can increase your speed endurance and delay the onset of muscle fatigue. This will help with more powerful, longer strides and will help you maintain a faster turnover rate for the duration of the race. Make sure that your stride stays under your hips. If you are overstriding and your foot is striking the ground in front of your center of gravity, that action will cause a braking effect, essentially slowing down your running motion.

By maintaining good form and proper running mechanics, you should continue to have explosive knee drive, fast arm action, good body lean, and the ability to stay relaxed; also, you should continue to accelerate through the final ten yards. My advice on the forty-yard dash finish is to accelerate through the finish line. The reason I give this advice is because most pro scouts and coaches stop the clock as the players back foot comes across the finish line as opposed to when they break the surface of the finish line. The finish is not the same as the finish for the one-hundred-meter dash, where the sprinter crosses the electronic beam, thereby stopping the clock. The only consistencies in timing the forty are inconsistencies. Make sure you sprint all the way through. Don't stop until you have sprinted ten yards past the forty-yard line.

Chip's Tips from Start to Finish: A Checklist

1. Use the same stance every time.
2. Put your front foot on the starting line, and put your back foot four to six inches behind the front foot.
3. Keep your elbow cocked and raised slightly above your back.
4. Raise your hips above your head.
5. Keep 80 percent of your weight on the ball of your front foot.

6. Stay focused, with your head down.

7. Stay relaxed.

8. Inhale on your start, and remember the Valsalva maneuver.

9. Drive your knees to your chest.

10. Explode off both feet, pushing the ground.

11. Stay in a straight line.

12. Remember, your arm swings should come from your shoulder.

13. Your stride count should be ten yards at six steps, twenty yards at four steps, thirty yards at four steps, and the last ten yards at four steps, for a total of eighteen strides.

14. Maintain stride length.

15. Maintain a good butt kick by cycling your legs.

16. Accelerate all the way past the finish line.

17. Practice the ten- and forty-yard dashes.

18. Remember, you are competing against yourself. Improve in all phases of the forty and you will shave your time.

19. Have fun!

Running Mechanics

Over the last sixteen years, I have seen just about every form of bad running mechanics, from improper arm action to bad body posture, from running flat-footed to overstriding, and from sitting back on the haunches to running tense and slowing up. I need to point out a couple of things that I have observed over my years of training professional athletes. Most of the time when I take on a new client, the client is between the ages of twenty-three and twenty-five years. I am constantly being asked by young coaches how I teach running mechanics to the pros. That is a great question. The fact is that I teach them very little technique. The reason for this is, at the age of most professional football players, their running mechanics have been permanently embedded into their muscle memory. The way they run is the way they have been running since they were little kids. I'm talking about twenty-three years of either proper running mechanics and positive reinforcement or negative running mechanics and negative reinforcement. It would be almost impossible for me to change their running style. I just don't have enough time to force positive motor patterns. The first time they take off running, they revert back to what they learned when they were young because that's what feels natural.

Champ Bailey is arguably one of the very best athletes in the National Football League and certainly one of the greatest athletes that I have been blessed to have trained. Champ had been a two-way player on offense and on defense at the University of Georgia. He had won the SEC indoor title for the fifty-five-meter dash and was a Jim Thorpe Award winner in football as the top defensive back in the country. Champ was already blessed with natural God-given talent by the time he got to me; he was simply "a freak of nature."

When I first started working with Champ, his running gait was terrible. He barely picked his feet up off the ground, he would swing his arms across his body in an ice-skating motion, he bent at the waist, and he had an incredibly inefficient running style. But somehow, that unconventional running style worked for Champ. I trained him without trying to change his natural running mechanics, by making him more explosive in his natural running style. That's what my training philosophy is all about—taking great athletes and helping them maximize their potential.

Chip's Tips

1. Maintain a good body lean that comes from the ground and not by bending at the waist.
2. Use fast arm action from cheek to cheek.
3. Make sure your lead foot hits under your center of gravity, or your hips.
4. Stay relaxed.

The Pool Workout

Get Wet, Get Wild, and Get Whipped

At Competitive Edge Sports, the pool workout is anything but a fun day in the water. In fact, you might see grown men on the verge of puking. Some lay on the pool deck, looking like beached whales and swearing like sailors. The record time for a player losing his breakfast was less than two minutes. Pool day at CES is "no joke," as Alvin Porter, former defensive back of the Baltimore Ravens, so eloquently stated. In fact, when Brian Urlacher signed his first NFL contract and bought a house, his wife wanted him to buy one with a pool. He adamantly told her, "If I ever see a swimming pool again, it will be too soon for me!"

Torture and Recovery Go Hand in Hand

The pool is part of that regeneration process, which is your body's process of repairing itself using different modalities for recovery. Some of these modalities include hot and cold treatment, massage therapy, active release, hyperbaric chamber, and the pool. And even though I use the pool for its aerobic benefit, the pool plays an even bigger role in improving the overall performance of my athletes. I know that the heavy volume of work that I prescribe over the first two days of training will cause a buildup of lactic acid in the player's system. Wednesday's pool workout will help flush out that excess lactic acid. The pool has such a soothing effect on the body because of the water temperature. The cool water speeds the recovery process and gets the players ready for the remainder of the demanding workouts at the end of the week. My players say that some of the best sleep they have ever experienced is after my pool workout!

The Benefits of Pool Work

The most obvious benefit of training in the pool is increasing your heart and lung capacity. Swimming not only builds your lung capacity, but it also builds endurance and burns calories at a tremendous rate. Three calories per mile per pound of body weight is the formula by which improvement is measured. If you weigh 250 pounds and you swim a total of two miles in one hour, you burn around 1,500 calories. What a great way for big offensive linemen to drop weight without the stress that most types of distance work can cause on their ankles, knees, hips, and lower back. Another great benefit of working in water is that it is a no-impact aerobic exercise. The buoyancy of the water helps support, invigorate, and assist with rehabilitation.

Water offers twelve times the resistance of air with constant multidirectional resistance for all your muscles. This happens in much the same way that gravity applies resistance to your entire body during the rebound phase on a trampoline. Try to bound laterally while chest deep in water. The muscles used to stabilize your core are recruited, and the water supplies the resistance equilaterally.

Another great benefit of the pool workout if you are injured is that the water is extremely forgiving. If you can't run because of a knee, ankle, or hip injury, you still can see gains from the pool workout. In deep water, your joints are cushioned from constant pounding. This no-impact pool workout is a welcome relief for all of your weight-bearing body parts. You can increase your intensity without fear of reinjuring your sensitive areas. One of the hydrostatic effects of working in deep water is increased blood flow. The cool water has an extremely soothing massagelike effect on your body.

Pool Workout Benefit Summary

1. Offers no-impact training
2. Involves all muscle groups
3. Aids with injury recovery
4. Increases lung and heart capacity
5. Speeds up your metabolism
6. Improves training recovery
7. Provides stress relief and relaxation
8. Offers training despite injury
9. Provides workout environment variety
10. Bumps up the fun factor
11. Builds life skills

The Eight-Phase Pool Workout Program

This workout day is an aerobic and recovery day.

1. Warm-Up

Just like running on the field, you need to warm the core before you start with high-intensity work in the pool. The first thing I have our athletes do is swim the length of the pool with a kickboard. The kickboard helps keep the upper body out of the water and keeps the focus on warming up the lower body. Try to keep your legs straight and flutter kick from the hips. Our pool is fifty meters, so one lap down and back is enough to get you ready to start your pool workout.

2. Deep-Water Sprints

I make all our athletes wear an aqua jogger belt. It's a light flotation device that will make the athlete remain upright as he swims. Some of our bigger athletes need to wear two belts to keep their heads above the water. Most athletes have so much muscle mass that they have a difficult time staying afloat. The more body fat you have, the easier it is to float. Some of the athletes that I train are scared to death of the water, so I try and make sure they feel as comfortable as possible before I start the workout. I have athletes who need to stay in the shallow end, where their feet can still touch, or hang close to the lane ropes, which they can grab if they feel threatened. (See Figure 9.1.)

Figure 9.1. Deep-Water Sprints with Flotation Device and Cord

I attach a rubber cord to their belts to give them resistance in the running motion. Your body needs to maintain a good running posture with a forward lean. Stay perpendicular as you drive your hip flexors up and down. Remember to alternate elbow snaps with alternate leg drive. The faster you drive your legs up and down, the more resistance will be generated by the water. Always maintain a chest-over-knees posture. The reps and sets I use are as follows:

Exercise	Set	Time	Rest
Sprints	1	40 seconds	40 seconds
Sprints	2	40 seconds	40 seconds
Sprints	3	40 seconds	40 seconds
Sprints	4	40 seconds	40 seconds

Start the drill by sprinting for forty seconds, followed by forty seconds of rest. Repeat this sequence for four sets. In between the exercises, you should rest about one minute.

3. Breaststroke

For the breaststroke, the coach should add hand paddles for resistance in the arm motion. He should add the resistance cord to the belt. (See Figures 9.2a and 9.2b.) Let me caution coaches about expecting proper swim mechanics and stroke technique from your athletes. Most of the time, there is none. These are football players in training, not Olympic swimmers. Sometimes the player is struggling just to survive and keep from drowning. The object of the breaststroke is to extend your arms up and out, continuing past the front of your face with your hands together, then around in a circular motion, all the while kicking your legs like a frog. If your rhythm is right, you should be stretching the cord out as far as possible for the duration of the drill. I have had players who reverse the stroke and actually start backing up. I take every opportunity to affirm my players and I brag on their efforts, even when their technique is suspect.

Figure 9.2a. Breaststroke

b.

Exercise	Set	Time	Rest
Breaststroke	1	40 seconds	40 seconds
Breaststroke	2	40 seconds	40 seconds
Breaststroke	3	20 seconds	20 seconds
Breaststroke	4	20 seconds	20 seconds
Breaststroke	5	20 seconds	20 seconds

You should start the drill after the player has stretched the cord out. He will swim for forty seconds, followed by a forty-second rest. He will next complete another set of forty seconds with forty second's rest, finishing up with three twenty-second swims with three twenty-second rest periods. At the end of this cycle, the athlete should rest one minute.

4. Freestyle

The freestyle is probably the hardest stroke for most football players. They spend so much of their time developing their traps and shoulder area that taking those muscles through a full range of motion is extremely difficult. As a result, most football players struggle with this movement. The freestyle technique also raises your heart rate faster than any other swim stroke. This phase is where you should take extra time to check the athlete's heart rate. Again, I routinely add resistance with the rubber cords.

The freestyle is an all-out sprint where you are alternating arm strokes while kicking your legs as fast as you can. Some swim experts will tell you how to breathe in on recovery and exhale on exertion. I tell my players to breathe, not just to hold their breath. The freestyle works every muscle in the body and forces you to suck in tremendous amounts of oxygen. As with any of these swimming strokes, you get out of the workout what you put into it.

Heart rate will usually tell the tale of how much effort a player actually put into his workout. Low heart rate equals low intensity; elevated heart rate means maximum output of effort. I like for my players' target heart rate to be in the 150 to 180 range.

Exercise	Set	Time	Rest
Freestyle	1	40 seconds	40 seconds
Freestyle	2	40 seconds	40 seconds
Freestyle	3	20 seconds	40 seconds
Freestyle	4	20 seconds	40 seconds
Freestyle	5	20 seconds	40 seconds

Start out swimming as hard as you can go for forty seconds, followed by a rest of forty seconds. The first two sets are done at a pace of forty seconds and the last three are done at intervals of twenty seconds with forty seconds of rest.

5. Combo Freestyle and Breaststroke

This set is a combination of the freestyle and breaststroke techniques. You will start out with breaststroke first and then switch to the freestyle. These movements provide two extremes at once, upper body resistance and lower body resistance. The heart rate is elevated and the body starts to sweat. I know that some of you think I'm crazy by stating that you'll sweat. But trust me, you will break a sweat in the pool, so make sure you stay hydrated before and after your session. You will need to replenish the lost fluids, so keep some water handy; the pool water that you have swallowed during your workout does not count toward staying hydrated.

Exercise	Set	Time	Rest
Freestyle/Breaststroke	1	20 seconds each	40 seconds
Freestyle/Breaststroke	2	20 seconds each	40 seconds
Freestyle/Breaststroke	3	20 seconds each	40 seconds
Freestyle/Breaststroke	4	20 seconds each	40 seconds

You will start out swimming the breaststroke for twenty seconds. Then switch to freestyle after twenty seconds, for a total swim time of forty seconds. You will rest forty seconds, and then repeat the same sequence for three more sets. After the last set, if you are able to get out of the pool, report to the shallow end to finish with abdominals and strength work.

6. Abdominals

I begin the strength workout phase by starting with the core. Make sure that you keep your flotation device on while doing your crunches. The flotation device keeps you in a crunch position. Have your partner hold your legs over the side of the pool, with your back floating and your body in an L shape. Keep your hands behind your head and bring your elbows up to your knees in a crunch position. Hold each crunch for a count of one thousand and one. You can alternate your elbows to the opposite knee for variation.

Exercise	Set	Reps	Rest
Crunches	1	25	30 seconds
Crunches	2	25	30 seconds
Crunches	3	25	30 seconds
Crunches	4	AMCD*	2 minutes

*As many as you can do.

7. Strength Work

The great thing about finishing with strength work in the pool is that the water resistance while swimming has prefatigued the athlete's muscles. It doesn't take long to get a serious pump in the upper body using little aerobic cords. The swimming motion uses many of the upper body muscles, such as the chest, deltoids, traps, back, biceps, triceps, and abdominals. With a little cord work, the athlete feels like the Incredible Hulk. I train mostly upper body on pool day and I use one continuous set. Some days I use twenty-five-second reps, where the athlete does as many reps as he can in twenty-five seconds. In that amount of time, you should get about fifteen to eighteen reps.

Giant Set 1

Exercise	Set	Reps	Time	Rest
Upright Row	1	15–18	25 seconds	None
Side Laterals	1	15–18	25 seconds	None
Front Raises	1	15–18	25 seconds	None
Biceps Curls	1	15–18	25 seconds	None
Triceps Extension	1	15–18	25 seconds	None
Shoulder Press	1	15–18	25 seconds	None

This group of exercise constitutes one giant set. Once you start this group of exercises, you will not stop until you are finished with all the exercises in this group. You will then rest two minutes before beginning the second giant set.

Giant Set 2

Exercise	Set	Reps	Time	Rest
Upright Row	2	15–18	25 seconds	None
Side Laterals	2	15–18	25 seconds	None
Front Raises	2	15–18	25 seconds	None
Biceps Curls	2	15–18	25 seconds	None
Triceps Extension	2	15–18	25 seconds	None
Shoulder Press	2	15–18	25 seconds	None

Note: Rest two minutes before beginning the third giant set.

Giant Set 3

Exercise	Set	Reps	Time	Rest
Upright Row	3	15–18	25 seconds	None
Side Laterals	3	15–18	25 seconds	None
Front Raises	3	15–18	25 seconds	None
Biceps Curls	3	15–18	25 seconds	None
Triceps Extension	3	15–18	25 seconds	None
Shoulder Press	3	15–18	25 seconds	None

Note: Rest two minutes before beginning the fourth giant set.

Giant Set 4

Exercise	Set	Reps	Time	Rest
Upright Row	4	15–18	25 seconds	None
Side Laterals	4	15–18	25 seconds	None
Front Raises	4	15–18	25 seconds	None
Biceps Curls	4	15–18	25 seconds	None
Triceps Extension	4	15–18	25 seconds	None
Shoulder Press	4	15–18	25 seconds	None

8. Cooldown

The cooldown consists of having the player swim a lap (down and back) in the pool with a kickboard. This workout should take about an hour and can be done with groups of athletes. The great thing about this pool workout is that you are only limited by your imagination. Technically, you can do any exercises that you can do on dry land. The main focus is to have as much fun as possible. There have been times when I have finished the pool workout with a diving board game called Jump or Dive. It's a hilarious sight, because I've seen everything from belly flops to swan dives.

Chip's Tips for Pool Workouts

1. Have fun and be safe.
2. Keep your body in the proper position when doing deep-water sprints.
3. Remember, you get out of it what you put into it.
4. Stay hydrated—you do sweat in the pool.
5. Keep the workout fresh, changing reps and sets of each exercise. Remember, anything you can do on dry land, you can do in the pool.

10

Strength Training

Getting Bigger and Stronger, Faster

Strength training is an integral part of the success of my program. I believe that the integration of proper explosive weight work with the explosive speed program is a key factor in the continued success I have come to expect. Strength is the ability of a muscle to exert force against resistance. There are three types of strength.

1. **Maximum strength (absolute strength).** The amount of weight the muscle can lift for one maximum contraction (one rep max). One of the very first questions that most athletes ask each other is how much they can bench press, as well as what their max is for one rep in the power clean and squats.

2. **Elastic strength.** The muscle's ability to overcome a resistance through fast contraction.

3. **Strength endurance.** The muscle's ability to contract with force many times over.

Progressive overload is a term used to explain how to make your muscles grow and get stronger. Your muscles will only get stronger by increasing the load with increased resistance, number of reps, and number of sets. By progressing one of these loads, the muscle fibers will tear down and build back stronger fibers to accommodate the extra load. This breaking down and building up causes the muscle to grow bigger and stronger. The resulting increase is called hypertrophy.

Reps and Sets

A repetition, or rep, is what you can lift and lower in a controlled manner one time. Six reps might constitute one set, depending on what you want to accomplish. Sets of one to five reps would develop general strength. Sets of six to twelve reps will develop your muscles and increase your strength. Sets of twelve to twenty reps will help increase muscle endurance. Sets of twenty or more reps will increase aerobic capacity. Most of the athletes that I train will stay in the four- to eight-rep range because that has been shown to produce the greatest strength gains. You should reach muscle failure somewhere between six and eight reps for upper body and eight and ten reps for lower body.

Repetitions to Percentages

Most of the strength programs that I use are based on the training loads built on the following percentage chart. This chart is based on the percentage of weight that can be lifted in one repetition as it equates to the number of repetitions to failure. The amount of weight lifted is based on the one max repetition, and the reps that can be completed correspond to the percentage chart. For example, if you can lift 225 pounds only five times, or five reps, then this would represent 90 percent of your one-rep max.

```
 60% of 1 RM = 17 reps
 65% of 1 RM = 14 reps
 70% of 1 RM = 12 reps
 75% of 1 RM = 10 reps
 80% of 1 RM =  8 reps
 85% of 1 RM =  6 reps
 90% of 1 RM =  5 reps
 95% of 1 RM =  3 reps
100% of 1 RM =  1 rep
```

A Variety of Training Systems

Over the past fifty years, new training programs and techniques have progressed to increase the rate of muscle growth faster than earlier training techniques could do. Joe Weider's bodybuilding magazines educated the world of bodybuilding and strength training with information and research concerning training techniques and methodologies that have been proven to accelerate muscle development. The training principles that I use with my players are but a few of the total number of training principles available to athletes.

My training system is certainly not the only way to train. In fact, I have used just about every conceivable training method out there with my athletes over the past thirty years. A wide variety of training systems are used today by strength coaches; most systems will give the player and the coach their desired results. The one training principle that I use the most is SAID (specific adaptations to imposed demands). What SAID really means is that by changing the reps, sets, weight, and exercises, your body will have to adapt to the new stresses, which will force the muscles to respond in a favorable way through added strength, growth, muscle endurance, and flexibility. In other words, it's beneficial to change up your workouts frequently!

Rest

By dividing my strength program up into a four-day split, I'm giving my athletes ample recovery time between sessions. Most coaches use the rule of forty-eight hours of rest between same body part training. It takes about twenty-four hours for your body to restore the adenosine triphosphate/creatine phosphate (ATP/CP) energy pathways and forty-eight hours to restore glycogen levels back in your muscles.

The recovery time that I recommend between sets and reps will vary, depending on the type of lifting program that the athlete is doing.

When training in the low-rep range of singles and up to the four-rep range, I want my athletes to rest three to five minutes between exercises and anywhere from forty-five seconds to one and a half minutes between sets. I have had athletes rest as little as twenty-five seconds between sets if I'm working on muscle endurance. This rest period represents huddle time. It takes about forty-five seconds to recover about 80 percent of your muscle fibers, so you can see how fast you would fatigue with twenty-five seconds of rest.

In my training program, there are three components that are of the utmost importance: intensity, volume, and frequency. Intensity is the amount of weight you lift during your training session. Volume refers to the number of reps, sets, and exercises done in your training session. Last is the frequency, or the number of sessions, you do per week. All three can impact each other.

If you constantly train without getting the proper rest time between sessions, you will be overtraining, which can result in injuries. Make sure that you get plenty of rest between workout days and be on the lookout for signs of overtraining.

Signs of Overtraining

- General fatigue
- Decrease in strength
- Loss of energy
- Weight loss
- Muscle soreness

Terminology

- **Drop sets.** When you have reached failure in your lift, the weight is stripped off the bar, making each subsequent lift progressively lighter.
- **Superset.** This consists of performing two or three exercises that work the muscles without any rest between sets. I typically superset the flat bench press with one-arm rows. Most of my supersets involve what I call a push-pull technique.
- **Push-pull.** On days that I do chest and back, I will superset using the push-pull technique. This technique is done by alternating a pushing exercise with a pulling exercise (for example, leg extension followed by leg curl), with no rest between sets. The exercises that are chosen work opposing muscle groups.
- **Pyramid.** This technique is used by most athletes at the highest level of training because of the intensity of the work. The load is increased and the repetitions are decreased. Here is an example of how this type of system would be applied to your bench press:

  200 pounds × 12 reps
  225 pounds × 10 reps
  235 pounds × 8 reps
  245 pounds × 6 reps
  255 pounds × 4 reps
  235 pounds × 8 reps

The first two reps are warm-up sets, and the middle three are for strength gains using the heaviest weight that you can handle for the four-to six-rep range. That is to fatigue the muscle, to take the muscle close to failure.

- **Giant sets.** On pool days, I always finish the pool workout with a giant set. Giant sets consist of four or five exercises performed without rest between each exercise. I use rubber tubing in the pool for resistance. An example of this type of system would be this shoulder routine:

  Upright Row × 15 reps
  Front Raises × 15 reps
  Side Laterals × 15 reps
  Shoulder Press × 15 reps

- **Forced reps.** When you have reached muscle failure, your spotter will assist you by helping you lift the bar through the sticking point. You will be able to complete a few more repetitions with this training technique.

Strength-Training Program

My strength-training program is based on a couple of basic principles. The first states that the strength-training program will complement the speed work program. On Mondays, players are lifting upper body in the weight room and completing heavy resistance running on the field. On Tuesdays, players are lifting heavy legs while doing overspeed and reaction training out on the field. This special combination of weight and speed work has produced results that, I would venture to say, have been unmatched on the professional level. The second point that I want to stress is that this program has been tried and tested by more than six hundred professional football players over the last twenty years. If this strength-training program is done in conjunction with my speed program, an athlete will experience tremendous gains in strength, muscle endurance, and speed and will enjoy a decrease in body fat composition.

The weight on the bar should always match the repetitions that are being performed. If the lifter is performing an eight-rep set, then the workload should be as close to 100 percent as possible. You should not be able to perform ten or twelve reps with the weight designated for an eight-rep set. Your results, if any, would not reflect those deserved. You should never sacrifice proper and safe technique or form in order to lift more weight. Always perform a warm-up set before starting your workout. It is recommended that you perform at least one warm-up set at the beginning of each lift. For example, if you finish the flat bench press and are now moving to the incline bench press, you should do at least one warm-up incline set to properly warm up these muscles and tendons.

I've included a six-week day-by-day and position-by-position program in Appendix A. What follows here is an explanation of some of the less traditional activities, as well as a rundown of proper form and routine for more common weight room exercises.

Flat Bench Press with Bar

A flat bench press station must be used for this exercise. The athlete will lie on the bench and adjust his positioning to ensure no movement problems during the set. He must select his grip, which tends to be slightly more narrow for football players, and make sure to grasp the bar evenly for proper balance. Using a spotter's assistance, the athlete should unrack the bar and begin the bench press. At the bottom position of the movement, the athlete will pinch his shoulder blades together to help put his chest into a prestretched mode; the bar should come in contact with the chest at about three inches above the sternum. The athlete's upper arm should be set at around a 45-degree angle from the upper torso. The elbows should be directly under the bar, and both should remain in that angle all the way through the press to help make sure the chest receives the bulk of the work. The bar should then be driven straight off the chest with a slight angle toward the head near the top of the movement until the arms are fully extended. The athlete will then lower the bar back to the starting position via the same motion with a slow, controlled manner.

Chip's Tips

1. Set your feet firmly and press them into the ground on every concentric stroke of the press and allow no movement of them during the set.
2. Ensure proper breathing. Breathe out as you press up, and breathe in as you bring the weight back to the starting position.
3. Make sure you lower the bar all the way down until it lightly touches your chest to help with complete range of motion and muscular development.
4. Keep your buttocks in contact with the bench while arching your back on the concentric phase.
5. At the top of the press, the bar should be over the targeted area of the chest—in this case, the middle of the chest and only slightly toward the head.
6. Avoid pushing the bar too far up toward the head or too low near the bottom of the chest. (See Figures 10.1a and 10.1b.)

Figure 10.1a. Flat Bench Press with Bar   b.

Warm-Ups, Top Sets, and Drop Sets. Complete at least three sets, increasing the weight on each set for warm-ups. Add more weight as your max weight increases with time.

The value of this routine is to perform the first set, or top set, with a weight that can be lifted for a total of five reps with maximal effort without sacrificing correct form. After completing the top set, all of the remaining sets will be lighter than the previous set by 10 pounds to 25 pounds, depending on the starting weight. From this point, there will be four drop sets. Each one of these drop sets will be performed for the maximal number of repetitions the lifter can obtain with correct form. Once the lifter reaches this point, the spotter will help the lifter perform two additional forced repetitions. It is important that the spotter never allow the weight to stall during the concentric phase of these two repetitions.

Top Set—Max Rep (Five)

Drop set #1 max reps and 2 forced reps
Drop set #2 max reps and 2 forced reps
Drop set #3 max reps and 2 forced reps
Drop set #4 max reps and 2 forced reps

If the top set is in the range of 310 to 350 pounds or more, then each of the drop sets will be decreased by 25 pounds per set.

If the top set is in the range of 275 to 310 pounds, each drop set will be decreased by 15 pounds.

If the top set is less than 275 pounds, each drop set will be decreased by 10 pounds.

When beginning this routine, it is common that an athlete will be unable to complete more than about five reps, regardless of the fact that the workload is being decreased each set.

The results may resemble this example:

Set	Workload Pounds	Unassisted Reps
Top set	315	5
Drop set #1	295	5
Drop set #2	275	4
Drop set #3	255	4
Drop set #4	235	3

These results are not uncommon in the first two to three weeks of the program. Once the top set goal of five reps has been reached, then the workload should be increased five pounds before the next drop set workout the following week. Remember, if the top set workload is increased, then each drop set (1 through 4) will be increased also. Each time the top set goal is reached, the workload is raised 5 pounds for the next workout. Here is an example:

Set	Workload Pounds	Unassisted Reps	Next Workout
Top set	315	5	320
Drop set #1	295	5	300
Drop set #2	275	4	280
Drop set #3	255	4	260
Drop set #4	235	3	240

Your strength should be increasing by about 2 percent per week, and your unassisted reps for drop sets will increase. Here is an example:

Top Sets (should always remain at five, adjusting the weight as needed)

Drop set #1	5- to 7-rep range
Drop set #2	7- to 9-rep range
Drop set #3	9- to 12-rep range
Drop set #4	12- to 15-rep range

Low Rows

On seated low rows, legs should be slightly bent to relieve pressure from the hamstrings. Start with the back straight, sitting upright, with arms stretched out in front of the body, holding the cable handle. It is acceptable to have a forward lean at the waist as long as the back remains straight and the head does not lower. This will allow more stretch on the targeted back muscles. From this starting position, the back should move backward until the body is upright, with the angle between the chest and leg at 90 degrees. Once the body has reached this position, the lats and the biceps are contracted until the handle of the low row machine touches the upper abdominal area. The weight is then returned to the starting point with arms outstretched. This should be performed in a smooth, continuous motion. There should be no jerking or snatching motions. (See Figures 10.2a, 10.2b, and 10.2c.)

Figure 10.2a. Low Rows   b.   c.

Incline Dumbbell Bench Press

The incline bench must be set to an angle between 30 and 45 degrees unless the bench is at a premade and unadjustable angle. The athlete should use a set of dumbbells that he can handle for the desired number of repetitions. It is recommended that at least two warm-up sets with increased workload be performed before starting the incline routine. Once proper warm-up has been completed, each of the sets should be performed with maximal workload for all reps in that set. It is common for workload to be increased as targeted muscles adjust to the workload. However, as the targeted muscles fatigue, it may be necessary to lower the workload. Each set should be performed with as close to 100 percent intensity as possible, while always maintaining proper technique.

The athlete will lie back onto the bench and move the dumbbells into the starting position. At the bottom position of the movement, the athlete will pinch his shoulder blades together to help put the chest into a pre-stretched mode. The hands should grip the dumbbell handles evenly to help with proper balance. The dumbbells should be centered over the top of the elbows during the entire pressing movement to help ensure good balance and proper movement of the weight. The athlete's upper arm should be set at about a 45-degree angle from the upper torso and remain at that angle all the way through the press to help make sure the chest receives the bulk of the work. The dumbbells should be driven up in a slightly arcing motion until they can be brought together lightly at the top of the press with the arms fully extended. The athlete will then lower the dumbbells back to the starting position via the same arcing motion with a slow, controlled manner.

Chip's Tips

1. Set your feet firmly and press them into the ground on every concentric stroke of the press with no movement during the set.
2. Ensure proper breathing technique. Breathe out as you press up, and breathe in as you bring the weight back to the starting position.
3. Make sure you get a good stretch at the bottom position on every repetition to help with a complete development of the muscle.
4. At the top of the press, the dumbbells should be over the targeted area of the chest—in this case, the upper chest. Avoid pushing the dumbbells too far up toward the head or too low near the bottom of the chest. (See Figures 10.3a, 10.3b, and 10.3c.)

One-Arm Dumbbell Rows

One-arm dumbbell rows should be performed from a standing position. The lifter will hold a dumbbell in one hand while he leans forward, resting

Figure 10.3a. Incline Dumbell
Bench Press

b.

c.

his opposite hand on a support (an incline bench, a wall, etc.). The foot on the side of the support arm should be positioned about three feet away from the support. The foot on the lifting side should be placed about two feet behind the support foot. With this arm and foot placement, the angle between the chest and front leg should be approximately 135 degrees. From this position, start with the back straight and the head up, with the lifting arm fully extended. From here, the lifter will pull weight upward until the weight touches the waist. The waist is then lowered back to the starting position. The lifter should keep his back straight for the duration of the exercise and repeat for the other arm. (See Figures 10.4a and 10.4b.)

Biceps Curls with the EZ Curl Bar

The athlete should use the appropriate weight that will allow him to complete the desired number of repetitions while maintaining proper form. First, the athlete should be using the two outside grips on the bar to achieve a wide grip. The proper way to grip the bar is to have the palms facing up toward the ceiling and to be on the inside of the bends of the bar so the wrists are in a natural position. The athlete should stand straight up and stagger his feet, one slightly in front of the other, and maintain a slight bend in his knees to help with balance and to avoid swinging the upper body during the movement. At the bottom position, the arms should be completely extended, and the athlete should flex his triceps to put the biceps into a fully stretched position. He then should begin curling the weight upward. During this part of the lift, he must keep his elbows close to his sides without "winging" them out. Also, the elbows should

Figure 10.4a. One-Arm Dumbell Rows   b.

not move backward at all and, in fact, should move slightly forward near the top of the lift to help with a complete contraction of the biceps. After a slight pause at the top for an extra squeeze of the biceps, he then should lower the weight back down to the starting, fully stretched position with absolute control to avoid swinging.

One variation on this exercise is the closed grip curl. Taking advantage of the EZ curl bar's unique shape, use the inside grips to emphasize the outer portion of the biceps.

Reverse Curls with Straight Bar

The athlete should use an appropriate weight to be able to complete the desired number of repetitions. The athlete should grip the straight bar with an overhand, palms-down grip that is about as wide as his shoulders. Then he should stand straight up with his feet staggered slightly, one foot in front of the other, and maintain a slight bend in the knees to achieve good balance and avoid swinging the upper body. The athlete should keep the elbows tight to his sides and avoid "winging" them outward. The elbows should also stay completely still without moving forward or backward. At the bottom position, the arms should be completely straight, and the athlete should flex the triceps to fully stretch the biceps and forearm muscles. The athlete should then begin to reverse curl the weight upward. During this part of the movement, the athlete should concentrate on his form and flick his wrist backward at the top of the movement to help with a maximal contraction. After a brief pause at the top for an extra squeeze, the athlete should then lower the weight downward in a controlled manner to the fully stretched starting position. (See Figures 10.5a, 10.5b, and 10.5c.)

Figure 10.5a. Reverse Curls with Straight Bar

b.

c.

Quick Hands

As previously discussed, quick hands are a basic clip belt with surgical tubing connected to the back. The tubing is fed through a ring device that adjusts according to an athlete's height and arm length. The role of quick hands is to provide resistance in punching, which aids in the development of the chest, triceps, and front deltoids. Quick hands are used at the end of the upper body workout to further fatigue the chest and triceps while recruiting the use of fast-twitch muscle fibers.

Once the quick hands are properly adjusted, the athlete will sit with his back against the wall. Holding a 25-pound plate with both hands, the athlete will start with the weight touching the floor on his right side. From this position, he will punch the weight upward, fully contracting the chest and triceps, with arms locked out at a 45-degree angle. The athlete then lowers the weight down to the floor on the left side of the body. This action will count as one repetition. The athlete will do two sets of twenty reps. (See Figure 10.6.)

Ts and Ys

This is an exercise I use mostly with my quarterbacks. The player takes a light dumbbell in each hand and stands with his arms straight out at his sides, so his arms and body form a capital "T." For

Figure 10.6. Quick Hands

the Ts, the player lowers the weights to his sides and then lifts them back to the starting T position. For the Ys, the player starts from the T position and lifts the weights over his head at a 45-degree angle, forming the letter "Y." The player's grip on the dumbbells should always be such that his thumb is pointing in the direction that the weight is moving. If the player is lifting the dumbbells from his side to the T or from the T to the Y, his palms should be under the weight with his thumbs pointing up. If the player is lowering the weight, he should have more of an overhand grip, with his thumb pointing down.

Flat Bench Press with Dumbbells

Adjustable benches must be laid completely flat and parallel to the ground or an already molded flat bench should be used. The athlete uses a set of dumbbells that he can handle for the desired number of repetitions. He will lie back onto the bench and move the dumbbells into the starting position. At the bottom position of the movement, the athlete will pinch his shoulder blades together to help put the chest into a prestretched mode. The hands should grip the handles evenly on the dumbbells to help with proper balance. The dumbbells also should be centered over the top of the elbows during the entire pressing movement to help ensure good balance and proper movement of the weight. The athlete's upper arm should be set at about a 45-degree angle from the upper torso and remain at that angle all the way through the press to help make sure the chest receives the bulk of the work. The dumbbells should be driven up in a slightly arcing motion until they can be brought together lightly at the top of the press with the arms fully extended. The athlete will then lower the dumbbells back to the starting position via the same arcing motion with a slow, controlled manner.

Chip's Tips

1. Set your feet firmly and press them into the ground on every concentric stroke of the press with no movement during the set.
2. Ensure proper breathing technique. Breathe out as you press up, and breathe in as you bring the weight back to the starting position.
3. Make sure you get a good stretch at the bottom position on every repetition to help with a complete development of the muscle.
4. At the top of the press, the dumbbells should be over the targeted area of the chest—in this case, the middle chest and only slightly toward the head. Avoid pushing the dumbbells too far up toward the head or too low near the bottom of the chest. (See Figures 10.7a, 10.7b, and 10.7c.)

Figure 10.7a. Flat Bench Press
with Dumbbells
b.
c.

Hang Cleans

The first step in performing the hang clean is for the athlete to select the proper weight to use. The athlete must use a weight he can control or handle or lift comfortably and be explosive while maintaining proper form. The athlete must make sure that the weight is enough to be challenging for the number of repetitions he is trying to complete.

Stance and Posture. Feet should be hip width apart at the start of the clean. The grip should be about shoulder width. An easy way for the athlete to select his grip is to set his feet first and then squat down to the bar resting on the platform. He then should reach just outside of his knees and grasp the bar; that should be approximately the right grip. The athlete should then stand up with the weight in hand and assume the correct stance before attempting to clean the weight. Before the attempt, the athlete's head should be up and facing forward, shoulders back, chest out, arms straight and locked, and elbows turned outward with the knuckles facing down. (See Figure 10.8a.)

Eccentric Phase. To initiate the eccentric phase of the hang clean, the athlete needs to start moving the weight downward toward his knees. To do this, he must push his hips back and let the shoulders come forward and must maintain a slight bend in his knees. The bar should remain in contact with the thighs during the entire descent and stop just above the kneecaps. The athlete should keep his posture the same during this part of the movement. The head should be up and shoulders back while the arms are still straight and locked. Also, the athlete's shoulders should be in line with or slightly past the bar. Having the shoulders behind the bar will result in his not being able to properly drive his hips and will decrease his explosive power and compromise the lift. Taking a deep breath on this phase will help start the concentric phase. (See Figure 10.8b.)

Concentric Phase. During this phase, the athlete will forcefully drive his hips and start the upward movement of the weight. After the proper descent is accomplished, the athlete then explosively drives his hips up and into the bar, essentially performing a vertical jump with the weight. He must make sure the bar travels straight upward along his body and not in an outward arcing motion. What the athlete is trying to accomplish here is what's called the triple extension. The ankles, knees, and hips must be completely and forcefully extended to help with the acceleration of the weight. The athlete should be standing completely straight up and even on his toes if this is done properly. At the top of the extension, the athlete will then bend his arms in an upright row motion, as opposed to a reverse curl motion, to help assist the weight even higher for the catch phase of the hang clean. (See Figure 10.8c.)

The Catch. After the concentric phase is completed, the athlete must then catch the weight. To complete the lift, he must be completely extended and must drive his elbows rapidly under the bar and think about pulling himself under the bar instead of the bar into him. His hands will remain in contact with the bar but will loosen so they can rotate around it to get into the proper position. The athlete can also widen his stance from hip width to shoulder width and slightly flex his knees to help drop under the bar to assist the catch. The bar should come to rest on the front deltoids, along the upper chest near the clavicle, and the hands should still be grasping the bar with the fingers slightly extended. The elbows should be up and pointing forward at the end of the catch. (See Figure 10.8d.)

After all phases are complete, the athlete will lower the weight down, reset his feet, and adjust his posture so that he can properly perform the next repetition. Due to the nature of this lift, the athlete will probably need to use straps to help secure his grip on the bar, especially while he is resetting himself to complete the next rep.

Power Cleans

The power clean is like the hang clean, except instead of starting the eccentric phase from the thighs, the athlete starts with the weight on the

Figure 10.8a. Hang Cleans   b. Eccentric Phase   c. Concentric Phase   d. The Catch

floor, squats to it with his back straight and butt low, and uses the same explosive drive from the hips to bring the weight up the body, through the concentric phase, and into the catch.

Chip's Tips for Hang Cleans and Power Cleans

1. Keep the arms straight and locked all the way through the lift until the catch. Letting the arms bend during the lift leads to the athlete performing more of a reverse curl action instead of a rowing motion at the top and can disrupt the power production.
2. Keep the head straight and looking forward, and don't throw it backward during the hip drive.
3. Make sure the hips have been completely extended and driven hard through. This exercise is all about hip drive and explosion; to leave any flexion in the hips just leads to less overall development. One way to tell if the hips are driving all the way through is to see if the athlete has hopped backward. If his feet are farther back on the platform than when he started, then he has not driven his hips completely and has compensated by pulling the weight backward and into himself during the catch instead of pulling himself under it.

Shrugs

Stand tall with your feet about hip width apart. Your grip on the bar should be shoulder width or slightly wider apart. You can choose to have your grip with your hands over the bar, facing toward you, or alternated, one hand over and one hand under. With the arms and back completely straight, shrug the weight upward and back as high as you can, using the muscles of your upper back. After pausing at the top for a maximal muscle contraction, lower the weight down until it stretches the muscles you are working.

Back Squats

Place the bar across the upper back and not across the base of the neck. Hold the bar firmly, making sure it does not shift during exercise. Feet should be about shoulder width apart, with toes pointing straight or slightly outside. Keeping the head facing forward and slightly upward, bend the knees until the thighs are parallel to the floor. Return to the starting position. The back must remain straight throughout the exercise. Keep the chest out to help in keeping the back straight. As the knees bend, the hips must also bend so that undue pressure will not be placed on the knees. (See Figures 10.9a, 10.9b, and 10.9c.)

Figure 10.9a. Back Squats   b.   c.

Vertimax

The Vertimax is a platform-based piece of training equipment that uses a pulley system with a specifically engineered bungee system. To enhance explosive jumping techniques, the Vertimax has the ability to be adjusted from low- to high-intensity by shortening the length of the bungee cords. The athlete starts by firmly fitting the specially designed belt around his waist. Depending on the desired intensity level, the cord will then be adjusted. Standing in the middle of the platform, the athlete fastens the cords to the belt and then performs explosive jumps that simulate those of a vertical jump. It is recommended that the athlete start out with eight single jumps (putting a short time between each jump to make sure he is properly set and balanced). After the athlete is comfortable with the way the cord's pull affects his jumping and landing, he will perform eight consecutive explosive jumps per set.

Chip's Tips

1. The desired depth or starting point of each jump is the same depth as you would have at the most down position of a testing vertical jump.
2. Do not sacrifice depth for speed of jump.
3. Upon landing, there should be no hesitation between landing in a squatted position and starting the upward movement.

Figure 10.10a. Vertimax   b

4. Do not bend at the waist and back to get depth. Depth should be obtained in the hips.
5. Your back should remain straight and upright throughout the entire motion. This will ensure that power is generated through the hips, not the swing of the back.
6. During the up phase, both hands should be extended above the body, and the head should be tilted upward. This will help ensure that the hips are fully extended. (See Figures 10.10a and 10.10b.)

Negatives with Vertimax

Negatives are performed by placing all four cords of the Vertimax on the belt of the athlete. The athlete will then hold a weight extended out in front of the body with both hands. From this point, the athlete will start a slow, deliberate motion down to the point at which the thighs are parallel to the floor. It should take about ten seconds to reach this point. The athlete then returns to the starting position at the same rate of movement. Each set of negatives consists of five repetitions. Once these five reps are complete, the athlete performs one set of five tuck jumps without resistance. (See Figures 10.11a and 10.11b.)

Figure 10.11a. Negatives with Vertimax   b.

Explosive Step-Ups

Step-ups are used to develop explosive power in the hips, quads, glutes, and hamstrings. A solidly built step-up box is needed for this exercise. The box should be at a height that allows the quad to be no higher than parallel to the floor (anything higher will put undue stress on the knees). Standing with toes about two inches from the box with the bar and weight across the upper back, place one foot approximately two inches above the box. From this point, with one explosive movement, drive the foot and leg down on the box, lifting the body upward onto the box. At the same time, lift the opposite leg up into the chest.

Figure 10.12. Explosive Step-Ups

If done properly, hips should be driven forward, resulting in the heel of the planted foot lifting off of the box as the weight is shifted onto the ball of the foot. From this point, carefully step down and off the box with both legs, and then repeat with the other leg. It is very important that the contact foot be entirely placed on the box. Do not hang the heel off, as this may cause injury. (See Figure 10.12.)

Pullover Press

Pullover press is an exercise that we primarily use to develop the triceps. However, it is classified as a multijoint exercise. This means that more than one muscle group is used to perform this exercise.

You'll need a flat bench press and an EZ curl bar to perform this exercise. The lifter will start by lying on the bench with his feet flat on the floor. The lifter's head should be even with the end of the bench. The hand placement on the bar should be with the outside of the palms placed in the innermost curves on the bar (hands should be about a thumb's width apart). The starting position of the bar should be behind the lifter's head at about bench level. The elbows are bent and placed as close to the center line of the body as possible. They should remain as close as possible throughout the entire exercise. From this position, the bar is pulled in a sweeping motion over the lifter's head until it touches his chest. From this point, he should extend his arms upward until the triceps are completely contracted. He then lowers the weight back to his chest and, in the same sweeping motion, returns it to the starting position behind the head. During both sweeping phases, the lifter should keep the bar close to the head to take undue stress off his shoulders. This exercise will be completed for ten reps. At that point, the lifter will perform ten close-grip bench press movements (bar starts by resting on the chest, arms are then extended until triceps are completely contracted). (See Figure 10.13.)

Figure 10.13. Pullover Press

Leg Press

Leg press is a great alternative to squats if the lifter has had shoulder or back problems. Leg press is also a great variance in a leg routine. Start by lying on the machine with your back against the back pad. Place your feet on the foot tray. Extend your legs forward while pushing up the sled and rotate the sled locks to allow the weight to be lowered. Lower the weight as far as possible without rotating your hips off of the seat. Your lower back and hips should always remain in contact with the seat pads. From this point, extend legs until the sled is returned to starting position. Be careful not to fully extend your legs due to the risk of knee hyperextension. (See Figures 10.14a and 10.14b.)

Figure 10.14a. Leg Press   b.

Foot Placement

When your feet are on the top of the foot plate, the emphasis is on the hamstrings and buttocks. When your feet are on the bottom of the foot plate, the emphasis is on the quadriceps. When the feet are on the outside edge of the foot plate, the emphasis is on the abductors. Some leg press machines may come with range limits for assistance with rehab.

Shoulder Raises

The following exercises will assist with shoulder muscle growth.

Seated Bent-Over Raises—Rear Dumbbell Flies. This version stresses the rear portion of the shoulder using dumbbells. Seated at the end of a bench, the athlete should place his feet out far enough where he can start with the dumbbells under his legs. He should lean forward until his upper torso is almost parallel to the ground and then grasp the dumbbells. Starting with a slight bend in the elbow and the palms facing each other, the athlete should begin raising the dumbbells in a widening, arcing motion and at the same time moving them slightly forward toward the head. The bend in the elbow will remain constant throughout the motion, and the stopping point of the dumbbells will be even with the upper back and in line with the forehead. At the top of the movement, the palms should have been rotated until they are facing toward the floor. After a brief pause for a maximal muscle contraction, the athlete should lower the dumbbells, controlling them to avoid swinging, in the same exact motion they were raised to the starting point.

Standing Lateral Raises—Medial Dumbbell Flies. This version stresses the middle portion of the shoulder using dumbbells. Standing completely straight and feet hip width apart, the athlete will grasp a set of dumbbells and start with them at his sides, with the palms facing his body. Putting a slight bend in the elbow, the athlete then raises the dumbbells up directly on his sides until the arms are shoulder height and parallel to the ground. At this point, the athlete will have kept the same bend in his elbow throughout the entire movement and rotated his palms so that they now are facing the floor. The athlete should lower the dumbbells, controlling them to avoid swinging, in the same exact motion they were raised, and the palms are rotated back toward the body.

Standing Front Raises—Front Flies. This version stresses the front portion of the shoulder using dumbbells. Standing completely straight with feet hip width apart, the athlete will grasp a set of dumbbells and start with them at his sides with the palms facing his body. Putting a slight bend in the elbow, the athlete then raises the dumbbells up directly in front of his shoulder until they are even with the shoulder; the palms will have been rotated until they are facing the ground at the top of the movement. After a brief pause for a maximal muscle contraction, the athlete should lower the dumbbells, controlling them to prevent swinging, until they reach the starting position. The athlete can choose whether to alternate the arms or raise them both together.

Combination Movement—Combination Flies. This version stresses all three parts of the shoulder that have previously been worked. Standing completely straight with the feet hip width apart, the athlete will grasp a pair of dumbbells and start with them at his sides with the palms facing his body. The athlete will then raise the dumbbells up in a front raise while rotating his palms toward the floor, using both arms at the same time, until they are shoulder height, at which point he should pause for a brief moment. Then he will pull his arms backward while keeping them shoulder height and put a slight bend in the elbow. Once the arms and dumbbells are pulled all the way back until they are in a lateral raise position, the athlete will then pause briefly again. The last part of the movement will have the athlete slowly lowering his arms back to his sides and into the starting position. A slow, controlled manner on this exercise is imperative to help completely fatigue the shoulders.

Chip's Rules to Lift By

Whether you're frosh-meat, someone who suffers from senioritis, or a perennial Pro Bowl player in the NFL, the basics of strength training apply to you.

1. **Have fun.** Make the weight room a fun place, and you'll never want to leave. That's rule number one because the key to making huge gains is lifting regularly, week in and week out. And it's a lot easier to keep to this schedule when you're having fun.

2. **Freshman or new lifters must learn proper technique with the bar and no weights.** Your coach should judge your technique. Once you're dialed in, you can start slapping on the weight. When Brian Urlacher came to me, he had had excellent technique drilled into him by his junior high and high school coach. All these years later, he's stronger because of it.

3. **Increase weight at your own pace.** That senior squatting 450 pounds today wasn't squatting 445 pounds as a freshman. He was probably struggling with just the bar. But he was consistent and committed. He made big gains year after year by having the discipline to make small gains day after day. He didn't get distracted by what his other teammates were doing or by simply trying to overdo it himself.

4. **If you want to be slow, train slowly.** You want to be fast, so train fast. Most weight lifting must be done at a controlled speed. But moves on the football field are explosive. So, we superset core lifts with plyometric exercises:

Lift	Plyo
Squats	Tuck Jumps
Bench Press	Power Ball Chest Pass (lying on bench)
Lat Pull-Down	Russian Twist
Lunges	Box Jumps

5. **Learn to fail.** Pushing yourself until muscle failure improves your strength. You should really struggle—even fail—to finish the last two reps of your final set. If you're failing before the final set, you're either lifting too much or doing too many reps. If you're popping out extra reps on your final set, you're ready to go up at least five pounds.

6. **Don't be "that guy."** During core lifts—or lifts where muscle failure could lead to you getting squashed—get a teammate to spot you. Don't be that guy everyone laughs at for getting stuck under the bar. And don't show off with more weight than you're used to. Injuries from the field have honor; injuries from the weight room are moronic.

7. **Your coach can make your life miserable if he wants, so you better take good care of his weight room.** Rerack your weights. If you're strong enough to put the weight on, then you're strong enough to take it off. And if you sweat on a piece of equipment, towel it off.

8. **Don't focus on your "show muscles."** Focus on your "go muscles." Triceps and biceps are mostly for show. Quads, hamstrings, and glutes make you go. Think of it this way: no matter how great your guns look, you'll still look like a chump if some guy outruns you.

Little Words for Heavy Lifters

Superset. Switching between exercises inside the set. For example, twelve reps of bench followed by twelve reps of pull-ups; repeat both three times.

Plyometric. An explosive exercise, typically where you're jumping, landing, bounding, or throwing.

Core lift. A lift that engages more than one muscle set. Biceps curls use just your guns. But bench uses your pectorals and your triceps.

Spotter. A teammate who helps you with the weight when you've achieved muscle failure.

Muscle failure. After a certain number of reps at a given weight, muscles just stop working. It could be five reps with twenty pounds or fifty reps with twenty pounds.

11

The Tahoe Experience

Training Brian Urlacher at High Altitude

Not too long ago, I received a call from Brian Urlacher's agent, Bryce Karger, about the possibility of training Brian at high altitude in Lake Tahoe, California. Bryce asked me if I would consider spending at least four weeks in Lake Tahoe, getting Brian ready for the 2004 season. Keep in mind that Brian usually comes to Competitive Edge Sports in Atlanta for his off-season training, but this year he wanted to do something different. This would be my fifth year training Brian, and he is certainly one of only a very few clients whom I would consider training outside of our complex in Atlanta for that extended amount of time.

Training in High Altitude

Training at high altitude causes a condition called hypoxia, which occurs when the muscle tissue doesn't have enough oxygen. The higher up you go, the thinner the air and the less oxygen that is delivered to the blood. Because of the lack of oxygen, your muscles fatigue more quickly. The flip side to this phenomenon, and the reason Brian wanted to train at high altitude, is that while your body does go into a hypoxia state, the effects are only temporary. It takes only a short period of time for your body to adapt, and during this time your kidneys release a hormone called erythropoietin. This causes your body to produce additional red blood cells that can carry oxygen-rich blood to your muscles for additional energy and work. When Brian comes back down to sea level, his extra red blood cells can transport more oxygen than what's normal and allow him to delay muscle fatigue. This is exactly what he wants to do in the fourth quarter: play longer and harder and recover quicker!

Program by Design

Brian wanted me to design a program that would help him with his endurance in the fourth quarter. He felt the effects of fatigue and believed he was running out of gas. I have always used position-specific training for Brian, with him working on scraping and filling, pursuit drills, first-step explosion, pass drops, change of direction, and any other drills that would benefit his play at the mike linebacker position.

The first challenge in designing a program for Brian was trying to figure out exactly what was happening in the third and fourth quarters to fatigue him. The first thing I did was ask Brian to send me film from four of his games. I then began to break down the film into different segments. I charted each play, starting with the first series, then included the quarter, down, and distance, Brian's position on the field, and the actual play that was run (for example, "blitzed the A gap from the right side"). I then broke down each game into four quarters, with each quarter representing the actual game movements from one of the four games Brian had played. I also put twenty-five seconds between each play, along with TV time-outs and fifteen minutes for halftime.

The first thing that I noticed about Brian's game film was the amount of running that he did on each play. I circled the end of each play and put a stopwatch on the length of the play. I quickly discovered that Brian was running to the ball each play, no matter whether it was a three-yard run or pass play twenty yards down the field. He would show up in the circle within three seconds of every play. This confirmed in my mind that the amount of sprinting from the start of the play to the end of the play was substantial. I could also see how fatigued he was at the end of each game. These are the actual defensive plays taken from four Bears football games in which Brian participated. Note the abbreviations for the following table are as follows: M = middle of the field, where he lined up; L = left; R = right; E/R = end of line of scrimmage on the right side.

Play-Based Training Schedule

Reps	Quarter	Down	Position	Play	Equipment	Pattern
1	1	1	M	Blitz A	2 cords	LB-21
2	1	2	L	Toss Away	QRH	LB-7
3	1	3	R	Hook/Curl	—	LB-3
4	1	1	M	45 Lead	2 cords	LB-21
5	1	2	M	Toss Away	QRH	LB-3
6	1	3	E/R	Blitz BS	2 cords	LB-20
7	1	1	R	PA H/C	—	LB-11
8	1	2	R	Hook/Curl Settle	—	LB-8
9	1	3	R	Scrape/Fill L	2 cords	LB-2

4-minute rest   9-play drive

Reps	Quarter	Down	Position	Play	Equipment	Pattern
10	1	1	R	Wheel RT	—	LB-18
11	1	2	L	Blitz A	2 cords	LB-21
12	1	3	L	ISO-FB	2 cords	LB-21
13	1	1	L	TE-3	—	LB-3
14	1	2	L	ISO	2 cords	LB-21
15	1	3	E/R	Blitz	2 cords	LB-20
16	1	1	L	Blitz A RT	2 cords	LB-21
17	1	2	M	Scrap R Shuffle	40 yards	LB-22
18	1	3	L	Toss Sweep	QRH	LB-3

2-minute rest   9-play drive

Reps	Quarter	Down	Position	Play	Equipment	Pattern
19	1	1	L	Blitz A	2 cords	LB-18
20	1	2	M	Hook/Curl	—	LB-21
21	1	3	E/R	Blitz BS	QRH	LB-21
22	1	1	R	ISO-FB	2 cords	LB-3
23	1	2	L	Flat RT	—	LB-21
24	1	3	R	Blitz C	2 cords	LB-20

5-minute rest   6-play drive   24 plays in QTR 1

Note: This is only an example of one quarter. Brian finished with four quarters, averaging about eighty plays and lasting about two hours ten minutes.

After watching game cuts for days, I decided to come up with a game-specific and movement-specific program that was both aerobic, because of the duration, and anaerobic, because of the short explosive bursts required. I also wanted to take into consideration the resistance that Brian faced on each play, the effects and weight of his football equipment, and, last but not least, his nutritional needs. I had to make sure that he was taking in enough calories to maintain his lean muscle mass.

In addressing the resistance part of Brian's training, I used a quick-release handle (QRH) to add resistance to Brian in his movements without impeding them. (See Figure 11.1.) When he blitzed or played the run, I would give him resistance for four or five steps, as though he were taking on a center or guard. Next I would make him get upfield three yards and then turn and run fifteen yards down the field, at which time I would release him from my resistance and he would turn and sprint. I also had my good friends at X-Vest make me a custom shoulder pad–style weight vest that we loaded up with eight pounds of weight (which is two times the normal weight of shoulder pads). This was important in acclimatizing Brian to the weight of his pads and the summer heat of two-a-days.

Week 1

I decided that I needed to be able to monitor Brian's heart rate during his training so that I could adjust his intensity based on that reading. Brian wore a polar heart rate monitor. I was able to set his target zone based on his age, height, and weight. The monitor also gave me additional information, including total training time, average heart rate, total calories burned, heart rate zone, and percent of calories from fat. This information was invaluable and turned out to be right on in terms of fat lost after my calculations.

On week 1, we started out with one quarter that was twenty-four total plays. The first series was nine plays with twenty-five seconds of rest between each play. The total time for series 1 was eleven minutes, with Brian's heart rate at 162 beats per minute. He then had a four-minute rest period. Series 2 was nine plays and lasted eleven minutes, with Brian's heart rate at 164 beats per minute, followed by a two-minute rest. The third series was six total plays and lasted seven and a half minutes, with

Figure 11.1. Quick-Release Handle

Brian's heart rate at 166 beats per minute. The total training time for the first quarter was twenty-nine minutes thirty seconds, and the grand total training time was one hour fifty minutes. Brian's average heart rate was 143 beats per minute. He was in his target zone for one hour eleven minutes, and his total calories burned were 2,200 calories, with 50 percent of those calories from fat.

I must note that we did not only do the first quarter; we always started out with a ballistic warm-up that consisted of fifteen to twenty movements to warm up the core. We also used the quick foot ladders and the reaction drills for our warm-ups. For the first two weeks, we did position-specific work, in addition to game situations, and used resistance forties for the two-minute drill. Brian would run ten forty-yard dashes in less than seven seconds with ten seconds of recovery. This was by far the hardest thing that Brian did during his workouts. We finished up each workout with me stretching Brian for fifteen minutes (halftime).

Weight Work

The next consideration for Brian's summer program was his weight work. Not only did I want to increase his aerobic endurance, but I needed to be able to increase his muscle endurance as well. I also wanted him to maintain the strength gains he had made during his off-season workouts in Chicago. Brian is extremely strong and has power cleaned more than 400 pounds while training with me in Atlanta. At 6′4″, he has a long way to pull that kind of weight. He has some of the most explosive hips I have ever trained, translating into a 4.49 forty, a thirty-eight-inch vertical leap, and unmatched athleticism at a body weight of almost 260 pounds.

The main goal of Brian's weight program was to increase muscle endurance, as was the case with his running. I had to figure out at what intensity we could train without overtraining. To keep it simple, I broke Brian's workouts into a push-pull regimen. I constantly changed the reps, sets, and exercises. I tried to keep Brian's rest time at twenty-five seconds (huddle time) between each set and one minute between each exercise. I felt that this type of high-volume training would assist in helping to achieve the desired results for Brian: muscle endurance and fat burning. Keep in mind that these are extreme results in such a short period of time.

Slow-twitch muscle fibers contract slowly, but they can sustain their contractions for long periods of time without fatiguing. Slow-twitch fibers get most of their energy from burning fat. Pure fast-twitch fibers can contract rapidly, but they fatigue quickly. Their energy comes from burning glycogen. Brian definitely has a greater number of fast-twitch fibers than slow-twitch. However, as with the slow-twitch fiber type, fat can be burned by the fast-twitch fiber. By training with high volume, you can change pure fast-twitch fibers into fast-twitch oxidative fibers that burn fat at a faster rate. With the combination of explosive running and high-volume weight work, Brian's body literally became a fat-burning machine.

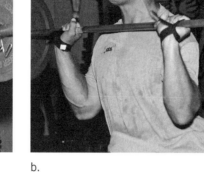

Figure 11.2a. Brian Power Cleaning   b.

We were able to achieve tremendous results with Brian. (see the before and after testing results at the end of the chapter). I firmly believe that you can burn fat with high-rep work using heavy poundage. (See Figures 11.2a and 11.2b.)

Chest, Back, and Biceps

Day 1

Bench Press	Superset	Seated Row
4 × max – max + 2		4 × 8 – 8 – 8 – 8
– max + 2 – max + 2		
Incline Press	Superset	One-Arm Row
4 × 8 – 8 – 8 – 8		4 × 8 – 8 – 8 – 8
Dips	Superset	Lat Pull-Down
3 × AMCD		3 × 12 – 12 – 12
Straight Bar Curl	Superset	Seated DB Curls
5 × 10 – 8 – 6 – 6 – 6		3 × 8 – 8 – 8
Crunches	Superset	Knee-Ups
3 × 30 – 30 – 30		3 × 30 – 30 – 30

Terms

> **Max + 2:** maximum reps you can perform plus two additional forced reps
> **Supersets:** the completion of consecutive sets without a rest
> **AMCD:** as many as you can do
> **Rollovers:** push-ups and then sit-ups
> **CGBP:** close-grip bench press

Note: Rest for twenty-five seconds between sets and one minute between each exercise.

Triceps, Shoulders, and Legs

Day 2

Power Cleans	Superset	Shrugs
5 × 10 – 8 – 6 – 6 – 6		4 × 8 – 8 – 8 – 8
Leg Extension	Superset	Squats
3 × 12 – 12 – 12		4 × 6 – 6 – 6 – 6
Seated Military Press	Superset	Front Raises
4 × 10 – 10 – 10 – 10		4 × 8 – 8 – 8 – 8
Upright Row	Superset	Side Lateral
4 × 8 – 8 – 8 – 8		4 × 8 – 8 – 8 – 8
Triceps Extension	Superset	CGBP
4 × 10 – 8 – 6 – 4		4 × 10 – 8 – 6 – 4
Rollovers		
3 × AMCD		

Results: Pre- and Posttesting, Chicago Bears Training Center

26 June 2004

Body weight	256 lbs.
Bod-pod (body comp)	6.9%

10 July 2004

Body weight	255.6 lbs.
Bod-pod (body comp)	5.2%
Bod-pod loss	−1.7%
Fat loss	−4.35 lbs.

26 July 2004

Body weight	255.3 lbs.
Bod-pod (body comp)	4.9%
Bod-pod loss	−2.0%
Fat loss	−5.10 lbs.
Lung capacity	Increased

Heart Rate Recovery

Week 1 exercising heart rate	173 BPM
3-minute recovery	118 BPM
Week 4 exercising heart rate	172 BPM
3-minute recovery	80 BPM

Weight Work

29 June	Muscular endurance, pretesting
Day 1	315 lbs. bench press × 8 reps
22 July	Training, 4 weeks
Last workout	315 lbs. bench press, posttesting × 13 reps
Increase	+ 5 reps in 4 weeks

Diet

I am not a registered dietitian; however, I feel that with twenty-five years of elite-level training, I do have some insight into the dietary needs of my athletes. That being said, the last challenge to contend with was Brian's diet. I had to make sure that this training program, along with the altitude, would not result in a loss of lean muscle. I based Brian's dietary needs on a couple of factors. I considered both his overall caloric needs and his protein needs. The first thing I needed to figure out was Brian's basal metabolic rate (BMR).

The BMR is the minimum number of calories required to sustain life in a waking state. Diet has a profound effect on your body composition. Either too much or not enough body fat can impact your performance in your sport. The benefits of speed and strength training can be maximized by proper nutrition. By decreasing your body fat, you can enhance your speed and endurance and aid in overall improved sports performance. Your body needs nutrients for recovery after hard workouts; bad nutrition can affect your training results in a negative manner if you do not replenish your body with the right fuels. You especially need to maintain a high caloric intake to generate the type of energy needed for sports such as football. When you shortchange your caloric intake, you will very quickly become tired and weak. You have essentially run out of gas. Let me show you how to calculate your basal metabolic rate.

There are different formulas and charts that you can use to calculate your BMR. I have found most of my professional football players have different caloric needs. So there will be variations in BMR, depending on a player's workout and weight needs as well as whether he wants to gain or lose weight. The basic formula I use to estimate BMR is to multiply the player's weight by 15, which is the number of calories that it takes to maintain 1 pound. I have also seen different numbers of calories used for different levels of needs. For example, I've seen 12 calories used for projections of players with extremely slow metabolisms and 18 calories used for the lucky player whose metabolism runs at mach one speed. Fifteen calories per pound is what I use to get a rough estimate of the player's BMR at a sedentary state. If the athlete is active, I'll add in extra calories to his BMR to calculate his actual caloric needs. I usually add an additional 500 calories per day for active players.

At the time, Brian weighed about 256 pounds. Based on that, Brian's weight of 256 pounds multiplied by 15 calories gave me his BMR of 3,840 calories. I added another 1,000 calories per day for his activity level, bringing his daily intake to around 5,800 calories per day.

Another consideration was Brian's protein needs. I needed to make sure he was getting enough protein to offset the effects of high-volume training and explosive running. I based his protein needs on 1 gram of protein per pound of body weight. That meant he needed at least 256 grams per day. The problem with consuming that much protein is that your body can only assimilate 30 grams per meal. Since I don't cook, I had to figure out how to make sure Brian received all his daily requirements for protein. I went to the store and bought EAS Myoplex ready-to-drink protein shakes. EAS is the only nutrition company whose products are currently certified by the National Football League. There are numerous reasons why those credentials are of utmost importance for my athletes. The main reason is that every supplement I recommend has been rigorously tested and ensures that approved products, those bearing the label certification program's logo, fully comply with the NFL's banned substances requirements. The protein shakes have 42 grams of protein and only 2 grams of sugar. About every three hours, Brian would drink a shake or would eat a meal.

After the second week of training, Brian went back to Chicago and was retested in the Bod-pod for body comp, making sure that my calculations about his diet and training program were right. After two weeks of training, Brian weighed in at 255.6 pounds and had lost 1.7 percent body fat, or 4 pounds of fat. He started at 256 pounds and 6.9 percent body fat. Even better news was the fact that he had increased his lung capacity, which validated the results I had imagined with this new type of training. Needless to say, Brian was pleased. (See Figure 11.3.)

Figure 11.3. Brian Urlacher Taking a Breather

APPENDIX A

Weight Program and Record Keeping

The following tables outline separate six-week programs for quarterbacks and players in all other positions. The recommended exercises come from the preceding chapters. Refer to Chapter 10 to determine how to distribute the weight across the recommended sets.

Weight Work: Quarterbacks

Mondays	Week 1	Week 2	Week 3	Week 4	Week 5	Week 6
Exercise	Sets × Reps	Sets × Reps	Sets × Reps	Sets × Reps	Sets × Reps	Sets × Reps
Ts and Ys	2 × 10	2 × 10	2 × 10	2 × 10	2 × 10	2 × 10
Flat DB Bench Press	4 × 10	4 × 10	4 × 10	4 × 10	4 × 10	4 × 10
Low Rows	4 × 8	4 × 8	4 × 8	4 × 8	4 × 8	4 × 8
Incline DB Bench Press	4 × 10	4 × 10	4 × 10	4 × 10	4 × 10	4 × 10
One-Arm Rows	4 × 8	4 × 8	4 × 8	4 × 8	4 × 8	4 × 8
EZ Bar Curls	10 × 8 × 6 × 6 × 6 × 6	10 × 8 × 6 × 6 × 6 × 6	10 × 8 × 6 × 6 × 6 × 6	10 × 8 × 6 × 6 × 6 × 6	10 × 8 × 6 × 6 × 6 × 6	10 × 8 × 6 × 6 × 6 × 6
EZ Bar Close Grip	2× max	2× max	2× max	2× max	2× max	2× max
Reverse Curls	2× max	2× max	2× max	2× max	2× max	2× max
Rollovers*	6–10	6–10	6–10	6–10	6–10	6–10

*Add one set of rollovers each week up to ten sets max.

Tuesdays	Week 1	Week 2	Week 3	Week 4	Week 5	Week 6
Exercise	Sets × Reps	Sets × Reps	Sets × Reps	Sets × Reps	Sets × Reps	Sets × Reps
Power Cleans	4 × 5	4 × 5	4 × 5	4 × 5	4 × 5	4 × 5
Shrugs	4 × 15	4 × 15	4 × 15	4 × 15	4 × 15	4 × 15
Squats	3 × 8	3 × 8	3 × 8	3 × 8	3 × 8	3 × 8
Vertimax (1 cord)	3 × 8	3 × 8	3 × 8	3 × 8	3 × 8	3 × 8
Step-Ups	3 × 6	3 × 6	3 × 6	3 × 6	3 × 6	3 × 6

continued

Weight Work: Quarterbacks, *continued*

		Week 1	Week 2	Week 3	Week 4	Week 5	Week 6
Vertimax			3 × 6	3 × 6	3 × 6	3 × 6	3 × 6
ABS #1			ABS #1	ABS #1	ABS #1	ABS #1	ABS #1

Wednesdays

Weeks 1–6: Pool Workout

Thursdays

Exercise	Week 1	Week 2	Week 3	Week 4	Week 5	Week 6
	Sets × Reps	*Sets × Reps*	*Sets × Reps*	*Sets × Reps*	*Sets × Reps*	*Sets × Reps*
Inversion/Eversion	2 × 10	2 × 10	2 × 10	2 × 10	2 × 10	2 × 10
Flat DB Bench Press	4 × 10	4 × 10	4 × 10	4 × 10	4 × 10	4 × 10
Low Rows	4 × 8	4 × 8	4 × 8	4 × 8	4 × 8	4 × 8
Incline DB Bench Press	4 × 10	4 × 10	4 × 10	4 × 10	4 × 10	4 × 10
One-Arm Incline Rows	4 × 8	4 × 8	4 × 8	4 × 8	4 × 8	4 × 8
Pullover Press	3 × 10	3 × 10	3 × 10	3 × 10	3 × 10	3 × 10
EZ Bar Curls	3 × 10	3 × 10	3 × 10	3 × 10	3 × 10	3 × 10
EZ Bar Close Grip	2× max	2× max	2× max	2× max	2× max	2× max
Reverse Curls	2× max	2× max	2× max	2× max	2× max	2× max
Rollovers	6 × 10	6 × 10	6 × 10	6 × 10	6 × 10	6 × 10

Fridays

Exercise	Week 1	Week 2	Week 3	Week 4	Week 5	Week 6
	Sets × Reps	*Sets × Reps*	*Sets × Reps*	*Sets × Reps*	*Sets × Reps*	*Sets × Reps*
Hang Cleans	4 × 5	4 × 5	4 × 5	4 × 5	4 × 5	4 × 5
Shrugs	4 × 15	4 × 15	4 × 15	4 × 15	4 × 15	4 × 15
Leg Press	4 × 12	4 × 12	4 × 12	4 × 12	4 × 12	4 × 12
Vertimax	4 × 8	4 × 8	4 × 8	4 × 8	4 × 8	4 × 8
Upright Rows	3 × 12	3 × 12	3 × 12	3 × 12	3 × 12	3 × 12
Rear Delt Flies	3 × 10	3 × 10	3 × 10	3 × 10	3 × 10	3 × 10
Medial Delt Flies	3 × 10	3 × 10	3 × 10	3 × 10	3 × 10	3 × 10
Front Delt Flies	3 × 10	3 × 10	3 × 10	3 × 10	3 × 10	3 × 10
Combo Flies	2 × 10	2 × 10	2 × 10	2 × 10	2 × 10	2 × 10

Weight Work: Running Backs, Offensive Linemen, Tight Ends, Defensive Linemen, Linebackers, and Defensive Backs

Mondays	Week 1	Week 2	Week 3	Week 4	Week 5	Week 6
Exercise	Sets × Reps	Sets × Reps	Sets × Reps	Sets × Reps	Sets × Reps	Sets × Reps
Flat Bench Press	Drop Set	Drop Set	Drop Set	Drop Set	Drop Set	Drop Set
Low Rows	5 × 8	5 × 8	5 × 8	5 × 8	5 × 8	5 × 8
Incline DB Bench Press	4 × 8	4 × 8	4 × 8	4 × 8	4 × 8	4 × 8
One-Arm Rows	4 × 8	4 × 8	4 × 8	4 × 8	4 × 8	4 × 8
EZ Bar Curls	10 × 8 × 6 × 6 × 6 × 6	10 × 8 × 6 × 6 × 6 × 6	10 × 8 × 6 × 6 × 6 × 6 × 6	10 × 8 × 6 × 6 × 6 × 6 × 6	10 × 8 × 6 × 6 × 6 × 6 × 6	10 × 8 × 6 × 6 × 6 × 6 × 6
EZ Bar Close Grip	2× max	2× max	2× max	2× max	2× max	2× max
Reverse Curls	2× max	2× max	2× max	2× max	2× max	2× max
Rollovers	6 × 10	6 × 10	8 × 10	8 × 10	8 × 10	8 × 10

*Add one set a week for rollovers up to ten sets.

Weeks 3–6: drop set—add one set of a half extension and whole extension, two max, each week; use the weight of the last set of drop set routine, 50 lbs.

Tuesdays	Week 1	Week 2	Week 3	Week 4	Week 5	Week 6
Exercise	Sets × Reps	Sets × Reps	Sets × Reps	Sets × Reps	Sets × Reps	Sets × Reps
Power Cleans	5 × 5	5 × 5	5 × 5	5 × 5	5 × 5	5 × 5
Shrugs	5 × 15	5 × 15	5 × 15	5 × 15	5 × 15	5 × 15
Squats	4 × 8	4 × 8	4 × 8	4 × 8	4 × 8	4 × 8
Vertimax (1 cord)	4 × 8	4 × 8	4 × 8	4 × 8	4 × 8	4 × 8
Step-Ups	3 × 6	3 × 6	3 × 6	3 × 6	3 × 6	3 × 6
Vertimax	3 × 6	3 × 6	3 × 6	3 × 6	3 × 6	3 × 6
Negatives (8 seconds)	NA	NA	1 × 5	2 × 5	2 × 5	2 × 5
ABS #1	ABS #1	ABS #1	ABS #1	ABS #1	ABS #1	ABS #1

continued

Weight Work: Running Backs, Offensive Linemen, Tight Ends, Defensive Linemen, Linebackers, and Defensive Backs, *continued*

Wednesdays

Weeks 1–6: Pool Workout

Thursdays

Exercise	Week 1	Week 2	Week 3	Week 4	Week 5	Week 6
	Sets × Reps	Sets × Reps	Sets × Reps	Sets × Reps	Sets × Reps	Sets × Reps
Flat Bench Press	5 × 5	5 × 5	5 × 5	5 × 5	5 × 5	5 × 5
Low Rows	5 × 6	5 × 6	5 × 6	5 × 6	5 × 6	5 × 6
Incline DB Bench Press	4 × 6	4 × 6	4 × 6	4 × 6	4 × 6	4 × 6
One-Arm Incline Rows	4 × 6	4 × 6	4 × 6	4 × 6	4 × 6	4 × 6
Pullover Press	3 × 10	3 × 10	3 × 10	3 × 10	3 × 10	3 × 10
EZ Bar Curls	3 × 10	3 × 10	3 × 10	3 × 10	3 × 10	3 × 10
EZ Bar Close Grip	2× max	2× max	2× max	2× max	2× max	2× max
Reverse Curls	2× max	2× max	2× max	2× max	2× max	2× max
Rollovers	6 × 10	7 × 10	8 × 10	8 × 10	8 × 10	8 × 10

Weeks 4–6: add on Thursdays two repetitions every eight seconds to max rep; use weight from last set, 60lbs.

Fridays

Exercise	Week 1	Week 2	Week 3	Week 4	Week 5	Week 6
	Sets × Reps	Sets × Reps	Sets × Reps	Sets × Reps	Sets × Reps	Sets × Reps
Hang Cleans	5 × 5	5 × 5	5 × 5	5 × 5	5 × 5	5 × 5
Shrugs	5 × 15	5 × 15	5 × 15	5 × 15	5 × 15	5 × 15
Leg Press	5 × 12	5 × 12	5 × 12	5 × 12	5 × 12	5 × 12
Vertimax	5 × 8	5 × 8	5 × 8	5 × 8	5 × 8	5 × 8
Upright Rows	4 × 12	4 × 12	4 × 12	4 × 12	4 × 12	4 × 12
Rear Delt Flies	4 × 10	4 × 10	4 × 10	4 × 10	4 × 10	4 × 10
Medial Delt Flies	4 × 10	4 × 10	4 × 10	4 × 10	4 × 10	4 × 10
Front Delt Flies	4 × 10	4 × 10	4 × 10	4 × 10	4 × 10	4 × 10
Combo Flies	3 × 10	3 × 10	3 × 10	3 × 10	3 × 10	3 × 10

It is most important that you record your results in a journal or spreadsheet to track your progress. For each exercise, each day, write down the number of sets and reps completed total, the percentage of your maximum lifted, the weight, and reps for each set. See the following sample.

Weight Work

Week _____

Day _____

Exercise _____ Sets × Reps _____ % of Max _____ Weight Reps _____

Use the following chart to estimate your one-rep max. For any exercise, take your best set at a given weight (left column) for a given number of reps (top row), and the corresponding number should be about your one-rep max. For example, if your best complete bench press set is eight reps of 200 pounds, your one-rep max should be about 250.

Weight/Reps

Best Weight	2	3	4	5	6	7	8	9	10
95	100	105	105	110	110	115	115	120	125
100	105	110	110	115	120	120	125	125	130
105	110	115	115	120	125	125	130	135	135
110	115	120	125	125	130	135	135	140	145
115	120	125	130	130	135	140	140	145	150
120	125	130	135	140	140	145	150	150	155
125	130	135	140	145	145	150	155	160	160
130	135	140	145	150	155	155	160	165	170
135	145	145	150	155	160	165	165	170	175
140	150	150	155	160	165	170	175	175	180
145	155	160	160	165	170	175	180	185	190
150	160	165	170	170	175	180	185	190	195
155	165	170	175	180	180	185	190	195	200
160	170	175	180	185	190	195	200	205	210
165	175	180	185	190	195	200	205	210	215

continued

Weight/Reps, *continued*

Best Weight	2	3	4	5	6	7	8	9	10
170	170	185	190	195	200	205	210	215	220
175	185	190	195	200	205	210	215	220	225
180	190	195	200	205	210	215	225	230	235
185	195	200	205	210	220	225	230	235	240
190	200	205	210	220	225	230	235	240	245
195	205	210	220	225	230	235	240	245	255
200	210	220	225	230	235	240	250	255	260
205	215	225	230	235	240	250	255	260	265
210	220	230	235	240	245	255	260	265	275
215	225	235	240	245	255	260	265	275	280
220	235	240	245	255	260	265	270	280	285
225	240	245	250	260	265	270	280	285	290
230	245	250	255	265	270	280	285	290	300
235	250	255	265	270	275	285	290	300	305
240	255	260	270	275	285	290	295	305	310
245	260	265	275	280	290	295	305	310	320
250	265	270	280	285	295	300	310	315	325
255	270	275	285	295	300	310	315	325	330
260	275	285	290	300	305	315	320	330	340
265	280	290	295	305	310	320	330	335	345
270	285	295	300	310	320	325	335	340	350
275	290	300	310	315	325	330	340	350	355
280	295	305	315	320	330	340	345	355	365
285	300	310	320	325	335	345	355	360	370
290	305	315	325	335	340	350	360	370	375

295	310	320	330	340	350	355	365	375	385
300	320	325	335	345	355	365	370	380	390
305	325	330	340	350	360	370	380	385	395
310	330	335	345	355	365	375	385	395	405
315	335	345	350	360	370	380	390	400	410
320	340	350	360	370	375	385	395	405	415
325	345	355	365	375	385	395	405	410	420
330	350	360	370	385	390	400	410	420	430
335	355	365	375	385	395	405	415	425	435
340	360	370	380	390	400	410	420	430	440
345	365	375	385	395	405	415	425	440	450
350	370	380	390	400	415	425	435	445	455
355	375	385	395	410	420	430	440	450	460
360	380	390	405	415	425	435	445	455	470
365	385	395	410	420	430	440	450	465	475
370	390	405	415	425	435	445	460	470	480
375	395	410	420	430	440	455	465	475	485
380	400	415	425	435	450	460	470	480	495
385	410	420	430	440	455	465	475	490	500
390	415	425	435	450	460	470	485	495	505
395	420	430	440	455	465	475	490	500	515
400	425	435	450	460	470	485	495	510	520
405	430	440	455	465	475	490	500	515	525
410	435	445	460	470	485	495	510	520	535
415	440	450	465	475	490	500	515	525	540
420	445	455	470	485	495	510	520	535	545
425	450	465	475	490	500	515	525	540	550

continued

Weight/Reps, *continued*

Best Weight	2	3	4	5	6	7	8	9	10
430	455	470	480	495	505	520	535	545	560
435	460	475	485	500	515	525	540	550	565
440	465	480	490	505	520	530	545	560	570
445	470	485	500	510	525	540	550	565	580
450	475	490	505	515	530	545	560	570	585
455	480	495	510	525	535	550	565	575	590
460	485	500	515	530	540	555	570	585	600
465	490	505	520	535	550	560	575	590	605
470	500	510	525	540	555	570	580	595	610
475	505	515	530	545	560	575	590	605	615
480	510	525	535	550	565	580	595	610	625
485	515	530	545	555	570	585	600	615	630
490	520	535	550	565	580	590	605	620	635
495	525	540	555	570	585	600	615	630	645
500	530	545	560	575	590	605	620	635	650
505	535	550	565	580	595	610	625	640	655
510	540	555	570	585	600	615	630	645	665
515	545	560	575	590	605	625	640	655	670
520	550	565	580	600	615	630	645	660	675
525	555	570	590	605	620	635	650	665	680
530	560	575	595	610	625	640	655	675	690
535	565	585	600	615	630	645	665	680	695
540	570	590	605	620	635	655	670	685	700
545	575	595	610	625	645	660	675	690	710
550	585	600	615	630	650	665	680	700	715

580	615	630	650	665	685	700	720	735	755
585	620	635	655	670	690	705	725	740	760
590	625	645	660	680	695	715	730	750	765
595	630	650	665	685	700	720	735	755	775
600	635	655	670	690	710	725	745	760	780
605	640	660	675	695	715	730	750	770	785
610	645	665	685	700	720	740	755	775	795

APPENDIX B

Six-Week Program Speed and Position Work

Six-Week Program Speed and Position Work

Position: Quarterbacks (Week 1)

Player: Charlie Whitehurst

Monday	Tuesday	Wednesday	Thursday	Friday
Day 1	Day 2	Day 3	Day 4	Day 5
Resistance	**Overspeed**	**Recovery Day**	**Resistance**	**Overspeed**
Ballistics	**Ballistics**	Pool	**Ballistics**	**Ballistics**
2 × 20 yards	Chip-O-Meters		2 × 20 yards	Chip-O-Meters
Ladders	**Ladders**		**Ladders**	**Ladders**
8 drills	Chip-O-Meters		8 drills	Chip-O-Meters
	8 drills			8 drills
Static Stretch	2 × Contrast		**Static Stretch**	2 × Contrast
Partner			Partner	
	Static Stretch			**Static Stretch**
	Partner			Partner
Reaction Drills	**Reaction Drills**		**Reaction Drills**	**Reaction Drills**
Bounds 1 × 8	Sandwich Drill		Bounds 1 × 8	Sandwich Drill
Shuffles 1 × 8	3 × 8 reps		Shuffles 1 × 8	3 × 8 reps
Sprint Outs 1 × 8	1 × 6 Contrast		Sprint Outs 1 × 8	1 × 6 Contrast
Quarter Turns 1 × 8	**Linear Overspeed**		Quarter Turns 1 × 8	**Linear Overspeed**
Scramble 1 × 8	1 × 5 reps		Scramble 1 × 8	1 × 5 reps
Shackles and Quick Hands	40-Yard Sprints		**Shackles and Quick Hands**	40-Yard Sprints
High Knee March			High Knee March	
Walking Lunge	**Position Overspeed**		Walking Lunge	**Position Overspeed**
Step, Squat & Punch	Pass Drops		Step, Squat & Punch	Pass Drops
Backward S, S & Punch	Right 1 × 5		Backward S, S & Punch	Right 1 × 5
Lateral Shuffle	Left 1 × 5		Lateral Shuffle	Left 1 × 5
2 × 15-Yard Contrast			2 × 15-Yard Contrast	

continued

Six-Week Program Speed and Position Work

Position: Quarterbacks (Week 2)

Player: Charlie Whitehurst

Monday Day 1	**Tuesday** Day 2	**Wednesday** Day 3	**Thursday** Day 4	**Friday** Day 5
Resistance	**Overspeed**	**Recovery Day**	**Resistance**	**Overspeed**
Ballistics 2 × 20 yards	**Ballistics** Chip-O-Meters	Pool	**Ballistics** 2 × 20 yards	**Ballistics** Chip-O-Meters
Ladders 8 drills	**Ladders** Chip-O-Meters, 8 drills, 2 × Contrast		**Ladders** 8 drills	**Ladders** Chip-O-Meters, 8 drills, 2 × Contrast
Static Stretch Partner	**Static Stretch** Partner		**Static Stretch** Partner	**Static Stretch** Partner
Reaction Drills Bounds 1 × 8, Shuffles 1 × 8, Sprint Outs 1 × 8, Quarter Turns 1 × 8, Scramble 1 × 8	**Reaction Drills** Sandwich Drill, 3 × 8 reps, 1 × 6 Contrast		**Reaction Drills** Bounds 1 × 8, Shuffles 1 × 8, Sprint Outs 1 × 8, Quarter Turns 1 × 8, Scramble 1 × 8	**Reaction Drills** Sandwich Drill, 3 × 8 reps, 1 × 6 Contrast
Position Resistance Pass Drops, Right 1 × 5, Left 1 × 5, Center 3 Step 1 × 5, 1 × 2 Contrast	**Position Resistance** Center 3 Step 1 × 5, 1 × 2 Contrast	Rest	**Position Resistance** Release Harness, Pass Drops, Right 1 × 5, Left 1 × 5, Center 1 × 5	**Position Resistance** Center 3 Step 1 × 5, 1 × 2 Contrast
Resistance Runs Up & Backs, Linear 1 × 8, Lateral Shuffle 1 × 8 R/L, Backpedal 1 × 8, 1 × 4 Contrasts each direction	**Weight Work**		**Resistance Runs** Long-Tow Sprints, 1 × 6 reps 40 yards, 2 × Contrast	**Weight Work**
Weight Work			**Weight Work**	

continued

Shackles and Quick Hands
High Knee March
Walking Lunge
Step, Squat & Punch
Backward S, S & Punch
Lateral Shuffle
2 × 15-Yard Contrast

Linear Overspeed
1 × 5 reps
40-Yard Sprints

Position Overspeed
Pass Drops
Sprint Out Right 1 × 5
Sprint Out Left 1 × 5
Contrast 1 × 2

Position Resistance
Shackles with cord
Pass Drops
Right 1 × 5
Left 1 × 5
Contrast 1 × 2

Release Harness
2 × 8 reps
1 × 5 Contrast

Resistance Runs
Long-Tow Sprints
1 × 6 reps 40 yards
2 × Contrast

Weight Work

Rest

Weight Work

Shackles and Quick Hands
High Knee March
Walking Lunge
Step, Squat & Punch
Backward S, S & Punch
Lateral Shuffle
2 × 15-Yard Contrast

Linear Overspeed
1 × 5 reps
40-Yard Sprints

Position Overspeed
Pass Drops
Right 1 × 5
Left 1 × 5
Center 3 Step 1 × 5
Sprint Out Right & Left 1 × 5
Contrast 1 × 2

Position Resistance
Contrast 1 × 2

Weight Work

Weight Work

Six-Week Program Speed and Position Work

Position: Quarterbacks (Week 3)

Player: Charlie Whitehurst

Monday	Tuesday	Wednesday	Thursday	Friday
Day 1	Day 2	Day 3	Day 4	Day 5
Resistance	**Overspeed**	**Recovery Day**	**Resistance**	**Overspeed**
Ballistics	**Ballistics**	Pool	**Ballistics**	**Ballistics**
2 × 20 yards	Chip-O-Meters		2 × 20 yards	Chip-O-Meters
Ladders	**Ladders**		**Ladders**	**Ladders**
Chip-O-Meters	Chip-O-Meters		8 drills	Chip-O-Meters
8 drills	8 drills			8 drills
	2 × Contrast			2 × Contrast
Static Stretch			**Static Stretch**	
Partner			Partner	

Static Stretch
Partner

Reaction Drills
Bounds 1 × 8
Shuffles 1 × 8
Sprint Outs 1 × 8
Quarter Turns 1 × 8
Scramble 1 × 8

Shackles and Quick Hands
High Knee March
Walking Lunge
Step, Squat & Punch
Backward S, S & Punch
Lateral Shuffle
2 × 15-Yard Contrast

Position Resistance
2 Cords
Pass Drops
Right 2 × 5
Left 2 × 5
Center 1 × 5
Contrast 1 × 2

Resistance Runs
Long-Tow Sprints
2 × 6 reps 40 yards
2 × Contrast

Weight Work

Static Stretch
Partner

Reaction Drills
Sandwich Drill
3 × 8 reps
1 × 6 Contrast

Linear Overspeed
2 × 5 reps
20-Yard Sprints

Position Overspeed
Up & Backs
With 3- and 5-Step Drops
2 × 8
Contrast 1 × 8

Weight Work

Static Stretch
Partner

Reaction Drills
Bounds 1 × 8
Shuffles 1 × 8
Sprint Outs 1 × 8
Quarter Turns 1 × 8
Scramble 1 × 8

Shackles and Quick Hands
High Knee March
Walking Lunge
Step, Squat & Punch
Backward S, S & Punch
Lateral Shuffle
2 × 15-Yard Contrast

Position Resistance
Shackles
X-Vest
Pass Drops
Right 2 × 5
Left 2 × 5
Center 3 Step 2 × 5
Contrast 1 × 2

Weight Work

Reaction Drills
Sandwich Drill
3 × 8 reps
1 × 6 Contrast

Linear Overspeed
1 × 5 reps
20-Yard Sprints

Position Overspeed
Pass Drops
Right 2 × 5
Left 2 × 5

Overspeed Progression
2 × 4 reps
1 × 4 Contrast

Center 1 × 5
Contrast 1 × 2

Weight Work

Rest

Six-Week Program Speed and Position Work

Position: Quarterbacks (Week 4)

Player: Charlie Whitehurst

Monday
Day 1

Resistance
Ballistic with X-Vest
2 × 20 yards
Ladders with X-Vest
8 drills

Static Stretch
Partner

Reaction Drills
Bounds 1 × 8
Shuffles 1 × 8
Sprint Outs 1 × 8
Quarter Turns 1 × 8
Scramble 1 × 8

Shackles and Quick Hands
High Knee March
Walking Lunge
Step, Squat & Punch
Backward S, S & Punch
Lateral Shuffle
2 × 15-Yard Contrast

Position Resistance
Pass Drops
Release Harness
Right & Left 2 × 5
Reaction Belts
3 × 15 second runs

Tuesday
Day 2

Overspeed
Ballistics
Chip-O-Meters
Ladders
Chip-O-Meters
8 drills
2 × Contrast

Static Stretch
Partner

Reaction Drills
Sandwich Drill
3 × 8 reps
1 × 6 Contrast

Linear Overspeed
2 × 5 reps
40-Yard Sprints

Position Overspeed
Pass Drops
Right 2 × 5
Left 2 × 5

Position Resistance
Center 1 × 5
Contrast 1 × 2

Wednesday
Day 3

Recovery Day
Pool

Thursday
Day 4

Resistance
Ballistics with X-Vest
2 × 20 yards
Ladders with X-Vest
8 drills

Static Stretch
Partner

Reaction Drills
Bounds 1 × 8
Shuffles 1 × 8
Sprint Outs 1 × 8
Quarter Turns 1 × 8
Scramble 1 × 8

Shackles and Quick Hands
High Knee March
Walking Lunge
Step, Squat & Punch
Backward S, S & Punch
Lateral Shuffle
2 × 15-Yard Contrast

Position Resistance
Quick Hands Drill 2 × 3 minutes

Friday
Day 5

Overspeed
Ballistics
Chip-O-Meters
Ladders
Chip-O-Meters
8 drills
2 × Contrast

Static Stretch
Partner

Reaction Drills
Sandwich Drill
3 × 8 reps
1 × 6 Contrast

Linear Overspeed
2 × 5 reps
40-Yard Sprints

Position Overspeed
Shackles
X-Vest
Drops
Right & Left 2 × 5
Contrast 1 × 2
Pattern Run
Passing Tree

Position Resistance
Quick Hands Drill 2 × 3 minutes

continued

Quick Hands Drill
3 × 15 seconds

Resistance
Up & Backs
Linear 1 × 8 reps
Lateral R/L 1 × 8 reps
Backpedal 1 × 8 reps
1 × 2 Contrasts each direction

Weight Work

Weight Work

Rest

Resistance Runs
Long-Tow Sprints
2 × 6 reps 40 yards
2 × Contrast

Weight Work

1 × 15 reps

Weight Work

Six-Week Program Speed and Position Work

Position: Quarterbacks (Week 5)

Player: Charlie Whitehurst

Monday
Day 1
Resistance
Ballistics with X-Vest
2 × 20 yards
Ladders with X-Vest
8 drills

Static Stretch
Partner

Reaction Drills
Bounds 1 × 8
Shuffles 1 × 8
Sprint Outs 1 × 8
Quarter Turns 1 × 8
Scramble 1 × 8
Shackles and Quick Hands with Weighted Bag
High Knee March
Walking Lunge

2 × 5 reps
40-Yard Sprints

Tuesday
Day 2
Overspeed
Ballistics
Chip-O-Meters
Ladders
Chip-O-Meters
8 drills
2 × Contrast

Static Stretch
Partner

Reaction Drills
Sandwich Drill
3 × 8 reps
1 × 6 Contrast
Linear Overspeed

2 × 5 reps
40-Yard Sprints

Wednesday
Day 3
Recovery Day
Pool

Thursday
Day 4
Resistance
Ballistics with X-Vest
2 × 20 yards
Ladders with X-Vest
8 drills

Static Stretch
Partner

Reaction Drills
Bounds 1 × 8
Shuffles 1 × 8
Sprint Outs 1 × 8
Quarter Turns 1 × 8
Scramble 1 × 8
Shackles and Quick Hands with Weighted Bag
High Knee March
Walking Lunge

Friday
Day 5
Overspeed
Ballistics
Chip-O-Meters
Ladders
Chip-O-Meters
8 drills
2 × Contrast

Static Stretch
Partner

Reaction Drills
Sandwich Drill
3 × 8 reps
1 × 6 Contrast
Linear Overspeed

2 × 5 reps
20-Yard Sprints

Step, Squat & Punch
Backward S, S & Punch
Lateral Shuffle
2 × 15-Yard Contrast

Position Resistance
Release Harness
Sprint Out Right & Left 1 × 5
Contrast 1 × 2

Mirror Drill
Resistance
3 × 15 seconds

Weight Work

Position Overspeed
Pass Drops
Right 2 × 5 reps
Left 2 × 5 reps
Center 2 × 5 reps
1 × 2 reps Contrast

3-Cone Pattern Runs
3 × 3 Progression Runs

In and Outs
1 × 10 reps
Sprint, Jog, Sprint
100 yards

Rest

Weight Work

Step, Squat & Punch
Backward S, S & Punch
Lateral Shuffle
2 × 15-Yard Contrast

Position Resistance
Shackles
X-Vest
Pass Drops
Right 2 × 5 reps
Left 2 × 5 reps
Center 2 × 5 reps
1 × 2 reps Contrast

Resistance Runs
Long-Tow Sprints
2 × 6 reps 40 yards
2 × Contrast
Weight Work

Step, Squat & Punch
Backward S, S & Punch
Lateral Shuffle
2 × 15-Yard Contrast

Position Overspeed
Pass Drops
2 × 5 reps
Right 2 × 5 reps
Left 2 × 5 reps
1 × 2 reps Contrast

Weight Work

continued

Six-Week Program Speed and Position Work

Position: Quarterbacks (Week 6)

Player: Charlie Whitehurst

Monday	Tuesday	Wednesday	Thursday	Friday
Day 1	Day 2	Day 3	Day 4	Day 5
Resistance	**Overspeed**	**Recovery Day**	**Resistance**	**Overspeed**
Ballistics with X-Vest	**Ballistics**	Pool	**Ballistics with X-Vest**	**Ballistics**
2 × 20 yards	Chip-O-Meters		2 × 20 yards	Chip-O-Meters
Ladders with X-Vest	**Ladders**		**Ladders with X-Vest**	**Ladders**
8 drills	Chip-O-Meters		8 drills	Chip-O-Meters
	8 drills			8 drills
Static Stretch	2 × Contrast		**Static Stretch**	2 × Contrast
Partner			Partner	
Weight Work	**Weight Work**		**Weight Work**	

Static Stretch
Partner

Reaction Drills
Sandwich Drill
3 × 8 reps
1 × 6 Contrast

Linear Overspeed
2 × 5 reps
20-Yard Sprints

Position Overspeed
Pass Drops
2 × 5 reps
Right 2 × 5 reps
Left 2 × 5 reps
1 × 2 reps Contrast

Reaction Drills
Bounds 1 × 8
Shuffles 1 × 8
Sprint Outs 1 × 8
Quarter Turns 1 × 8
Scramble 1 × 8

Shackles and Quick Hands with Weighted Bag
High Knee March
Walking Lunge
Step, Squat & Punch
Backward S, S & Punch
Lateral Shuffle
2 × 15-Yard Contrast

Position Resistance
Release Harness
With X-Vest
Pass Drops
Right 3 × 6 reps
Left 3 × 6 reps
Center 3 × 6 reps
1 × 2 reps each direction

Resistance Runs
Lateral, Shuffle, and Punch
2 × 6 reps
2 × Contrast

Weight Work

Rest

Static Stretch
Partner

Reaction Drills
Sandwich Drill
3 × 8 reps
1 × 6 Contrast

Linear Overspeed
2 × 5 reps
20-Yard Sprints

Position Overspeed
Pass Drops
Right 2 × 5 reps
Left 2 × 5 reps

Center 2 × 5 reps
1 × 2 reps Contrast

3-Cone Pattern Runs
3 × 3 Progression Runs
Backpedal Weaves

Reaction Drills
Bounds 1 × 8
Shuffles 1 × 8
Sprint Outs 1 × 8
Quarter Turns 1 × 8
Scramble 1 × 8

Shackles and Quick Hands with Weighted Bag
High Knee March
Walking Lunge
Step, Squat & Punch
Backward S, S & Punch
Lateral Shuffle
2 × 15-Yard Contrast

Position Resistance
Release Harness
Pass Drops
Right and Left 1 × 5

Mirror Drill
Resistance
3 × 15 seconds

Release Pulls
Right/Left
3 × 8 reps
1 × 2 Contrasts each direction

Weight Work

Six-Week Program Speed and Position Work

Position: Running Backs (Week 1)

Player: Garrison Hearst

Monday	Tuesday	Wednesday	Thursday	Friday
Day 1	Day 2	Day 3	Day 4	Day 5
Resistance	**Overspeed**	**Recovery Day**	**Resistance**	**Overspeed**
Ballistics	**Ballistics**	Pool	**Ballistics**	**Ballistics**
2 × 20 yards	Chip-O-Meters		2 × 20 yards	Chip-O-Meters
Ladders	**Ladders**		**Ladders**	**Ladders**
8 drills	Chip-O-Meters		8 drills	Chip-O-Meters
	8 drills			8 drills
Static Stretch	**Static Stretch**		**Static Stretch**	**Static Stretch**
Partner	2 × Contrast		Partner	2 × Contrast
	Static Stretch			**Static Stretch**
	Partner			Partner
Reaction Drills	**Reaction Drills**		**Reaction Drills**	**Reaction Drills**
Bounds 1 × 8	Bounds 1 × 8		Bounds 1 × 8	Sandwich Drill
Shuffles 1 × 8	Shuffles 1 × 8		Shuffles 1 × 8	3 × 8 reps
Sprint Outs 1 × 8	Sprint Outs 1 × 8		Sprint Outs 1 × 8	1 × 6 Contrast
Quarter Turns 1 × 8	Quarter Turns 1 × 8		Quarter Turns 1 × 8	**Linear Overspeed**
Scramble 1 × 8	Scramble 1 × 8		Scramble 1 × 8	1 × 5 reps
Shackles and Quick Hands	**Shackles and Quick Hands**		**Shackles and Quick Hands**	40-Yard Sprints
High Knee March	High Knee March		High Knee March	**Position Overspeed**
Walking Lunge	Walking Lunge		Walking Lunge	Zone Runs
Step, Squat & Punch	Step, Squat & Punch		Step, Squat & Punch	Right 1 × 5 reps
Backward S, S & Punch	Backward S, S & Punch		Backward S, S & Punch	Left 1 × 5 reps
Lateral Shuffle	Lateral Shuffle		Lateral Shuffle	**Position Resistance**
2 × 15-Yard Contrast	2 × 15-Yard Contrast		2 × 15-Yard Contrast	Center 1 × 5 reps
	Linear Overspeed			1 × 2 reps Contrast
	1 × 5 reps			
	40-Yard Sprints			
Position Resistance	**Position Overspeed**		**Position Resistance**	
Zone Runs	Zone Runs		Resistance Routes	
Right 1 × 5 reps	Right 1 × 5 reps		Right Flair 1 × 5 reps	
Left 1 × 5 reps	Left 1 × 5 reps		Left Flair 1 × 5 reps	
Center 1 × 5 reps	**Position Resistance**		Center Flat 1 × 5 reps	
Center Gap 1 × 5 reps				
1 × 2 reps Contrast				

continued

Six-Week Program Speed and Position Work

Position: Running Backs (Week 2)

Player: Garrison Hearst

Monday
Day 1
Resistance
Ballistics
2 × 20 yards
Ladders
8 drills
Static Stretch
Partner
Reaction Drills
Bounds 1 × 8
Shuffles 1 × 8
Sprint Outs 1 × 8
Quarter Turns 1 × 8
Scramble 1 × 8
Shackles and Quick Hands
High Knee March
Walking Lunge
Step, Squat & Punch
1 × 4 Contrasts each direction
Resistance Runs
Up & Backs
Linear 1 × 8
Lateral Shuffle 1 × 8 R/L
Backpedal 1 × 8
1 × 2 reps Contrast
Weight Work

Tuesday
Day 2
Overspeed
Ballistics
Chip-O-Meters
Ladders
Chip-O-Meters
8 drills
2 × Contrast
Static Stretch
Partner
Reaction Drills
Sandwich Drill
3 × 8 reps
1 × 6 Contrast
Linear Overspeed
1 × 5 reps
40-Yard Sprints
Weight Work

Wednesday
Day 3
Recovery Day
Pool

Rest

Thursday
Day 4
Resistance
Ballistics
2 × 20 yards
Ladders
8 drills
Static Stretch
Partner
Reaction Drills
Bounds 1 × 8
Shuffles 1 × 8
Sprint Outs 1 × 8
Quarter Turns 1 × 8
Scramble 1 × 8
Shackles and Quick Hands
High Knee March
Walking Lunge
Step, Squat & Punch

Weight Work

Friday
Day 5
Overspeed
Ballistics
Chip-O-Meters
Ladders
Chip-O-Meters
8 drills
2 × Contrast
Static Stretch
Partner
Reaction Drills
Sandwich Drill
3 × 8 reps
1 × 6 Contrast
Linear Overspeed
1 × 5 reps
40-Yard Sprints
1 × 2 reps Contrast
Resistance Runs
Long-Tow Sprints
1 × 6 reps 40 yards
2 × Contrast
Weight Work

continued

Backward S, S & Punch
Lateral Shuffle
2 × 15-Yard Contrast

Position Resistance
Bag Drill
Lateral Runs
3 × 8 reps
1 × 8 Contrasts

Resistance Catching Drill
Quick Hands
1 × 3 minutes
1 × set Contrast

Weight Work

Position Overspeed
Pass Routes
Right 1 × 5 reps
Left 1 × 5 reps
Center 1 × 5 reps
1 × 2 reps Contrast

8-Cone Overspeed
2 × 6 reps

Backward S, S & Punch
Lateral Shuffle
2 × 15-Yard Contrast

Position Resistance
Meadow Harness
Drive Block
Right 1 × 6 reps
Left 1 × 6 reps
Center 1 × 6 reps
1 × 2 reps each direction

Resistance Runs
Long-Tow Sprints
1 × 6 reps 40 yards
2 × Contrast

Weight Work

Position Overspeed
Zone Runs
Right 1 × 5 reps
Left 1 × 5 reps
Center 1 × 5 reps
1 × 2 reps Contrast

Release Harness
2 × 8 reps
1 × 5 Contrast

Weight Work

Rest

Six-Week Program Speed and Position Work

Position: Running Backs (Week 3)

Player: Garrison Hearst

Monday
Day 1
Resistance
Ballistics
2 × 20 yards
Ladders
Chip-O-Meters
8 drills

Static Stretch
Partner

Reaction Drills
Bounds 1 × 8

Tuesday
Day 2
Overspeed
Ballistics
Chip-O-Meters
Ladders
Chip-O-Meters
8 drills
2 × Contrast

Static Stretch
Partner

Wednesday
Day 3
Recovery Day
Pool

Thursday
Day 4
Resistance
Ballistics
2 × 20 yards
Ladders
8 drills

Static Stretch
Partner

Friday
Day 5
Overspeed
Ballistics
Chip-O-Meters
Ladders
Chip-O-Meters
8 drills
2 × Contrast

Static Stretch
Partner

Six-Week Program Speed and Position Work

Position: Running Backs (Week 4)

Player: Garrison Hearst

Monday
Day 1
Resistance
Ballistic with X-Vest
2 × 20 yards

Tuesday
Day 2
Overspeed
Ballistics
Chip-O-Meters

Wednesday
Day 3
Recovery Day
Pool

Thursday
Day 4
Resistance
Ballistics with X-Vest
2 × 20 yards

Friday
Day 5
Overspeed
Ballistics
Chip-O-Meters

Monday (Day 1)

Resistance Routes
Right Hitch 2 × 5 reps
Left Hitch 2 × 5 reps
1 × 2 Contrasts each direction

Position Resistance
Meadow Harness
5 Cord Drill
3 × 8 reps
1 × 8 Contrast

Quick Hands Drill
3 × 15 seconds

Weight Work

Position Overspeed
Pass Routes
Right 2 × 5 reps
Left 2 × 5 reps
Center 2 × 5 reps
1 × 2 reps Contrast

Overspeed Progression
2 × 4 reps
1 × 4 Contrast

Shackles and Quick Hands
High Knee March
Walking Lunge
Step, Squat & Punch
Backward S, S & Punch
Lateral Shuffle
2 × 15-Yard Contrast

Linear Overspeed
1 × 5 reps
40-Yard Sprints

Reaction Drills
Shuffles 1 × 8
Sprint Outs 1 × 8
Quarter Turns 1 × 8
Scramble 1 × 8
Sandwich Drill
3 × 8 reps
1 × 6 Contrast

Weight Work

Thursday (Day 4)

Rest

Weight Work

Resistance Runs
Long-Tow Sprints
2 × 6 reps 40 yards
2 × Contrast

Position Resistance
Quick Hands Drill
Zone Runs
Right 2 × 6 reps
Left 2 × 6 reps
Center 2 × 6 reps
1 × 2 reps each direction

Shackles and Quick Hands
High Knee March
Walking Lunge
Step, Squat & Punch
Backward S, S & Punch
Lateral Shuffle
2 × 15-Yard Contrast

Position Overspeed
Pass Routes
2 × 5 reps
Right 1 × 5 reps
Left 1 × 5 reps
1 × 2 reps Contrast

Linear Overspeed
2 × 5 reps
20-Yard Sprints

Reaction Drills
Shuffles 1 × 8
Sprint Outs 1 × 8
Quarter Turns 1 × 8
Scramble 1 × 8
Sandwich Drill
3 × 8 reps
1 × 6 Contrast

Weight Work

continued

Ladders
Chip-O-Meters
8 drills
2 × Contrast

Static Stretch
Partner

Reaction Drills
Sandwich Drill
3 × 8 reps
1 × 6 Contrast

Linear Overspeed
2 × 5 reps
40-Yard Sprints

Position Overspeed
Zone Runs
Right 2 × 5 reps
Left 2 × 5 reps
Center 2 × 5 reps
1 × 2 reps Contrast

Pattern Run
7-Cone Drill

Weight Work

Ladders with X-Vest
8 drills

Static Stretch
Partner

Reaction Drills
Bounds 1 × 8
Shuffles 1 × 8
Sprint Outs 1 × 8
Quarter Turns 1 × 8
Scramble 1 × 8

Shackles and Quick Hands
High Knee March
Walking Lunge
Step, Squat & Punch
Backward S, S, & Punch
Lateral Shuffle
2 × 15-Yard Contrast

Position Resistance
Quick Hands Drill
2 × 3 minutes

Pass Routes
Right 2 × 6 reps
Left 2 × 6 reps
Center 2 × 6 reps
1 × 2 reps each direction

Resistance Runs
Long-Tow Sprints
2 × 6 reps 40 yards
2 × Contrast

Weight Work

Rest

Ladders
Chip-O-Meters
8 drills
2 × Contrast

Static Stretch
Partner

Reaction Drills
Sandwich Drill
3 × 8 reps
1 × 6 Contrast

Linear Overspeed
2 × 5 reps
40-Yard Sprints

Position Overspeed
Pass Routes
Right 2 × 5 reps
Left 2 × 5 reps
Center 2 × 5 reps
1 × 2 reps Contrast

Reaction Belts
3 × 15 second runs

Ball Drills
Jug Machine

Weight Work

Ladders with X-Vest
8 drills

Static Stretch
Partner

Reaction Drills
Bounds 1 × 8
Shuffles 1 × 8
Sprint Outs 1 × 8
Quarter Turns 1 × 8
Scramble 1 × 8

Shackles and Quick Hands
High Knee March
Walking Lunge
Step, Squat & Punch
Backward S, S, & Punch
Lateral Shuffle
2 × 15-Yard Contrast

Position Resistance
Meadow Harness

5 Cone 3 × 6
1 × 4 Contrast

Quick Hands Drill
3 × 15 seconds

Resistance
Up & Backs
Linear 1 × 8 reps
Lateral R/L 1 × 8 reps
Backpedal 1 × 8 reps
1 × 2 Contrasts each direction

Weight Work

Six-Week Program Speed and Position Work

Position: Running Backs (Week 5)

Player: Garrison Hearst

Monday
Day 1

Resistance

Ballistics with X-Vest
2 × 20 yards

Ladders with X-Vest
8 drills

Static Stretch
Partner

Reaction Drills
Bounds 1 × 8
Shuffles 1 × 8
Sprint Outs 1 × 8
Quarter Turns 1 × 8
Scramble 1 × 8

Shackles and Quick Hands with Weighted Bag
High Knee March
Walking Lunge
Step, Squat & Punch
Backward S, S & Punch
Lateral Shuffle
2 × 15-Yard Contrast

Position Resistance
Bag Runs
Lateral 3 × 6
Linear 3 × 6

Tuesday
Day 2

Overspeed

Ballistics
Chip-O-Meters

Ladders
Chip-O-Meters
8 drills

Static Stretch
2 × Contrast

Static Stretch
Partner

Reaction Drills
Sandwich Drill
3 × 8 reps
1 × 6 Contrast

Linear Overspeed
2 × 5 reps
40-Yard Sprints

Position Overspeed
Pass Routes
Right Hitch 2 × 5 reps
Left Hitch 2 × 5 reps
Center Curl 2 × 5 reps
1 × 2 reps Contrast

3-Cone Pattern Runs
3 × 3 Progression Runs

Wednesday
Day 3

Recovery Day
Pool

Thursday
Day 4

Resistance

Ballistics with X-Vest
2 × 20 yards

Ladders with X-Vest
8 drills

Static Stretch
Partner

Reaction Drills
Bounds 1 × 8
Shuffles 1 × 8
Sprint Outs 1 × 8
Quarter Turns 1 × 8
Scramble 1 × 8

Shackles and Quick Hands with Weighted Bag
High Knee March
Walking Lunge
Step, Squat & Punch
Backward S, S & Punch
Lateral Shuffle
2 × 15-Yard Contrast

Position Resistance
Shackles & Hands
X-Vest
Zone Runs
Right 3 × 6 reps

Friday
Day 5

Overspeed

Ballistics
Chip-O-Meters

Ladders
Chip-O-Meters
8 drills

Static Stretch
2 × Contrast

Static Stretch
Partner

Reaction Drills
Sandwich Drill
3 × 8 reps
1 × 6 Contrast

Linear Overspeed
2 × 5 reps
20-Yard Sprints

Position Overspeed
Zone Runs
Right 2 × 5 reps
Left 2 × 5 reps
Center 2 × 5 reps
1 × 2 reps Contrast

Ball Drills
Jugs Machine

Mirror Drill
Resistance
3 × 15 seconds

Black Widows
2 × 5 reps
1 × 4 reps Contrast

Weight Work

In and Outs
1 × 10 reps
Sprint, Jog, Sprint
100 yards

Weight Work

Left 3 × 6 reps
Center 3 × 6 reps
1 × 2 reps Contrast

Resistance Runs
Long-Tow Sprints
2 × 6 reps 40 yards
2 × Contrast

Weight Work

Rest

Weight Work

Weight Work

Six-Week Program Speed and Position Work

Position: Running Backs (Week 6)

Player: Garrison Hearst

Monday	**Tuesday**	**Wednesday**	**Thursday**	**Friday**
Day 1	Day 2	Day 3	Day 4	Day 5
Resistance	**Overspeed**	**Recovery Day**	**Resistance**	**Overspeed**
Ballistics with X-Vest	**Ballistics**	Pool	**Ballistics with X-Vest**	**Ballistics**
2 × 20 yards	Chip-O-Meters		2 × 20 yards	Chip-O-Meters
Ladders with X-Vest	**Ladders**		**Ladders with X-Vest**	**Ladders**
8 drills	Chip-O-Meters		8 drills	Chip-O-Meters
	8 drills			8 drills
	2 × Contrast			2 × Contrast
Static Stretch	**Static Stretch**		**Static Stretch**	**Static Stretch**
Partner	Partner		Partner	Partner
Reaction Drills	**Reaction Drills**		**Reaction Drills**	**Reaction Drills**
Bounds 1 × 8	Sandwich Drill		Bounds 1 × 8	Sandwich Drill
Shuffles 1 × 8	3 × 8 reps		Shuffles 1 × 8	3 × 8 reps
Sprint Outs 1 × 8	1 × 6 Contrast		Sprint Outs 1 × 8	1 × 6 Contrast
Quarter Turns 1 × 8	**Linear Overspeed**		Quarter Turns 1 × 8	**Linear Overspeed**
Scramble 1 × 8	3 × 5 reps		Scramble 1 × 8	2 × 5 reps
Shackles and Quick Hands with Weighted Bag	40-Yard Sprints		**Shackles and Quick Hands with Weighted Bag**	40-Yard Sprints
High Knee March			High Knee March	

continued

Six-Week Program Speed and Position Work

Position: Offensive Linemen (Week 1)

Player: Le Charles Bentley

Monday
Day 1
Resistance
Ballistics
2 × 20 yards
Ladders
8 drills
Static Stretch
Partner

Walking Lunge
Step, Squat & Punch
Backward S, S & Punch
Lateral Shuffle
2 × 15-Yard Contrast

Position Resistance
Zigzag Drill
3 × 5 reps
1 × 4 Contrast

Mirror Drill
Resistance
3 × 15 seconds

Release 3-Cone Runs
Right/Left
3 × 8 reps
1 × 2 Contrasts each direction

Weight Work

Position Overspeed
Zone Runs
Right 2 × 5 reps
Left 2 × 5 reps
Center 2 × 5 reps
1 × 2 reps Contrast

3-Cone Pattern Runs
3 × 3 Progression Runs

Tuesday
Day 2
Overspeed
Ballistics
Chip-O-Meters
Ladders
Chip-O-Meters
8 drills
Static Stretch
2 × Contrast

Wednesday
Day 3
Recovery Day
Pool

Rest

Thursday
Day 4
Resistance
Ballistics
2 × 20 yards
Ladders
8 drills
Static Stretch
Partner

Walking Lunge
Step, Squat & Punch
Backward S, S & Punch
Lateral Shuffle
2 × 15-Yard Contrast

Position Resistance
Black Widow
With X-Vest
Pass Sets
Right 3 × 6 reps
Left 3 × 6 reps
Center 3 × 6 reps
1 × 2 reps each direction

Resistance Runs
Lateral, Shuffle, and Punch
2 × 6 reps
2 × Contrast

Weight Work

Friday
Day 5
Overspeed
Ballistics
Chip-O-Meters
Ladders
Chip-O-Meters
8 drills
2 × Contrast

Static Stretch
Partner

Walking Lunge
Step, Squat & Punch
Backward S, S & Punch
Lateral Shuffle
2 × 15-Yard Contrast

Position Overspeed
Zone Runs
2 × 5 reps
Right 2 × 5 reps
Left 2 × 5 reps
1 × 2 reps Contrast

Star Pattern Runs
3 × 1 rep

Weight Work

Static Stretch
Partner

Reaction Drills
Bounds 1 × 8
Shuffles 1 × 8
Sprint Outs 1 × 8
Quarter Turns 1 × 8
Scramble 1 × 8

Reaction Drills
Sandwich Drill
3 × 8 reps
1 × 6 Contrast

Shackles and Quick Hands
High Knee March
Walking Lunge
Step, Squat & Punch
Backward S, S & Punch
Lateral Shuffle
2 × 15-Yard Contrast

Linear Overspeed
1 × 5 reps
20-Yard Sprints

Position Overspeed
Pass Sets
Right 1 × 5 reps
Left 1 × 5 reps

Position Overspeed
Center 1 × 5 reps
1 × 2 reps Contrast

Position Resistance
Pass Sets
Right 1 × 5 reps
Left 1 × 5 reps
Center 1 × 5 reps
1 × 2 reps Contrast

Resistance Runs
Long-Tow Sprints
1 × 6 reps 40 yards
2 × Contrast

Weight Work

Rest

Static Stretch
Partner

Reaction Drills
Bounds 1 × 8
Shuffles 1 × 8
Sprint Outs 1 × 8
Quarter Turns 1 × 8
Scramble 1 × 8

Reaction Drills
Sandwich Drill
3 × 8 reps
1 × 6 Contrast

Shackles and Quick Hands
High Knee March
Walking Lunge
Step, Squat & Punch
Backward S, S & Punch
Lateral Shuffle
2 × 15-Yard Contrast

Linear Overspeed
1 × 5 reps
20-Yard Sprints

Position Overspeed
Pass Sets
Right 1 × 5 reps
Left 1 × 5 reps

Position Overspeed
Center 1 × 5 reps
1 × 2 reps Contrast

Position Resistance
Pass Sets
Right 1 × 5 reps
Left 1 × 5 reps
Center 1 × 5 reps
1 × 2 reps Contrast

Resistance Runs
Up & Backs
Linear 1 × 8
Lateral Shuffle 1 × 8 R/L
Backpedal 1 × 8
1 × 4 Contrasts each direction

Weight Work

continued

Six-Week Program Speed and Position Work

Position: Offensive Linemen (Week 2)

Player: Le Charles Bentley

Monday
Day 1

Resistance
Ballistics
2 × 20 yards
Ladders
8 drills

Static Stretch
Partner

2 × Contrast

Reaction Drills
Bounds 1 × 8
Shuffles 1 × 8
Sprint Outs 1 × 8
Quarter Turns 1 × 8
Scramble 1 × 8
Shackles and Quick Hands
High Knee March
Walking Lunge
Step, Squat & Punch
Backward S, S & Punch
Lateral Shuffle
2 × 15-Yard Contrast
Linear Overspeed
1 × 5 reps
20-Yard Sprints
Position Overspeed
Pass Sets
Right 1 × 5 reps
Left 1 × 5 reps
Position Resistance
Center 1 × 5 reps
1 × 2 reps Contrast

Position Resistance
Shackles & Hands
Lateral Shuffle & Punch

3 × 8 reps
1 × 8 Contrasts

Tuesday
Day 2

Overspeed
Ballistics
Chip-O-Meters
Ladders
Chip-O-Meters
8 drills

Static Stretch
Partner

Wednesday
Day 3

Recovery Day
Pool

Thursday
Day 4

Resistance
Ballistics
2 × 20 yards
Ladders
8 drills

Static Stretch
Partner

2 × Contrast

Reaction Drills
Bounds 1 × 8
Shuffles 1 × 8
Sprint Outs 1 × 8
Quarter Turns 1 × 8
Scramble 1 × 8
Shackles and Quick Hands
High Knee March
Walking Lunge
Step, Squat & Punch
Backward S, S, & Punch
Lateral Shuffle
2 × 15-Yard Contrast
Position Resistance
Shackles & Hands
Pass Sets
Right 1 × 6 reps
Left 1 × 6 reps
Center 1 × 6 reps
1 × 2 reps each direction

Friday
Day 5

Overspeed
Ballistics
Chip-O-Meters
Ladders
Chip-O-Meters
8 drills

2 × Contrast

Static Stretch
Partner

Reaction Drills
Sandwich Drill
3 × 8 reps
1 × 6 Contrast
Linear Overspeed
1 × 5 reps
20-Yard Sprints
Position Overspeed
Pass Sets
Right 1 × 5 reps
Left 1 × 5 reps

continued

Six-Week Program Speed and Position Work

Position: Offensive Linemen (Week 3)

Player: Le Charles Bentley

Monday	**Tuesday**	**Wednesday**	**Thursday**	**Friday**
Day 1	Day 2	Day 3	Day 4	Day 5
Resistance	**Overspeed**	**Recovery Day**	**Resistance**	**Overspeed**
Ballistics	**Ballistics**	Pool	**Ballistics**	**Ballistics**
2 × 20 yards	Chip-O-Meters		2 × 20 yards	Chip-O-Meters
Ladders	**Ladders**		**Ladders**	**Ladders**
8 drills	Chip-O-Meters		8 drills	Chip-O-Meters
2 × Contrast	8 drills		2 × Contrast	8 drills
Static Stretch	2 × Contrast		**Static Stretch**	2 × Contrast
Partner	**Static Stretch**		Partner	**Static Stretch**
Reaction Drills	Partner		**Reaction Drills**	Partner
Bounds 1 × 8	**Reaction Drills**		Bounds 1 × 8	**Reaction Drills**
Shuffles 1 × 8	Sandwich Drill		Shuffles 1 × 8	Sandwich Drill
Sprint Outs 1 × 8	3 × 8 reps		Sprint Outs 1 × 8	3 × 8 reps
Quarter Turns 1 × 8	1 × 6 Contrast		Quarter Turns 1 × 8	1 × 6 Contrast
Scramble 1 × 8	**Linear Overspeed**		Scramble 1 × 8	**Linear Overspeed**
Shackles and Quick Hands	1 × 5 reps		**Shackles and Quick Hands**	2 × 5 reps
High Knee March	20-Yard Sprints		High Knee March	20-Yard Sprints
Walking Lunge			Walking Lunge	
Step, Squat & Punch			Step, Squat & Punch	
Linear Overspeed				
1 × 5 reps				
20-Yard Sprints				
Resistance Pulls	**Weight Work**	**Rest**	**Resistance Runs**	**Weight Work**
Right/Left			Long-Tow Sprints	
1 × 8 reps			1 × 6 reps 40 yards	
1 × 2 Contrasts each direction			2 × Contrast	
Weight Work			**Weight Work**	

Six-Week Program Speed and Position Work

Position: Offensive Linemen (Week 4)

Player: Le Charles Bentley

Monday
Day 1

Resistance

Ballistic with X-Vest
2 × 20 yards

Ladders with X-Vest
8 drills

Static Stretch
Partner

Reaction Drills
Bounds 1 × 8

Backward S, S & Punch
Lateral Shuffle
2 × 15-Yard Contrast

Position Resistance
Shackles & Hands
Lateral Shuffle & Punch
3 × 8 reps
1 × 8 Contrast

Quick Hands Drill
3 × 15 seconds

Resistance Pulls
Right/Left
2 × 8 reps
1 × 2 Contrasts each direction

Weight Work

Position Overspeed
Pass Sets
Right 2 × 5 reps
Left 2 × 5 reps
Center 2 × 5 reps
1 × 2 reps Contrast

Weight Work

Tuesday
Day 2

Overspeed

Ballistics
Chip-O-Meters

Ladders
Chip-O-Meters
8 drills

Static Stretch
2 × Contrast

Static Stretch
Partner

Weight Work

Rest

Weight Work

Wednesday
Day 3

Recovery Day
Pool

Thursday
Day 4

Resistance

Ballistics with X-Vest
2 × 20 yards

Ladders with X-Vest
8 drills

Static Stretch
Partner

Reaction Drills
Bounds 1 × 8

Backward S, S & Punch
Lateral Shuffle
2 × 15-Yard Contrast

Position Resistance
Shackles and Quick Hands
Pass Sets
Right 2 × 6 reps
Left 2 × 6 reps
Center 2 × 6 reps
1 × 2 reps each direction

Resistance Runs
Long-Tow Sprints
2 × 6 reps 40 yards
2 × Contrast

Weight Work

Friday
Day 5

Overspeed

Ballistics
Chip-O-Meters

Ladders
Chip-O-Meters
8 drills

Static Stretch
2 × Contrast

Static Stretch
Partner

Reaction Drills
Bounds 1 × 8

Position Overspeed
Pass Sets
2 × 5 reps
Right 1 × 5 reps
Left 1 × 5 reps
1 × 2 reps Contrast

Weight Work

continued

Six-Week Program Speed and Position Work

Position: Offensive Linemen (Week 5)

Player: Le Charles Bentley

Monday	**Tuesday**	**Wednesday**	**Thursday**	**Friday**
Day 1	Day 2	Day 3	Day 4	Day 5
Resistance	**Overspeed**	**Recovery Day**	**Resistance**	**Overspeed**
Ballistics with X-Vest	**Ballistics**	Pool	**Ballistics with X-Vest**	**Ballistics**
2 × 20 yards	Chip-O-Meters		2 × 20 yards	Chip-O-Meters

Monday (Day 1)

Reaction Drills
Shuffles 1 × 8
Sprint Outs 1 × 8
Quarter Turns 1 × 8
Scramble 1 × 8
Sandwich Drill
3 × 8 reps
1 × 6 Contrast

Shackles and Quick Hands
High Knee March
Walking Lunge
Step, Squat & Punch
Backward S, S & Punch
Lateral Shuffle
2 × 15-Yard Contrast

Linear Overspeed
1 × 5 reps
20-Yard Sprints

Position Overspeed
Pass Sets
Right 2 × 5 reps
Left 2 × 5 reps
Center 2 × 5 reps
1 × 2 reps Contrast

Position Resistance
Meadow Harness
Drive Block 2 × 6
Angle Block 2 × 6
Pattern Run
1 × 12 runs

Quick Hands Drill
3 × 15 seconds

Resistance Pulls
Right/Left
2 × 8
1 × 2 Contrasts each direction

Weight Work

Wednesday (Day 3)

Rest

Thursday (Day 4)

Reaction Drills
Shuffles 1 × 8
Sprint Outs 1 × 8
Quarter Turns 1 × 8
Scramble 1 × 8
Sandwich Drill
3 × 8 reps
1 × 6 Contrast

Shackles and Quick Hands
High Knee March
Walking Lunge
Step, Squat & Punch
Backward S, S & Punch
Lateral Shuffle
2 × 15-Yard Contrast

Linear Overspeed
2 × 5 reps
20-Yard Sprints

Position Overspeed
Pass Sets
Right 2 × 5 reps
Left 2 × 5 reps
Center 2 × 5 reps
1 × 5 reps Contrast

Position Resistance
Shackles & Hands
Pass Sets
Right 2 × 6 reps
Left 2 × 6 reps
Center 2 × 6 reps
1 × 2 reps each direction

Resistance Runs
Long-Tow Sprints
2 × 6 reps 40 yards
2 × Contrast

Weight Work

Ladders with X-Vest
8 drills

Static Stretch
Partner

Reaction Drills
Bounds 1 × 8
Shuffles 1 × 8
Sprint Outs 1 × 8
Quarter Turns 1 × 8
Scramble 1 × 8

Shackles and Quick Hands with Weighted Bag
High Knee March
Walking Lunge
Step, Squat & Punch
Backward S, S & Punch
Lateral Shuffle
2 × 15-Yard Contrast

Position Resistance
Shackles & Hands
X-Vest
Pass Sets
Right 3 × 6 reps
Left 3 × 6 reps
Center 3 × 6 reps
1 × 2 reps Contrast

Resistance Runs
Long-Tow Sprints
2 × 6 reps 40 yards
2 × Contrast

Weight Work

Ladders
Chip-O-Meters
8 drills
2 × Contrast

Static Stretch
Partner

Reaction Drills
Sandwich Drill
3 × 8 reps
1 × 6 Contrast

Linear Overspeed
2 × 5 reps
20-Yard Sprints

Position Overspeed
Pass Sets
Right 2 × 5 reps
Left 2 × 5 reps
Center 2 × 5 reps
1 × 2 reps Contrast

Rest

Ladders with X-Vest
8 drills

Static Stretch
Partner

Reaction Drills
Bounds 1 × 8
Shuffles 1 × 8
Sprint Outs 1 × 8
Quarter Turns 1 × 8
Scramble 1 × 8

Shackles and Quick Hands with Weighted Bag
High Knee March
Walking Lunge
Step, Squat & Punch
Backward S, S & Punch
Lateral Shuffle
2 × 15-Yard Contrast

Position Resistance
Meadow Harness
Drive Block 3 × 6 reps
Angle Block 3 × 6 reps

Mirror Drill
Resistance
3 × 15 seconds

Resistance Pulls
Right/Left
3 × 8 reps
1 × 2 Contrasts each direction

Weight Work

Ladders
Chip-O-Meters
8 drills
2 × Contrast

Static Stretch
Partner

Reaction Drills
Sandwich Drill
3 × 8 reps
1 × 6 Contrast

Linear Overspeed
2 × 5 reps
20-Yard Sprints

Position Overspeed
Pass Sets
Right 2 × 5 reps
Left 2 × 5 reps
Center 2 × 5 reps
1 × 2 reps Contrast

3-Cone Pattern Runs
3 × 3 Progression Runs
Backpedal Weaves

Weight Work

Six-Week Program Speed and Position Work

Position: Offensive Linemen (Week 6)

Player: Le Charles Bentley

Monday	**Tuesday**	**Wednesday**	**Thursday**	**Friday**
Day 1	Day 2	Day 3	Day 4	Day 5
Resistance	**Overspeed**	**Recovery Day**	**Resistance**	**Overspeed**
Ballistics with X-Vest	**Ballistics**	Pool	**Ballistics with X-Vest**	**Ballistics**
2 × 20 yards	Chip-O-Meters		2 × 20 yards	Chip-O-Meters
Ladders with X-Vest	**Ladders**		**Ladders with X-Vest**	**Ladders**
8 drills	Chip-O-Meters		8 drills	Chip-O-Meters
	8 drills			8 drills
Static Stretch	2 × Contrast		**Static Stretch**	2 × Contrast
Partner	**Static Stretch**		Partner	**Static Stretch**
	Partner			Partner
Reaction Drills	**Reaction Drills**		**Reaction Drills**	**Reaction Drills**
Bounds 1 × 8	Sandwich Drill		Bounds 1 × 8	Sandwich Drill
Shuffles 1 × 8	3 × 8 reps		Shuffles 1 × 8	3 × 8 reps
Sprint Outs 1 × 8	1 × 6 Contrast		Sprint Outs 1 × 8	1 × 6 Contrast
Quarter Turns 1 × 8	**Linear Overspeed**		Quarter Turns 1 × 8	**Linear Overspeed**
Scramble 1 × 8	2 × 5 reps		Scramble 1 × 8	2 × 5 reps
Shackles and Quick Hands with Weighted Bag	20-Yard Sprints		**Shackles and Quick Hands with Weighted Bag**	20-Yard Sprints
High Knee March	**Position Overspeed**		High Knee March	**Position Overspeed**
Walking Lunge	Pass Sets		Walking Lunge	Pass Sets
Step, Squat & Punch	Right 2 × 5 reps		Step, Squat & Punch	2 × 5 reps
Backward S, S & Punch	Left 2 × 5 reps		Backward S, S & Punch	Right 2 × 5 reps
Lateral Shuffle	Center 2 × 5 reps		Lateral Shuffle	Left 2 × 5 reps
2 × 15-Yard Contrast	1 × 2 reps Contrast		2 × 15-Yard Contrast	1 × 2 reps Contrast
Position Resistance	**3-Cone Pattern Runs**		**Position Resistance**	
Meadow Harness	3 × 3 Progression Runs		Black Widow	
Drive Block 3 × 6	Backpedal Weaves		With X-Vest	
Angle Block 3 × 6			Pass Sets	
			Right 3 × 6 reps	

continued

Mirror Drill
Resistance
3 × 15 seconds

Release Harness
3 × 8 reps
2 × 5 Release reps
1 × 2 Contrasts each direction

Weight Work

Left 3 × 6 reps
Center 3 × 6 reps
1 × 2 reps each direction

Resistance Runs
Lateral, Shuffle, and Punch
2 × 6 reps
2 × Contrast

Weight Work

Rest

Weight Work

Weight Work

Six-Week Program Speed and Position Work

Position: Tight Ends (Week 1)

Player: Alge Crumpler

Monday — Day 1
Resistance
Ballistics
2 × 20 yards
Ladders
8 drills
Static Stretch
Partner
Reaction Drills
Bounds 1 × 8
Shuffles 1 × 8
Sprint Outs 1 × 8
Quarter Turns 1 × 8
Scramble 1 × 8
Shackles and Quick Hands
High Knee March
Walking Lunge
Step, Squat & Punch

Tuesday — Day 2
Overspeed
Ballistics
Chip-O-Meters
Ladders
Chip-O-Meters
8 drills
Static Stretch
2 × Contrast
Reaction Drills
Sandwich Drill
3 × 8 reps
1 × 6 Contrast
Linear Overspeed
1 × 5 reps
40-Yard Sprints

Wednesday — Day 3
Recovery Day Resistance
Pool

Thursday — Day 4
Overspeed
Ballistics
2 × 20 yards
Ladders
8 drills
Static Stretch
Partner
Reaction Drills
Bounds 1 × 8
Shuffles 1 × 8
Sprint Outs 1 × 8
Quarter Turns 1 × 8
Scramble 1 × 8
Shackles and Quick Hands
High Knee March
Walking Lunge
Step, Squat & Punch

Friday — Day 5
Ballistics
Chip-O-Meters
Ladders
Chip-O-Meters
8 drills
2 × Contrast
Static Stretch
Partner
Reaction Drills
Sandwich Drill
3 × 8 reps
1 × 6 Contrast
Linear Overspeed
1 × 5 reps
40-Yard Sprints

continued

(continued from previous page)

Monday
- Backward S, S & Punch
- Lateral Shuffle
- 2 × 15-Yard Contrast

Position Resistance
- Get-Offs
- Right 1 × 5 reps
- Left 1 × 5 reps
- Center 1 × 5 reps
- 1 × 2 reps Contrast

Resistance Runs
- Up & Backs
- Linear 1 × 8
- Lateral Shuffle 1 × 8 R/L
- Backpedal 1 × 8
- 1 × 4 Contrasts each direction

Weight Work

Tuesday

Position Overspeed
- Get-Offs
- Right 1 × 5 reps
- Left 1 × 5 reps
- Center 1 × 5 reps
- 1 × 2 reps Contrast

Weight Work

Wednesday

Rest

Thursday
- Backward S, S & Punch
- Lateral Shuffle
- 2 × 15-Yard Contrast

Position Resistance
- Resistance Routes
- Right Hitch 1 × 5 reps
- Left Hitch 1 × 5 reps
- Center Curl 1 × 5 reps
- 1 × 2 reps Contrast

Resistance Runs
- Long-Tow Sprints
- 1 × 6 reps 40 yards
- 2 × Contrast

Weight Work

Friday

Position Overspeed
- Get-Offs
- Right 1 × 5 reps
- Left 1 × 5 reps
- Center 1 × 5 reps
- 1 × 2 reps Contrast

Weight Work

Six-Week Program Speed and Position Work

Position: Tight Ends (Week 2)

Player: Alge Crumpler

Monday
Day 1
Resistance
Ballistics
2 × 20 yards
Ladders
8 drills

Static Stretch
Partner

Tuesday
Day 2
Overspeed
Ballistics
Chip-O-Meters
Ladders
Chip-O-Meters
8 drills
2 × Contrast

Wednesday
Day 3
Recovery Day
Pool

Thursday
Day 4
Resistance
Ballistics
2 × 20 yards
Ladders
8 drills

Static Stretch
Partner

Friday
Day 5
Overspeed
Ballistics
Chip-O-Meters
Ladders
Chip-O-Meters
8 drills
2 × Contrast

Static Stretch
Partner

Reaction Drills
Sandwich Drill
3 × 8 reps
1 × 6 Contrast

Linear Overspeed
1 × 5 reps
40-Yard Sprints

Position Overspeed
Get-Offs
Right 1 × 5 reps
Left 1 × 5 reps

Position Resistance
Center 1 × 5 reps
1 × 2 reps Contrast

Release Harness
2 × 8 reps
1 × 5 Contrast

Weight Work

Reaction Drills
Bounds 1 × 8
Shuffles 1 × 8
Sprint Outs 1 × 8
Quarter Turns 1 × 8
Scramble 1 × 8

Shackles and Quick Hands
High Knee March
Walking Lunge
Step, Squat & Punch
Backward S, S & Punch
Lateral Shuffle
2 × 15-Yard Contrast

Position Resistance
Meadow Harness
Drive Block
Right 1 × 6 reps
Left 1 × 6 reps
Center 1 × 6 reps
1 × 2 reps each direction

Resistance Runs
Long-Tow Sprints
1 × 6 reps 40 yards
2 × Contrast

Weight Work

Rest

Static Stretch
Partner

Reaction Drills
Sandwich Drill
3 × 8 reps
1 × 6 Contrast

Linear Overspeed
1 × 5 reps
40-Yard Sprints

Position Overspeed
Pass Routes
Right 1 × 5 reps
Left 1 × 5 reps

Position Resistance
Center 1 × 5 reps
1 × 2 reps Contrast

Weight Work

Reaction Drills
Bounds 1 × 8
Shuffles 1 × 8
Sprint Outs 1 × 8
Quarter Turns 1 × 8
Scramble 1 × 8

Shackles and Quick Hands
High Knee March
Walking Lunge
Step, Squat & Punch
Backward S, S & Punch
Lateral Shuffle
2 × 15-Yard Contrast

Position Resistance
Shackles & Hands
Lateral Shuffle & Punch
3 × 8 reps
1 × 8 Contrasts

Resistance Catching
Quick Hands Drill
1 × 3 minutes
1 × set Contrast

Weight Work

Six-Week Program Speed and Position Work

Position: Tight Ends (Week 3)

Player: Alge Crumpler

Monday
Day 1
Resistance
Ballistics
2 × 20 yards
Ladders
8 drills
Static Stretch
Partner
Reaction Drills
Bounds 1 × 8
Shuffles 1 × 8
Sprint Outs 1 × 8
Quarter Turns 1 × 8
Scramble 1 × 8
Shackles and Quick Hands
High Knee March
Walking Lunge
Step, Squat & Punch
Backward S, S & Punch
Lateral Shuffle
2 × 15-Yard Contrast
Position Resistance
Meadow Harness
5 Cord Drill

Tuesday
Day 2
Overspeed
Ballistics
Chip-O-Meters
Ladders
Chip-O-Meters
8 drills
2 × Contrast
Static Stretch
Partner
Reaction Drills
Sandwich Drill
3 × 8 reps
1 × 6 Contrast
Linear Overspeed
1 × 5 reps
20-Yard Sprints
Position Overspeed
Pass Routes
Right 2 × 5 reps
Left 2 × 5 reps
Position Resistance
Center 2 × 5 reps
1 × 2 reps Contrast

Wednesday
Day 3
Recovery Day
Pool

Thursday
Day 4
Resistance
Ballistics
2 × 20 yards
Ladders
8 drills
Static Stretch
Partner
Reaction Drills
Bounds 1 × 8
Shuffles 1 × 8
Sprint Outs 1 × 8
Quarter Turns 1 × 8
Scramble 1 × 8
Shackles and Quick Hands
High Knee March
Walking Lunge
Step, Squat & Punch
Backward S, S & Punch
Lateral Shuffle
2 × 15-Yard Contrast
Position Resistance
Quick Hands
Pass Routes

Friday
Day 5
Overspeed
Ballistics
Chip-O-Meters
Ladders
Chip-O-Meters
8 drills
2 × Contrast
Static Stretch
Partner
Reaction Drills
Sandwich Drill
3 × 8 reps
1 × 6 Contrast
Linear Overspeed
2 × 5 reps
20-Yard Sprints
Position Overspeed
Pass Routes
2 × 5 reps
Right 1 × 5 reps
Left 1 × 5 reps
1 × 2 reps Contrast

continued

Six-Week Program Speed and Position Work

Position: Tight Ends (Week 4)

Player: Alge Crumpler

Monday
Day 1
Resistance
Ballistic with X-Vest
2 × 20 yards
Ladders with X-Vest
8 drills
Static Stretch
Partner
Reaction Drills
Bounds 1 × 8
Shuffles 1 × 8
Sprint Outs 1 × 8
Quarter Turns 1 × 8
Scramble 1 × 8
Shackles and Quick Hands
High Knee March
3 × 8 reps
1 × 8 Contrast
Quick Hands Drill
3 × 15 seconds
Resistance Routes
Right Hitch 2 × 5 reps
Left Hitch 2 × 5 reps
1 × 2 Contrasts each direction
Weight Work

Overspeed Progression
2 × 4 reps
1 × 4 Contrast
Weight Work

Tuesday
Day 2
Overspeed
Ballistics
Chip-O-Meters
Ladders
Chip-O-Meters
8 drills
Static Stretch
2 × Contrast
Static Stretch
Partner
Reaction Drills
Sandwich Drill
3 × 8 reps
1 × 6 Contrast
Linear Overspeed
2 × 5 reps

Wednesday
Day 3
Recovery Day
Pool

Rest

Thursday
Day 4
Resistance
Ballistics with X-Vest
2 × 20 yards
Ladders with X-Vest
8 drills
Static Stretch
Partner
Reaction Drills
Bounds 1 × 8
Shuffles 1 × 8
Sprint Outs 1 × 8
Quarter Turns 1 × 8
Scramble 1 × 8
Shackles and Quick Hands
High Knee March

Right 2 × 6 reps
Left 2 × 6 reps
Center 2 × 6 reps
1 × 2 reps each direction
Resistance Runs
Long-Tow Sprints
2 × 6 reps 40 yards
2 × Contrast
Weight Work

Friday
Day 5
Overspeed
Ballistics
Chip-O-Meters
Ladders
Chip-O-Meters
8 drills
Static Stretch
2 × Contrast
Static Stretch
Partner
Reaction Drills
Sandwich Drill
3 × 8 reps
1 × 6 Contrast
Linear Overspeed
2 × 5 reps

Weight Work

continued

Six-Week Program Speed and Position Work

Position: Tight Ends (Week 5)

Player: Alge Crumpler

	Monday	**Tuesday**	**Wednesday**	**Thursday**	**Friday**
	Day 1	Day 2	Day 3	Day 4	Day 5
	Resistance	**Overspeed**	**Recovery Day**	**Resistance**	**Overspeed**
	Ballistics with X-Vest	Ballistics	Pool	Ballistics with X-Vest	Ballistics
	2 × 20 yards	Chip-O-Meters		2 × 20 yards	Chip-O-Meters
	Ladders with X-Vest	Ladders		Ladders with X-Vest	Ladders
	8 drills	Chip-O-Meters		8 drills	Chip-O-Meters
	Chip-O-Meters				

Monday (Day 1) — Resistance

Walking Lunge
Step, Squat & Punch
Backward S, S & Punch
Lateral Shuffle
2 × 15-Yard Contrast

Position Resistance
Meadow Harness
Drive Block 3 × 6
Angle Block 3 × 6

Quick Hands Drill
3 × 15 seconds

Reaction Belts
3 × 15 second runs

Ball Drills
Jug Machine

Resistance Runs
Up & Backs
Linear 1 × 8 reps
Lateral R/L 1 × 8 reps
Backpedal 1 × 8 reps
1 × 2 Contrasts each direction

Weight Work

Wednesday (Day 3) — Recovery Day

Rest

Thursday (Day 4) — Resistance

Walking Lunge
Step, Squat & Punch
Backward S, S & Punch
Lateral Shuffle
2 × 15-Yard Contrast

Position Resistance
Quick Hands Drill
2 × 3 minutes

Pass Routes
Right 2 × 6 reps
Left 2 × 6 reps
Center 2 × 6 reps
1 × 2 reps each direction

Resistance Runs
Long-Tow Sprints
2 × 6 reps 40 yards
2 × Contrast

Weight Work

Friday (Day 5) — Overspeed

40-Yard Sprints

Position Overspeed
Pass Routes
Right 2 × 5 reps
Left 2 × 5 reps
Center 2 × 5 reps
1 × 2 reps Contrast

Pattern Run
Passing Tree
1 × 15 reps

Weight Work

Static Stretch
Partner

8 drills
2 × Contrast

Reaction Drills
Bounds 1 × 8
Shuffles 1 × 8
Sprint Outs 1 × 8
Quarter Turns 1 × 8
Scramble 1 × 8

**Shackles and Quick Hands
with Weighted Bag**
High Knee March
Walking Lunge
Step, Squat & Punch
Backward S, S & Punch
Lateral Shuffle
2 × 15-Yard Contrast

Linear Overspeed
2 × 5 reps
40-Yard Sprints

Position Overspeed
Pass Routes
Right 2 × 5 reps
Left 2 × 5 reps
Center 2 × 5 reps
1 × 2 reps Contrast

3-Cone Pattern Runs
3 × 3 Progression Runs

In and Outs
1 × 10 reps
Sprint, Jog, Sprint
100 yards

Position Resistance
Meadow Harness
Drive Block 3 × 6 reps
Angle Block 3 × 6 reps

Mirror Drill
Resistance
3 × 15 seconds

Resistance Get-Offs
Right/Left
3 × 8 reps
1 × 2 Contrasts each direction

Weight Work

Static Stretch
Partner

Reaction Drills
Bounds 1 × 8
Shuffles 1 × 8
Sprint Outs 1 × 8
Quarter Turns 1 × 8
Scramble 1 × 8

**Shackles and Quick Hands
with Weighted Bag**
High Knee March
Walking Lunge
Step, Squat & Punch
Backward S, S & Punch
Lateral Shuffle
2 × 15-Yard Contrast

Position Resistance
Shackles & Hands
X-Vest
Pass Set
Right 3 × 6 reps
Left 3 × 6 reps
Center 3 × 6 reps
1 × 2 reps Contrast

Resistance Runs
Long-Tow Sprints
2 × 6 reps 40 yards
2 × Contrast
Weight Work

Rest

---

8 drills
2 × Contrast

Static Stretch
Partner

Reaction Drills
Sandwich Drill
3 × 8 reps
1 × 6 Contrast

Linear Overspeed
2 × 5 reps
20-Yard Sprints

Position Overspeed
Pass Routes
Right 2 × 5 reps
Left 2 × 5 reps
Center 2 × 5 reps
1 × 2 reps Contrast

Ball Drills
Jugs Machine

Weight Work

Six-Week Program Speed and Position Work

Position: Tight Ends (Week 6)

Player: Alge Crumpler

Monday	**Tuesday**	**Wednesday**	**Thursday**	**Friday**
Day 1	Day 2	Day 3	Day 4	Day 5
Resistance	**Overspeed**	**Recovery Day**	**Resistance**	**Overspeed**
Ballistics with X-Vest	**Ballistics**	Pool	**Ballistics with X-Vest**	**Ballistics**
2 × 20 yards	Chip-O-Meters		2 × 20 yards	Chip-O-Meters
Ladders with X-Vest	**Ladders**		**Ladders with X-Vest**	**Ladders**
8 drills	Chip-O-Meters		8 drills	Chip-O-Meters
	8 drills			8 drills
Static Stretch	**Static Stretch**		**Static Stretch**	**Static Stretch**
Partner	2 × Contrast		Partner	2 × Contrast
Reaction Drills	**Static Stretch**		**Reaction Drills**	**Static Stretch**
Bounds 1 × 8	Partner		Bounds 1 × 8	Partner
Shuffles 1 × 8			Shuffles 1 × 8	
Sprint Outs 1 × 8	**Reaction Drills**		Sprint Outs 1 × 8	**Reaction Drills**
Quarter Turns 1 × 8	Sandwich Drill		Quarter Turns 1 × 8	Sandwich Drill
Scramble 1 × 8	3 × 8 reps		Scramble 1 × 8	3 × 8 reps
	1 × 6 Contrast			1 × 6 Contrast
Shackles and Quick Hands	**Linear Overspeed**		**Shackles and Quick Hands**	**Linear Overspeed**
with Weighted Bag	2 × 5 reps		**with Weighted Bag**	2 × 5 reps
High Knee March	20-Yard Sprints		High Knee March	20-Yard Sprints
Walking Lunge			Walking Lunge	
Step, Squat & Punch	**Position Overspeed**		Step, Squat & Punch	**Position Overspeed**
Backward S, S & Punch	Pass Sets		Backward S, S & Punch	Pass Sets
Lateral Shuffle	Right 2 × 5 reps		Lateral Shuffle	2 × 5 reps
2 × 15-Yard Contrast	Left 2 × 5 reps		2 × 15-Yard Contrast	Right 2 × 5 reps
	Center 2 × 5 reps			Left 2 × 5 reps
Position Resistance	1 × 2 reps Contrast		**Position Resistance**	1 × 2 reps Contrast
Meadow Harness			Black Widow	
Drive Block 3 × 6	**3-Cone Pattern Runs**		With X-Vest	
Angle Block 3 × 6	3 × 3 Progression Runs		Pass Sets	
	Backpedal Weaves		Right 3 × 6 reps	

Six-Week Program Speed and Position Work

Position: Defensive Linemen (Week 1)

Player: Bobby Hamilton

Monday
Day 1
Resistance
Ballistics
2 × 20 yards
Ladders
8 drills

Static Stretch
Partner

Reaction Drills
Bounds 1 × 8
Shuffles 1 × 8
Sprint Outs 1 × 8
Quarter Turns 1 × 8
Scramble 1 × 8
Shackles and Quick Hands
High Knee March
Walking Lunge
Step, Squat & Punch
Mirror Drill
Resistance
3 × 15 seconds
Release Pulls
Right/Left
3 × 8 reps
1 × 2 Contrasts each direction
Weight Work

Tuesday
Day 2
Overspeed
Ballistics
Chip-O-Meters
Ladders
Chip-O-Meters
8 drills
2 × Contrast

Static Stretch
Partner

Reaction Drills
Sandwich Drill
3 × 8 reps
1 × 6 Contrast
Linear Overspeed
1 × 5 reps
20-Yard Sprints
Weight Work
Rest

Wednesday
Day 3
Recovery Day
Pool

Thursday
Day 4
Resistance
Ballistics
2 × 20 yards
Ladders
8 drills

Static Stretch
Partner

Reaction Drills
Bounds 1 × 8
Shuffles 1 × 8
Sprint Outs 1 × 8
Quarter Turns 1 × 8
Scramble 1 × 8
Shackles and Quick Hands
High Knee March
Walking Lunge
Step, Squat & Punch
Left 3 × 6 reps
Center 3 × 6 reps
1 × 2 reps each direction
Resistance Runs
Lateral, Shuffle, and Punch
2 × 6 reps
2 × Contrast
Weight Work

Friday
Day 5
Overspeed
Ballistics
Chip-O-Meters
Ladders
Chip-O-Meters
8 drills
2 × Contrast

Static Stretch
Partner

Reaction Drills
Sandwich Drill
3 × 8 reps
1 × 6 Contrast
Linear Overspeed
1 × 5 reps
20-Yard Sprints
Weight Work

continued

Backward S, S & Punch
Lateral Shuffle
2 × 15-Yard Contrast

Position Resistance
Get-Offs-Rip and Swim
Right 1 × 5 reps
Left 1 × 5 reps
Center 2 Gap 1 × 5 reps
1 × 2 reps Contrast

Position Overspeed
Get-Offs
Right 1 × 5 reps
Left 1 × 5 reps
Center 1 × 5 reps
1 × 2 reps Contrast

Resistance Runs
Up & Backs
Linear 1 × 8
Lateral Shuffle 1 × 8 R/L
Backpedal 1 × 8
1 × 4 Contrasts each direction

Weight Work

Backward S, S & Punch
Lateral Shuffle
2 × 15-Yard Contrast

Position Resistance
6 Cord Rip/Swim
Right 1 × 5 reps
Left 1 × 5 reps
Center 1 × 5 reps
1 × 2 reps Contrast

Resistance Runs
Long-Tow Sprints
1 × 6 reps 40 yards
2 × Contrast

Weight Work

Rest

Backward S, S & Punch
Lateral Shuffle
2 × 15-Yard Contrast

Position Overspeed
Get-Offs
Right 1 × 5 reps
Left 1 × 5 reps
Center 1 × 5 reps
1 × 2 reps Contrast

Weight Work

Six-Week Program Speed and Position Work

Position: Defensive Linemen (Week 2)

Player: Bobby Hamilton

Monday
Day 1
Resistance
Ballistics
2 × 20 yards
Ladders
Chip-O-Meters
8 drills

Static Stretch
Partner

Tuesday
Day 2
Overspeed
Ballistics
Chip-O-Meters
Ladders
Chip-O-Meters
8 drills
2 × Contrast

Wednesday
Day 3
Recovery Day
Pool

Thursday
Day 4
Resistance
Ballistics
2 × 20 yards
Ladders
8 drills

Static Stretch
Partner

Friday
Day 5
Overspeed
Ballistics
Chip-O-Meters
Ladders
Chip-O-Meters
8 drills
2 × Contrast

Static Stretch
Partner

Reaction Drills
Sandwich Drill
3 × 8 reps
1 × 6 Contrast

Linear Overspeed
1 × 5 reps
40-Yard Sprints

Position Overspeed
Get-Offs
Right 1 × 5 reps
Left 1 × 5 reps
1 × 2 reps Contrast
Release Harness
2 × 8 reps
1 × 5 Contrast

Weight Work

Reaction Drills
Bounds 1 × 8
Shuffles 1 × 8
Sprint Outs 1 × 8
Quarter Turns 1 × 8
Scramble 1 × 8

Shackles and Quick Hands
High Knee March
Walking Lunge
Step, Squat & Punch
Backward S, S & Punch
Lateral Shuffle
2 × 15-Yard Contrast

Position Resistance
Meadow Harness
Pop-Up Dummy
Right 2 × 6 reps
Left 2 × 6 reps
2 Gap 2 × 6 reps
1 × 2 reps each direction

Resistance Runs
Long-Tow Sprints
1 × 6 reps 40 yards
2 × Contrast
Weight Work

Rest

Static Stretch
Partner

Reaction Drills
Sandwich Drill
3 × 8 reps
1 × 6 Contrast

Linear Overspeed
1 × 5 reps
20-Yard Sprints

Position Overspeed
Circle Rush
Right 1 × 5 reps
Left 1 × 5 reps
1 × 2 reps Contrast

4 Bag Drill
4 × 1 rep

Weight Work

Reaction Drills
Bounds 1 × 8
Shuffles 1 × 8
Sprint Outs 1 × 8
Quarter Turns 1 × 8
Scramble 1 × 8

Shackles and Quick Hands
High Knee March
Walking Lunge
Step, Squat & Punch
Backward S, S & Punch
Lateral Shuffle
2 × 15-Yard Contrast

Position Resistance
Attack & React
2 Gap
3 × 8 reps
1 × 8 Contrasts

Resistance
Quick Hands Drills
1 × 3 minutes

Weight Work

Six-Week Program Speed and Position Work

Position: Defensive Linemen (Week 3)

Player: Bobby Hamilton

Monday
Day 1
Resistance
Ballistics
2 × 20 yards
Ladders
8 drills

Static Stretch
Partner

Reaction Drills
Bounds 1 × 8
Shuffles 1 × 8
Sprint Outs 1 × 8
Quarter Turns 1 × 8
Scramble 1 × 8
Shackles and Quick Hands
High Knee March
Walking Lunge
Step, Squat & Punch
Backward S, S & Punch
Lateral Shuffle
2 × 15-Yard Contrast

Position Resistance
Meadow Harness
5 Cord Drill
3 × 8 reps
1 × 8 Contrast

Tuesday
Day 2
Overspeed
Ballistics
Chip-O-Meters
Ladders
Chip-O-Meters
8 drills

Static Stretch
2 × Contrast

Static Stretch
Partner

Reaction Drills
Sandwich Drill
3 × 8 reps
1 × 6 Contrast
Linear Overspeed
2 × 5 reps
20-Yard Sprints

Position Overspeed
Rip/Swim
Right 2 × 5 reps
Left 2 × 5 reps

Position Resistance
Center 2 × 5 reps
1 × 2 reps Contrast

Overspeed Progression
2 × 4 reps

Wednesday
Day 3
Recovery Day
Pool

Thursday
Day 4
Resistance
Ballistics
2 × 20 yards
Ladders
8 drills

Static Stretch
Partner

Reaction Drills
Bounds 1 × 8
Shuffles 1 × 8
Sprint Outs 1 × 8
Quarter Turns 1 × 8
Scramble 1 × 8
Shackles and Quick Hands
High Knee March
Walking Lunge
Step, Squat & Punch
Backward S, S & Punch
Lateral Shuffle
2 × 15-Yard Contrast

Position Resistance
Shackles & Hands
Pop-Up Dummy
Right 2 × 6 reps
Left 2 × 6 reps

Friday
Day 5
Overspeed
Ballistics
Chip-O-Meters
Ladders
Chip-O-Meters
8 drills

Static Stretch
2 × Contrast

Static Stretch
Partner

Reaction Drills
Sandwich Drill
3 × 8 reps
1 × 6 Contrast
Linear Overspeed
2 × 5 reps
20-Yard Sprints

Position Overspeed
Release Harness
Backpedal 2 × 5 reps
Right 1 × 5 reps

Left 1 × 5 reps
1 × 5 reps Contrast

6-Cone Drill
1 × 12 reps

continued

Six-Week Program Speed and Position Work

Position: Defensive Linemen (Week 4)

Player: Bobby Hamilton

Monday — Day 1

Resistance
- Ballistic with X-Vest — 2 × 20 yards
- Ladders with X-Vest — 8 drills

Static Stretch
- Partner

Reaction Drills
- Bounds 1 × 8
- Shuffles 1 × 8
- Sprint Outs 1 × 8
- Quarter Turns 1 × 8
- Scramble 1 × 8

Shackles and Quick Hands
- High Knee March
- Walking Lunge
- Quick Hands Drill — 3 × 15 seconds

Resistance Runs
- Up & Backs
- 4-Directions — 1 × 8 reps
- 1 × 4 Contrast

Weight Work

Tuesday — Day 2

Overspeed

Ballistics
- Chip-O-Meters

Ladders
- Chip-O-Meters
- 8 drills

Static Stretch
- 2 × Contrast

Static Stretch
- Partner

Reaction Drills
- Sandwich Drill
- 3 × 8 reps
- 1 × 6 Contrast

Linear Overspeed
- 2 × 5 reps
- 20-Yard Sprints

Weight Work

Wednesday — Day 3

Recovery Day

Pool

Rest

Thursday — Day 4

Resistance

Ballistics with X-Vest
- 2 × 20 yards

Ladders with X-Vest
- 8 drills

Static Stretch
- Partner

Reaction Drills
- Bounds 1 × 8
- Shuffles 1 × 8
- Sprint Outs 1 × 8
- Quarter Turns 1 × 8
- Scramble 1 × 8

Shackles and Quick Hands
- High Knee March
- Walking Lunge

Resistance Runs
- Long-Tow Sprints
- 2 × 6 reps 40 yards
- 2 × Contrast

Weight Work

Friday — Day 5

Overspeed

Ballistics
- Chip-O-Meters

Ladders
- Chip-O-Meters
- 8 drills

Static Stretch
- 2 × Contrast

Static Stretch
- Partner

Reaction Drills
- Sandwich Drill
- 3 × 8 reps
- 1 × 6 Contrast

Linear Overspeed
- 2 × 5 reps
- 20-Yard Sprints

Center 2 × 6 reps
1 × 2 reps each direction

Weight Work

continued

Step, Squat & Punch
Backward S, S & Punch
Lateral Shuffle
2 × 15-Yard Contrast

Position Resistance
Meadow Harness
5-Cone 3 × 6
1 × 4 Contrast

Resistance Runs
Up & Backs
Linear 1 × 8
Lateral Shuffle 1 × 8 R/L
Backpedal 1 × 8
1 × 4 Contrasts each direction

Weight Work

Position Overspeed
Hoop Drill
Right 2 × 5 reps
Left 2 × 5 reps
5 × each direction

Reaction Belts
3 × 15 second runs

Mirror Drill

Step, Squat & Punch
Backward S, S & Punch
Lateral Shuffle
2 × 15-Yard Contrast

Position Resistance
Quick Hands Drill
2 × 3 minutes

Black Widow
2 × 6 rep 20 yards
1 × 2 Contrast
Resistance Runs
Long-Tow Sprints
2 × 6 reps 40 yards
2 × Contrast

Weight Work

Rest

Position Overspeed
Rip/Swim
Right 2 × 5 reps
Left 2 × 5 reps
Center2 × 5 reps
1 × 5 reps Contrast

Pattern Run
6-Cone Drill
1 × 6

Weight Work

Six-Week Program Speed and Position Work

Position: Defensive Linemen (Week 5)

Player: Bobby Hamilton

Monday
Day 1
Resistance
Ballistics with X-Vest
2 × 20 yards
Ladders with X-Vest
8 drills
Static Stretch
Partner

Tuesday
Day 2
Overspeed
Ballistics
Chip-O-Meters
Ladders
Chip-O-Meters
8 drills
2 × Contrast

Wednesday
Day 3
Recovery Day
Pool

Thursday
Day 4
Resistance
Ballistics with X-Vest
2 × 20 yards
Ladders with X-Vest
8 drills
Static Stretch
Partner

Friday
Day 5
Overspeed
Ballistics
Chip-O-Meters
Ladders
Chip-O-Meters
8 drills
2 × Contrast

Static Stretch
Partner

Reaction Drills
Bounds 1 × 8
Shuffles 1 × 8
Sprint Outs 1 × 8
Quarter Turns 1 × 8
Scramble 1 × 8

Shackles and Quick Hands with Weighted Bag
High Knee March
Walking Lunge
Step, Squat & Punch
Backward S, S & Punch
Lateral Shuffle
2 × 15-Yard Contrast

Position Resistance
Shackles & Hands
X-Vest
Meadow Harness
Right 3 × 6 reps
Left 3 × 6 reps
2 Gap 3 × 6 reps
1 × 2 reps Contrast

Resistance Runs
Long-Tow Sprints
2 × 6 reps 40 yards
2 × Contrast

Weight Work

Reaction Drills
Sandwich Drill
3 × 8 reps
1 × 6 Contrast

Linear Overspeed
2 × 5 reps
20-Yard Sprints

Position Overspeed
Get-Offs
Right 2 × 5 reps
Left 2 × 5 reps
Center 2 × 5 reps
1 × 2 reps Contrast

3-Cone Mirror
4 × 15 seconds

Rest

Static Stretch
Partner

Reaction Drills
Bounds 1 × 8
Shuffles 1 × 8
Sprint Outs 1 × 8
Quarter Turns 1 × 8
Scramble 1 × 8

Shackles and Quick Hands with Weighted Bag
High Knee March
Walking Lunge
Step, Squat & Punch
Backward S, S & Punch
Lateral Shuffle
2 × 15-Yard Contrast

Position Overspeed
Get-Offs
Right 2 × 5 reps
Left 2 × 5 reps
2 Gap 2 × 5 reps
1 × 2 reps Contrast

3-Cone L Drill
3 × 3 Progression Runs

In and Outs
1 × 10 reps
Sprint, Jog, Sprint
100 yards

Weight Work

Reaction Drills
Bounds 1 × 8
Shuffles 1 × 8
Sprint Outs 1 × 8
Quarter Turns 1 × 8
Scramble 1 × 8

Shackles and Quick Hands with Weighted Bag
High Knee March
Walking Lunge
Step, Squat & Punch
Backward S, S & Punch
Lateral Shuffle
2 × 15-Yard Contrast

Position Resistance
Attack & React
Rip 3 × 6 reps
Swim 3 × 6 reps

Mirror Drill
Resistance
3 × 15 seconds

Black Widows
2 × 5 reps
1 × 4 reps Contrast

Weight Work

Six-Week Program Speed and Position Work

Position: Defensive Linemen (Week 6)

Player: Bobby Hamilton

continued

Monday	Tuesday	Wednesday	Thursday	Friday
Day 1	Day 2	Day 3	Day 4	Day 5
Resistance	**Overspeed**	**Recovery Day**	**Resistance**	**Overspeed**
Ballistics with X-Vest	**Ballistics**	Pool	**Ballistics with X-Vest**	**Ballistics**
2 × 20 yards	Chip-O-Meters		2 × 20 yards	Chip-O-Meters
Ladders with X-Vest	**Ladders**		**Ladders with X-Vest**	**Ladders**
8 drills	Chip-O-Meters		8 drills	Chip-O-Meters
	8 drills			8 drills
Static Stretch	2 × Contrast		**Static Stretch**	2 × Contrast
Partner			Partner	
	Static Stretch			**Static Stretch**
	Partner			Partner
Reaction Drills	**Reaction Drills**		**Reaction Drills**	**Reaction Drills**
Bounds 1 × 8	Bounds 1 × 8		Bounds 1 × 8	Sandwich Drill
Shuffles 1 × 8	Shuffles 1 × 8		Shuffles 1 × 8	3 × 8 reps
Sprint Outs 1 × 8	Sprint Outs 1 × 8		Sprint Outs 1 × 8	1 × 6 Contrast
Quarter Turns 1 × 8	Quarter Turns 1 × 8		Quarter Turns 1 × 8	
Scramble 1 × 8	Scramble 1 × 8		Scramble 1 × 8	**Linear Overspeed**
Shackles and Quick Hands	**Shackles and Quick Hands**		**Shackles and Quick Hands**	2 × 5 reps
with Weighted Bag	**with Weighted Bag**		**with Weighted Bag**	20-Yard Sprints
High Knee March	High Knee March		High Knee March	
Walking Lunge	Walking Lunge		Walking Lunge	**Position Overspeed**
Step, Squat & Punch	Step, Squat & Punch		Step, Squat & Punch	Get-Offs
Backward S, S & Punch	Backward S, S & Punch		Backward S, S & Punch	2 × 5 reps
Lateral Shuffle	Lateral Shuffle		Lateral Shuffle	Right 2 × 5 reps
2 × 15-Yard Contrast	2 × 15-Yard Contrast		2 × 15-Yard Contrast	Left 2 × 5 reps
				1 × 2 reps Contrast
Linear Overspeed	**Linear Overspeed**		**Linear Overspeed**	
2 × 5 reps	2 × 5 reps		2 × 5 reps	**Position Resistance**
20-Yard Sprints	20-Yard Sprints		20-Yard Sprints	Black Widow
				With X-Vest
Position Overspeed	**Position Overspeed**		**Position Resistance**	Rip/Swim
Hoop Drill	Get-Offs		Black Widow	Right 3 × 6 reps
Right 2 × 5 reps	2 × 5 reps		With X-Vest	
Left 2 × 5 reps	Right 2 × 5 reps		Rip/Swim	Reaction Belts
1 × 2 reps Contrast	Left 2 × 5 reps		Right 3 × 6 reps	Mirror Drill
	1 × 2 reps Contrast			4 × 15 seconds
Position Resistance				
Meadow Harness	**Position Resistance**			
2 Gap 3 × 6 & Rip/Swim	7-Cone Pattern Runs			
3 × 6	3 × 7 Progression Run			

Six-Week Program Speed and Position Work

Position: Defensive Backs (Week 1)

Player: Champ Bailey

Monday	Tuesday	Wednesday	Thursday	Friday
Day 1	Day 2	Day 3	Day 4	Day 5
Resistance	**Overspeed**	**Recovery Day**	**Resistance**	**Overspeed**
Ballistics	**Ballistics**	Pool	**Ballistics**	**Ballistics**
2 × 20 yards	Chip-O-Meters		2 × 20 yards	Chip-O-Meters
Ladders	**Ladders**		**Ladders**	**Ladders**
8 drills	Chip-O-Meters		8 drills	Chip-O-Meters
	8 drills			8 drills
	2 × Contrast			2 × Contrast
Static Stretch	**Static Stretch**		**Static Stretch**	**Static Stretch**
Partner	Partner		Partner	Partner
Reaction Drills	**Reaction Drills**		**Reaction Drills**	**Reaction Drills**
Bounds 1 × 8	Sandwich Drill		Bounds 1 × 8	Sandwich Drill
Shuffles 1 × 8	3 × 8 reps		Shuffles 1 × 8	3 × 8 reps
Sprint Outs 1 × 8	1 × 6 Contrast		Sprint Outs 1 × 8	1 × 6 Contrast
Quarter Turns 1 × 8	**Linear Overspeed**		Quarter Turns 1 × 8	**Linear Overspeed**
Scramble 1 × 8	1 × 5 reps		Scramble 1 × 8	1 × 5 reps
Shackles and Quick Hands			**Shackles and Quick Hands**	
High Knee March			High Knee March	
Mirror Drill		Rest	Left 3 × 6 reps	
Resistance			2 Gap 3 × 6 reps	
Shackles & Quick Hands			1 × 2 Contrast	
3 × 15 seconds			**Resistance Runs**	
1 × 5 Contrast			Lateral, Shuffle, and Punch	
Release Harness			2 × 6 reps	
3 × 8 reps			2 × Contrast	
2 × 5 Release reps				
1 × 2 Contrasts each direction				
Weight Work	**Weight Work**		**Weight Work**	**Weight Work**

continued

40-Yard Sprints

Walking Lunge
Step, Squat & Punch
Backward S, S & Punch
Lateral Shuffle
2 × 15-Yard Contrast

Position Resistance
Backpedal
Turn to Right 1 × 5 reps
Turn to Left 1 × 5 reps
Center 2 Gap 1 × 5 reps
1 × 2 reps Contrast

Resistance Runs
Up & Backs
Linear 1 × 8
Lateral Shuffle 1 × 8 R/L
Backpedal 1 × 8
1 × 4 Contrasts each direction
Weight Work

Position Overspeed
Backpedal
Right 1 × 5 reps
Left 1 × 5 reps
Center 2 Gap 1 × 5 reps
1 × 2 reps Contrast

3-Cone Drill
Mirror Drill
3 × 15 seconds
Weight Work

Rest

20-Yard Sprints

Walking Lunge
Step, Squat & Punch
Backward S, S & Punch
Lateral Shuffle
2 × 15-Yard Contrast

Position Resistance
Backpedal
Turn to Right 1 × 5 reps
Turn to Left 1 × 5 reps
Center 2 Gap 1 × 5 reps
1 × 2 reps Contrast

Resistance Runs
Long-Tow Sprints
1 × 6 reps 40 yards
2 × Contrast
Weight Work

Position Overspeed
Backpedal
Right 1 × 5 reps
Left 1 × 5 reps
Center 2 Gap 1 × 5 reps
1 × 2 reps Contrast
Weight Work

Six-Week Program Speed and Position Work

Position: Defensive Backs (Week 2)

Player: Champ Bailey

Monday	**Tuesday**	**Wednesday**	**Thursday**	**Friday**
Day 1	Day 2	Day 3	Day 4	Day 5
Resistance	**Overspeed**	**Recovery Day**	**Resistance**	**Overspeed**
Ballistics	**Ballistics**	Pool	**Ballistics**	**Ballistics**
2 × 20 yards	Chip-O-Meters		2 × 20 yards	Chip-O-Meters
Ladders	**Ladders**		**Ladders**	**Ladders**
8 drills	Chip-O-Meters		8 drills	Chip-O-Meters
	8 drills			8 drills
2 × Contrast	2 × Contrast			2 × Contrast
Static Stretch			**Static Stretch**	
Partner			Partner	

Static Stretch
Partner

Reaction Drills
Sandwich Drill
3 × 8 reps
1 × 6 Contrast

Linear Overspeed
1 × 5 reps
20-Yard Sprints

Position Overspeed
Backpedal @45
Right 1 × 5 reps
Left 1 × 5 reps
1 × 2 reps Contrast

Release Harness
2 × 8 reps
1 × 5 Contrast

Weight Work

Reaction Drills
Bounds 1 × 8
Shuffles 1 × 8
Sprint Outs 1 × 8
Quarter Turns 1 × 8
Scramble 1 × 8

Shackles and Quick Hands
High Knee March
Walking Lunge
Step, Squat & Punch
Backward S, S & Punch
Lateral Shuffle
2 × 15-Yard Contrast

Position Resistance
Meadow Harness
5-Cone
1 × 4 Contrast

Resistance Runs
Long-Tow Sprints
1 × 6 reps 40 yards
2 × Contrast

Weight Work

Rest

Static Stretch
Partner

Reaction Drills
Sandwich Drill
3 × 8 reps
1 × 6 Contrast

Linear Overspeed
1 × 5 reps
40-Yard Sprints

Position Overspeed
Backpedal
Right 1 × 5 reps
Left 1 × 5 reps
1 × 2 reps Contrast

W-Drill
4 × 4 reps

Weight Work

Reaction Drills
Bounds 1 × 8
Shuffles 1 × 8
Sprint Outs 1 × 8
Quarter Turns 1 × 8
Scramble 1 × 8

Shackles and Quick Hands
High Knee March
Walking Lunge
Step, Squat & Punch
Backward S, S & Punch
Lateral Shuffle
2 × 15-Yard Contrast

Position Resistance
Backpedal Weave
2 × 8 reps
Backpedal
2 × 8 reps
1 × 8 Contrasts

Resistance Runs
Up & Backs
2 × sets

Weight Work

Six-Week Program Speed and Position Work

Position: Defensive Backs (Week 3)

Player: Champ Bailey

Monday
Day 1

Resistance

Ballistics
2 × 20 yards

Ladders
8 drills

Static Stretch
Partner

Reaction Drills
Bounds 1 × 8
Shuffles 1 × 8
Sprint Outs 1 × 8
Quarter Turns 1 × 8
Scramble 1 × 8

Shackles and Quick Hands
High Knee March
Walking Lunge
Step, Squat & Punch
Backward S, S & Punch
Lateral Shuffle
2 × 15-Yard Contrast

Position Resistance
Read & React
Break 90 2 × 5 reps
Break 45 2 × 5 reps
1 × 8 Contrast

Tuesday
Day 2

Overspeed

Ballistics
Chip-O-Meters

Ladders
Chip-O-Meters
8 drills

Static Stretch
2 × Contrast

Static Stretch
Partner

Reaction Drills
Sandwich Drill
3 × 8 reps
1 × 6 Contrast

Linear Overspeed
2 × 5 reps
40-Yard Sprints

Position Overspeed
Weave
Right 2 × 5 reps
Left 2 × 5 reps

Position Overspeed
Overspeed Progression
2 × 4 reps
1 × 4 Contrast

Wednesday
Day 3

Recovery Day
Pool

Thursday
Day 4

Resistance

Ballistics
2 × 20 yards

Ladders
8 drills

Static Stretch
Partner

Reaction Drills
Bounds 1 × 8
Shuffles 1 × 8
Sprint Outs 1 × 8
Quarter Turns 1 × 8
Scramble 1 × 8

Shackles and Quick Hands
High Knee March
Walking Lunge
Step, Squat & Punch
Backward S, S & Punch
Lateral Shuffle
2 × 15-Yard Contrast

Position Resistance
Black Widow
Backpedal
Left 2 × 6 reps
Right 2 × 6 reps
1 × 2 reps Contrast

Friday
Day 5

Overspeed

Ballistics
Chip-O-Meters

Ladders
Chip-O-Meters
8 drills
2 × Contrast

Static Stretch
Partner

Reaction Drills
Sandwich Drill
3 × 8 reps
1 × 6 Contrast

Linear Overspeed
2 × 5 reps
20-Yard Sprints

Position Overspeed
Release Harness
Backpedal 2 × 5 reps
Right 1 × 5 reps
Left 1 × 5 reps
1 × 5 reps Contrast

6-Cone Drill
1 × 12 reps

continued

Quick Hands Ball Receiving Drill
3 × 3 minutes/3 × 15 seconds

Resistance Runs
Up & Backs
4-Directions
1 × 8 reps
1 × 4 Contrast

Weight Work

3-Cone Drill Mirror Drill
4 × 15 seconds

Weight Work

Rest

Resistance Runs
Long-Tow Sprints
2 × 6 reps 40 yards
2 × Contrast

Weight Work

Weight Work

Six-Week Program Speed and Position Work

Position: Defensive Backs (Week 4)

Player: Champ Bailey

Monday	**Tuesday**	**Wednesday**	**Thursday**	**Friday**
Day 1	Day 2	Day 3	Day 4	Day 5
Resistance	**Overspeed**	**Recovery Day**	**Resistance**	**Overspeed**
Ballistic with X-Vest	**Ballistics**	Pool	**Ballistics with X-Vest**	**Ballistics**
2 × 20 yards	Chip-O-Meters		2 × 20 yards	Chip-O-Meters
Ladders with X-Vest	**Ladders**		**Ladders with X-Vest**	**Ladders**
8 drills	Chip-O-Meters		8 drills	Chip-O-Meters
	8 drills			8 drills
	2 × Contrast			2 × Contrast
Static Stretch	**Static Stretch**		**Static Stretch**	**Static Stretch**
Partner	Partner		Partner	Partner
Reaction Drills	**Reaction Drills**		**Reaction Drills**	**Reaction Drills**
Bounds 1 × 8	Sandwich Drill		Bounds 1 × 8	Sandwich Drill
Shuffles 1 × 8	3 × 8 reps		Shuffles 1 × 8	3 × 8 reps
Sprint Outs 1 × 8	1 × 6 Contrast		Sprint Outs 1 × 8	1 × 6 Contrast
Quarter Turns 1 × 8	**Linear Overspeed**		Quarter Turns 1 × 8	**Linear Overspeed**
Scramble 1 × 8	2 × 5 reps		Scramble 1 × 8	2 × 5 reps
Shackles and Quick Hands	20-Yard Sprints		**Shackles and Quick Hands**	20-Yard Sprints
High Knee March			High Knee March	
Walking Lunge			Walking Lunge	
Step, Squat & Punch			Step, Squat & Punch	

continued

Position Overspeed
W-Drill
2 × 5 reps

Reaction Belts
3 × 15-second runs

Mirror Drill

Position Resistance
Meadow Harness
5-Cone 3 × 6
1 × 4 Contrast

Resistance Runs
Up & Backs
Linear 1 × 8
Lateral Shuffle 1 × 8 R/L
Backpedal 1 × 8
1 × 4 Contrasts each direction

Weight Work

Backward S, S & Punch
Lateral Shuffle
2 × 15-Yard Contrast

Position Overspeed
Backpedal
Right 2 × 5 reps
Left 2 × 5 reps
Center 2 Gap 2 × 5 reps
1 × 5 reps Contrast

Pattern Run
6-Cone Drill
1 × 6

Position Resistance
Quick Hands Drill
2 × 3 minutes

Black Widow
2 × 6 rep 20 yards
1 × 2 Contrast

Resistance Runs
Long-Tow Sprints
2 × 6 reps 40 yards
2 × Contrast

Weight Work

Backward S, S & Punch
Lateral Shuffle
2 × 15-Yard Contrast

Rest

Weight Work

Six-Week Program Speed and Position Work

Position: Defensive Backs (Week 5)

Player: Champ Bailey

Monday
Day 1
Resistance
Ballistics with X-Vest
2 × 20 yards
Ladders with X-Vest
8 drills

Static Stretch
Partner

Tuesday
Day 2
Overspeed
Ballistics
Chip-O-Meters
Ladders
Chip-O-Meters
8 drills
2 × Contrast

Wednesday
Day 3
Recovery Day
Pool

Thursday
Day 4
Resistance
Ballistics with X-Vest
2 × 20 yards
Ladders with X-Vest
8 drills

Static Stretch
Partner

Friday
Day 5
Overspeed
Ballistics
Chip-O-Meters
Ladders
Chip-O-Meters
8 drills
2 × Contrast

Reaction Drills
Bounds 1 × 8
Shuffles 1 × 8
Sprint Outs 1 × 8
Quarter Turns 1 × 8
Scramble 1 × 8

Shackles and Quick Hands with Weighted Bag
High Knee March
Walking Lunge
Step, Squat & Punch
Backward S, S & Punch
Lateral Shuffle
2 × 15-Yard Contrast

Position Resistance
Backpedal
3 × 6 reps

Mirror Drill
Resistance
3 × 6 reps

Black Widows
2 × 5 reps
1 × 4 reps Contrast

Weight Work

Static Stretch
Partner

Reaction Drills
Sandwich Drill
3 × 8 reps
1 × 6 Contrast

Linear Overspeed
2 × 5 reps
40-Yard Sprints

Position Overspeed
Backpedal
Right 2 × 5 reps
Left 2 × 5 reps
1 × 2 reps Contrast

3-Cone L Drill
3 × 3 Progression Runs

In and Outs
1 × 10 reps
Sprint, Jog, Sprint
100 yards

Weight Work

Reaction Drills
Bounds 1 × 8
Shuffles 1 × 8
Sprint Outs 1 × 8
Quarter Turns 1 × 8
Scramble 1 × 8

Shackles and Quick Hands with Weighted Bag
High Knee March
Walking Lunge
Step, Squat & Punch
Backward S, S & Punch
Lateral Shuffle
2 × 15-Yard Contrast

Position Resistance
Shackles & Hands
X-Vest
Backpedal
Right 3 × 6 reps
Left 3 × 6 reps
1 × 2 reps Contrast

Resistance Runs
Long-Tow Sprints
2 × 6 reps 40 yards
2 × Contrast

Weight Work

Static Stretch
Partner

Reaction Drills
Sandwich Drill
3 × 8 reps
1 × 6 Contrast

Linear Overspeed
2 × 5 reps
40-Yard Sprints

Position Overspeed
Weave
Right 2 × 5 reps
Left 2 × 5 reps
1 × 2 reps Contrast

7-Cone Drill
Progression

Weight Work

Rest

Weight Work

Six-Week Program Speed and Position Work

Position: Defensive Backs (Week 6)

Player: Champ Bailey

Monday — Day 1

Resistance

Ballistics with X-Vest
2 × 20 yards

Ladders with X-Vest
8 drills

Static Stretch
Partner

Reaction Drills
Bounds 1 × 8
Shuffles 1 × 8
Sprint Outs 1 × 8
Quarter Turns 1 × 8
Scramble 1 × 8

Shackles and Quick Hands with Weighted Bag
High Knee March
Walking Lunge
Step, Squat & Punch
Backward S, S & Punch
Lateral Shuffle
2 × 15-Yard Contrast

Position Resistance
Break @ 45
3 × 5

Tuesday — Day 2

Overspeed

Ballistics
Chip-O-Meters
2 × 20 yards

Ladders
Chip-O-Meters
8 drills
2 × Contrast

Static Stretch
Partner

Reaction Drills
Sandwich Drill
3 × 8 reps
1 × 6 Contrast

Linear Overspeed
2 × 5 reps
40-Yard Sprints

Position Overspeed
W-Drill
2 × 4 reps

7-Cone Pattern Runs
3 × 7 Progression Run

Wednesday — Day 3

Recovery Day
Pool

Thursday — Day 4

Resistance

Ballistics with X-Vest
2 × 20 yards

Ladders with X-Vest
8 drills

Static Stretch
Partner

Reaction Drills
Bounds 1 × 8
Shuffles 1 × 8
Sprint Outs 1 × 8
Quarter Turns 1 × 8
Scramble 1 × 8

Shackles and Quick Hands with Weighted Bag
High Knee March
Walking Lunge
Step, Squat & Punch
Backward S, S & Punch
Lateral Shuffle
2 × 15-Yard Contrast

Position Resistance
Black Widow
Weaves
Backpedal

Friday — Day 5

Overspeed

Ballistics
Chip-O-Meters

Ladders
Chip-O-Meters
8 drills
2 × Contrast

Static Stretch
Partner

Reaction Drills
Sandwich Drill
3 × 8 reps
1 × 6 Contrast

Linear Overspeed
2 × 5 reps
20-Yard Sprints

Position Overspeed
Get-Offs
2 × 5 reps
Right 2 × 5 reps
Left 2 × 5 reps
1 × 2 reps Contrast

Reaction Belts
Mirror Drill

continued

Mirror Drill
Resistance
Shackles & Hands
3 × 15 seconds
1 × 5 Contrast

Right 3 × 6 reps
Left 3 × 6 reps
1 × 2 Contrast

4 × 15 seconds

Resistance Runs
Lateral, Shuffle, and Punch
2 × 6 reps
2 × Contrast

Release Harness
3 × 8 reps
2 × 5 Release reps
1 × 2 Contrasts each direction

Weight Work

Weight Work

Rest

Weight Work

Weight Work

INDEX